Culture and Conflict in Egyptian-Israeli Relations

CULTURE AND CONFLICT IN EGYPTIAN-ISRAELI RELATIONS

A DIALOGUE OF THE DEAF

RAYMOND COHEN

INDIANA UNIVERSITY PRESS
Bloomington and Indianapolis

The paper used in this publication meets the minimum requirements of American National Standard for Information Sciences—Permanence of Paper for Printed Library Materials, ANSI Z39.48-1984.

∞™

Manufactured in the United States of America

Library of Congress Cataloging-in-Publication Data

Cohen, Raymond
    Culture and conflict in Egyptian-Israeli relations : a dialogue of the deaf / Raymond Cohen.
       p.   cm.
    Includes bibliographical references.
    ISBN 0-253-31379-1 (alk. paper)
    1. Israel—Foreign relations—Egypt—Psychological aspects.
2. Egypt—Foreign relations—Israel—Psychological aspects.
I. Title.
DS119.8.E3C64   1990   89-45478
327.6205694—dc20   CIP

1 2 3 4 5   94 93 92 91 90

For Ronnie and his generation

CONTENTS

ACKNOWLEDGMENTS

This book was written with the assistance of a Ford Foundation grant administered by the Israel Foundations Trustees. I am grateful to Professor Robert F. Hunter of Tulane University and Professor Ann M. Lesch, Villanova University, for their helpful comments on the manuscript.

Culture and Conflict in Egyptian-Israeli Relations

I

CAIRO AND JERUSALEM
THE MYTH

Until President Sadat's journey to Jerusalem in November 1977, received truth has it, virtually the only contact or communication between Egypt and Israel was on the field of battle. When not engaged in full-scale war, border skirmishes, or undercover operations, the two sides glowered at each other across an impassable divide. Interest, ideology, and loyalty to the Palestinian cause conspired to ensure implacable Egyptian hostility to the Jewish state. Dedicated to the destruction of the usurper, it took thirty years of failed efforts for Egypt to realize Israel could not be vanquished. Israel, meanwhile, like a humble spinster, waited patiently for a partner. Once an Arab leader appeared, reconciled to the existence of Israel and willing to talk peace, a dialogue got under way which led rapidly to a settlement of the bilateral dispute. Following the March 1979 peace treaty and the opening of diplomatic relations, both sides lived happily ever after.

Actually, the historical reality of Egyptian-Israeli relations is rather different. Since the signing of the peace treaty, the inhibitions and vows of silence of diplomats and statesmen have given way to greater candor. A spate of fascinating material has begun to come to light. As archives in London, Washington, and Jerusalem are opened, as memoirs and diaries appear, as scraps of information are pieced together—in short, as the curtain is lifted—a totally different picture emerges. It becomes clear that, over the years, there were many contacts, direct and indirect, between the protagonists. Communication, far from being sparse, was, on the contrary, not infrequent. And what is even more thought-provoking is the accumulating evidence of overtures for peace—not just from Israel, but from the Egyptian side as well. The authorized version appears increasingly threadbare.

Between 1949 and 1956, we now know that there were secret meetings between representatives of the two sides in such places as Ankara, Brussels, Lausanne, London, Milan, New York, Paris, Rome, and Washington. The list is endless. Israelis and Egyptians dined together, talked at length, exchanged information—even, on one occasion, formed a partnership at canasta (they won, against a Swiss-Yugoslav pair). A number of mediation

1

efforts—including the remarkable Anglo-American "Alpha" project of 1955–56—were initiated by various parties, including the United States Central Intelligence Agency (CIA), the State Department, the British Foreign Office, the Quakers, and a large supporting cast of well-wishers. After the shock of the 1956 Suez War, Egyptian enthusiasm waned, although there was an important American initiative in 1963 (the McCloy mission) to defuse the Middle East arms race, and a curious Egyptian attempt to establish contact with Israel through the good offices of an American businessman in Portugal. With Egypt's catastrophic defeat in 1967 came the realization that there was no alternative to a peaceful settlement with Israel, and a spate of feelers and initiatives ensued. Nasser's acceptance, before his death, of the 1970 Rogers plan was a first step on the road to reconciliation. Sadat took the next step with his February 1971 initiative. Unfortunately, it took the 1973 Yom Kippur War to break up the logjam of prejudice and preconception and set in motion the series of interim agreements that were to lead up to the peace negotiations of 1977–79.

Ironically, Sadat's 1977 Jerusalem trip was not at all the prelude to a new era of unencumbered communication. Obviously, Israelis and Egyptians could now meet publicly, where once they had met surreptitiously, and could speak directly, where before they may have passed messages on through a third party. Yet it very quickly turned out that they were quite unable to get through to each other. There was conversation but there was no comprehension; not dialogue but a dialogue of the deaf. Within weeks they had almost entirely stopped talking to each other. The "peace process," as it was called by the Americans, then reverted from a two-sided negotiation to a three-sided mediation, with the United States acting the part of postman and marriage broker—a role it had played on and off since 1955.

Nor did the eventual signing of the peace treaty in March 1979, amidst pageant and fanfare, herald in a roseate dawn of sweetness and light. Serious bilateral contact soon petered out. The autonomy talks on the future of the West Bank spluttered and died. The Israeli ambassador in Cairo became a lone, rather pathetic figure. His Egyptian counterpart was withdrawn in protest from Tel Aviv—a diplomatic casualty of the 1982 Lebanon War. (A new ambassador was appointed in 1986.) Negotiations on Taba, a one-square-kilometer area of land on the Egyptian-Israeli border, whose ownership remained in dispute, dragged on interminably, embittering relations. Innumerable agreements to "normalize" relations, in the fields of trade, tourism, culture, scientific cooperation, and so on, had been concluded but remained dead letters. True, formal diplomatic ties persisted, but everyone knew that this was an Egyptian bow as much in the direction of Washington as of Jerusalem. Anyway, this was no sign or guarantee of an amicable and productive relationship; nothing more, indeed, than the bare bones of mutual sufferance like that existing, say, between the two superpowers during the chilliest period of the cold war. A new term, in fact, was added to the diplomatic lexicon: *cold peace*.

A nadir was reached in October 1985 when a "crazy" Egyptian guard opened fire without provocation on a party of Israeli tourists holidaying in the Sinai, killing seven people, including four children. Egypt's official reaction was self-righteous, its apology perfunctory at best. Tourism, never extensive despite the two countries' adjacency, plunged. During the following six months of 1986, only two thousand five hundred Egyptians visited their Israeli neighbors. Egyptian imports from Israel for 1985 stood at a mere $7.8 million. As for exports, under the terms of the 1979 treaty, the supply of Egyptian oil to Israel was guaranteed; non-oil exports came to a derisory $700,000.[1] Even the long-awaited resolution of the Taba dispute in 1989 came as an anticlimax, having little impact on these dismal trends. So communication in the wider sense of the movement of people, goods, and ideas remained rudimentary. Communication in the sense of the exchange of views resulting in greater understanding was as elusive as ever. Press comment in both countries was marked by suspicion and sometimes abuse. Cold peace might be better than no peace. But could things continue this way without Egypt slipping back into a hostile coalition against Israel?

How is one to account for this sorry pattern of missed opportunity, dislocation, and incomprehension, not to say of tragically unnecessary bloodshed? None of the theories put forward over the years provide a very satisfactory explanation for the puzzling and persistent inability of the parties to resolve their differences in a civilized manner. The classic, "realist" view of international disharmony, that it arises from an objective conflict of opposing interests, fails to explain the particular case of Egyptian-Israeli relations. Geography has separated the fertile, populous areas of the Nile Valley and the banks of the Jordan river by an immense, virtually uninhabited desert. Pointing this out in 1952, David Ben Gurion, Israel's founding father, went on to argue that there was no cause for political, economic, or territorial discord between the two neighbors. On the contrary, they could only benefit from mutual co-operation.[2]

Perhaps all the subsequent killing and destruction were unavoidable, the reader may object; a sort of prolonged course in the facts of international life necessary to demonstrate to Egypt that Israel was a permanent feature of the landscape. However, a wealth of diplomatic papers recently declassified in the Israel State Archives, the American National Archives, and the British Public Records Office shows this view to be untenable. Quite the reverse in fact. After the 1948 War, it was Israel that was feared as an irresistible, expansionist force by Egypt. As early as 1950, one senior Egyptian officer could describe Israeli power as "already immeasurably greater than that of all the Arab States put together." His conclusion, like that of other members of the elite, was that peace was unavoidable. During the last years of Farouk's reign, the air fairly buzzed with signals, open and covert, of a willingness in some Egyptian circles for a settlement with Israel. The Egyptian consul in Holland, Mohamed Ali Sadek, told his Israeli counterpart in October 1951 that there were "no essential conflicts of interest between Egypt and the State of Israel." Egypt was "interested in peace and quiet in the area." True, alongside these favorable auguries there were also more sober indications. Israel did have powerful enemies in the Egyptian establishment. Another Egyptian diplomat warned an Israeli colleague at the United Nations that as long as King Farouk persisted in his "stubborn hatred" for Israel, nobody in Egypt would dare speak out in favor of relations with Israel.[3]

However, the corollary of this was that after Farouk's departure, things might begin to get moving. Sure enough, in 1953 and 1954, after the Free Officers' coup, at least two letters were addressed by Colonel Nasser to Israeli Prime Minister Moshe Sharett. Sadly, it can now be seen that Israel's reprisal raids against Palestinian infiltration gravely damaged such promising developments. Massive retaliation, Israel's security strategy in the periods preceding both the 1956 and 1967 wars, neither brought peace any closer nor deterred Israel's enemies. It made war more, not less, likely. And if the 1982 invasion of the Lebanon is viewed as the last great reprisal raid, it could also be argued that that same policy seriously jeopardized the eventual peace.

If this was the case, critics of Israel will triumphantly exclaim, was it not Israel that had to do the learning—of the limits of power, not Israel that was the warmonger, eager to exploit the superiority of its "military machine"? Against this argument one can simply point out that, however irrational, Israel's perception of threat, its sense of impending disaster, was genuine, not feigned—a product of a military outlook derived more from the Warsaw ghetto uprising and the 1948 sieges of the kibbutzim of Yad Mordekhai and Degania than from the academies of Sandhurst and West Point. May 1967, the pivot of the conspiracy theorists' argument, is the story not of a cunning Israeli trap sprung for an unwary Nasser but of an Israeli failure of deterrence, a Nasser striding toward the precipice like a sleepwalker, an Israel, notwithstanding its paper advantage, overwhelmed by intimations of a new Holocaust. The wars of 1948, 1969–70 (the War of Attrition following the June War), and 1973 were, of course, initiated by Egypt. The 1956 Sinai campaign, a "war of choice" in Israeli parlance, was the outcome of a two-year spiral of tension along the Israeli-Egyptian border for which Cairo was not blameless, and an arms race that fueled and accompanied that escalation.

What, then, of the Palestinian issue—the wretched fate of the hundreds of thousands of Arab refugees displaced by the 1948 War? Did this not rule out of court any chance of accommodation? Shocking as it may seem, the evidence suggests that Egypt really only paid lip service to what, basically, was not its problem, although it was a rhetorical touchstone of Arab loyalty. At one of the secret meetings between Egyptian and Israeli officials at Lausanne in 1949, the Egyptian delegate candidly admitted his indifference:

"Last year thousands of people died of cholera in my country, and none of us cared. Why should we care about the refugees?" Egypt simply had "no interest in a Palestinian state," as another official put it. Nothing changed after King Farouk's deposal. In March 1955 Egyptian Foreign Minister Fawzi told the U.S. ambassador that his country was "realistic" on the refugee issue and realized quite clearly that "there was no question of the bulk of them returning to Israel." Egypt was prepared to accept the alternative of their resettlement on Arab territory with compensation for material losses. Nasser confirmed this, doubting that "the majority of refugees" would wish to become Israeli citizens anyway. He added to the CIA that Palestinians could be resettled with American assistance. In the end Sadat contented himself with even less: no provision whatsoever for repatriation or resettlement, and an ambiguous Israeli commitment to negotiate "autonomy"—whatever that meant—for the inhabitants of the West Bank.[4]

Another problem that appeared to weigh heavily at one time was the Egyptian demand for a land link between Egypt and Jordan. In this way the geographical continuity of the Arab world, disrupted by the establishment of Israel, might be restored. A genuine enough aspiration, it must be doubted whether this was the reef on which the ship of peace ran aground. If there were normal relations between Israel and the Arabs, there would be free transit across Israeli territory anyway. Had this been the critical obstacle in the way of a peace settlement, a way round would surely have been found. Israeli Foreign Minister Sharett had argued in an internal memorandum of 1952 that a compromise would have to be sought, while admitting that Israel liked the idea of territorial concessions in the Negev not one whit. "Were we to be faced with the choice of either peace with Egypt or the inviolability of the Eilat wedge, it would be difficult to maintain an absolutely negative position."[5] In the event, not even this was called for. At Camp David in 1978, the question was finally disposed of with the face-saving agreement to construct an extraterritorial highway between Egypt and Jordan at the very southernmost tip of the Negev in the vicinity of Eilat. Since then nothing more has been heard of the project, and the Egyptians rest content with a flourishing ferry service between the Sinai port of Nuweiba and Aqaba, Jordan's southern outlet to the sea, that bypasses Israel altogether.

A final argument heard at one time was that the ideology of Arab unity prevented Egypt from reconciling itself to the existence of the State of Israel. Israel was resented as a wedge in the heart of the Arab nation, its establishment seen as an indelible historical injustice—an intolerable affront which had to be expunged. No state aspiring to leadership of the Arab world could possibly accept it. The trouble with this case is that it hardly fits the evidence now available of extensive contact between the parties in the 1950s. The Egyptians were quite frank about it. If necessary, Fawzi informed the British ambassador in November 1955, Egypt would not shrink from being the "black sheep" of the Arab world; that is, take a lead which other Arab states would eventually follow.[6] After the Six Day War, Egypt actually stated its willingness in public, first implicitly, then explicitly, to recognize Israel. Virulent opposition by other Arab states was accepted philosophically. (Reference is made here to Egypt's acceptance of UN Resolution 242 and its more formal reply to UN mediator Gunnar Jarring of 15 February 1971.) Even in the early 1960s, when Nasser was at the height of his prestige, he displayed the utmost circumspection concerning Israel. Only the few, frenzied days preceding the 1967 War really provide any evidence to sustain the thesis. And, as I shall later demonstrate, this evidence is very far from conclusive.

Now that these various skittles have been knocked down, the question naturally arises as to what one is to put in their place. It is much easier and more reassuring for propagandists and apologists on both sides to anathematize their opponent, shifting all blame onto his shoulders and presenting their own champion as a paragon of virtue. If neither side was wicked or hell-bent on war, what are we left with? As I plodded through the material I was amazed by the rivals' ignorance of each other, the misperceptions and inadvertent distortions that marked their mutual appraisals—in a word, their self-centeredness. Hermann Eilts, United States ambassador to Egypt in 1973–79, greatly surprised me by his description not only of Egypt's feeling of centrality and superiority in the Arab world but also of its ignorance and misjudgment of other Arab states. How much more did this apply to Egypt's knowledge—or rather lack of it—of Israel. One of Israel's interlocutors in the 1950s, Mohamed Sarag el-Din (at the time inspector-general of the Egyptian Ministry of the Interior), admitted that one of the main obstacles to a peace settlement was his compatriots' "sense of the alien nature of this body that has intruded into the Middle East." Ismail Fahmy, former Egyptian foreign minister, has a bizarre passage in his memoirs in which he expresses his disgust and contempt that Begin had shown President Ceausescu a map of the Middle East with the place-names marked in Hebrew. What did he think, that Israeli-made maps are printed in Chinese?[7] The concomitant of this utter unfamiliarity was an Egyptian inability, blatant in 1967, to predict Israeli reactions. Israel was *terra incognita*, its citizens mysterious, demonic beings.

Israel, too, notwithstanding its legendary intelligence-gathering capacity, was basically ill informed about the human, qualitative attributes—rather than the technical and quantifiable facts—of its neighbors. This particularly struck Henry Kissinger in 1974 at the start of his "shuttle diplomacy" to separate the forces of the combatants in the recent war. Talking to Abba Eban, Israel's brilliant Arabic-speaking foreign minister, the American secretary of state realized that it was for him, a visitor from afar, to explain the "psychology" of the Arabs to his hosts. As far as the Israelis were concerned, Syria and Egypt might have been situated somewhere on the dark side of the moon. Years later, with Egypt and Israel linked by diplomatic ties and open borders, it was Eban's turn to shake his head at his compatriots' demonization of the Arabs, their failure to grasp Arab "ways of thought and reaction."[8]

Through war and peace, fruitless contact and stumbling negotiation, a clear pattern emerges. It is summed up by the subtitle of this book: between Israel and Egypt there was a dialogue of the deaf. Separating the two sides were not irreconcilable interests, megalomaniac ambitions, still less soaring ideals, but a cultural chasm. Each side imprisoned within the confines of its own habits, traditions, language, and, most important, assumptions about the way people think and behave, neither was able to make itself understood to the other or make sense of the other's equally futile attempts at communication. Like tourists caught on different sides of the Niagara Falls, Egyptians and Israelis could only mouth and gesticulate at each other across the roaring, spray-filled divide in grotesque and mutual incoherence.

Just why this cultural incompatibility was such a prominent factor in their relations and how it made itself felt are the subjects of this book. It is sufficient to say at this point that what finally convinced me I was on the right track was the testimony of the pilgrims themselves on the long and weary road of Egyptian-Israeli relations. While the various theories outlined above, with their emphasis on objective factors, tend to be put forward by outside observers, those who have actually trod the stony path are preoccupied with the practical, day-to-day, subjective barriers to diplomatic comprehension—what Harold Saunders calls "the other walls."

Moshe Dayan and Ezer Weizman, two old Israeli war-horses who became enthusiastic proponents of peace with Egypt and were key figures in the "peace process," both come up with the same telling image of incomprehension. Negotiating with Egypt, they write, was "a dialogue of the deaf." What the explanation for this might be is not ventured, though Ezer Weizman is on the way to an answer when he reiterates his conviction that Israelis are still stuck in the narrow confines of the ghetto. Drawing on his experience as United States ambassador in Tel Aviv during the "peace process," Samuel Lewis confirms that "Israelis couldn't get across the cultural divide." Hermann Eilts, his counterpart in Cairo, argues that it was the cultural gap between the two sides, not the shortcomings of either one of them in isolation, that hindered communication in the past and now threatens to undermine hard-won achievements.[9] Just as it takes two to tango, it takes two to tangle.

Were the symmetrical autism that one discerns in the Egyptian-Israeli case an unusual feature of human, let alone international, relations, one might hesitate to give it much overall emphasis. It might then be more convincingly viewed as a mere symptom or accompaniment of something else, perhaps the fact that the two countries were cut off from each other for so long. Now there is no doubt that an absence of relations did not help. On the other hand, the presence of relations has not helped much either. But there is no need to resort to this hypothesis. Recent research throughout the social sciences into the problem of *intercultural communication* or *cross-cultural relations*, as it is called, leaves little doubt that the Egypt-Israel case is not only not unique; it is, rather, typical of a broad class of phenomena. When individuals from disparate cultures come into contact, all too often the result is confusion and misunderstanding.

The Intercultural Approach to Human Affairs

Very briefly, the contention of this approach is that interaction and communication between people of different ethnic backgrounds raises the problem of cross-cultural misunderstanding. Some of the confusions arising from cross-cultural differences can be avoided by acquiring experience of the customs, mannerisms, and etiquette of the unfamiliar culture. However, the most significant incompatibilities work at a more profound level and are less easily surmounted.

Different cultures, we learn from the anthropologist, may perceive the world and man's place in the order of things in utterly incommensurate ways. Fundamental concepts such as space and time are grasped differently. Values and therefore goals may clash. Tools of communication, both linguistic and nonverbal, vary widely. Furthermore, members of contrasting cultures are conditioned to behave differently in the whole possible range of human interactions, from meeting and parting to bargaining and resolving conflict. Culture—that inbuilt system of thought, perception, belief, and expectation of right conduct shared by a community—is taken in by the individual with his mother's milk and during the long years of childhood. *Socialization*, an ugly but apt word, well describes that extended process of learning, formal and informal, by which a society slips the mantle of its way of life over its members. Culture permeates our behavior and relationships without our necessarily being aware of it. Indeed, the profounder an influence, the more likely it is to be taken for granted. In contacts across cultures, therefore, obstacles can arise to harmonious relations and unfettered understanding because of the working of incompatible assumptions which participants are oblivious to and quite unable to overcome.

Now international relations are, in many cases, a form of intercultural relations. Until recently this did not matter very much. For one thing, cultural differences were not very great within the European states system that dominated international life for so long. Members of this community belonged to a single, distinct civilization, and their habits and beliefs, as a result, were largely consistent. For another, the political elites in charge of foreign policy had more in common with each other than with the masses of their compatriots. They tended to speak a common language, whether Latin or French, enjoyed the same kind of education, had similar tastes, and were well acquainted with each other's countries. Finally, centuries of political contact had produced something like a common code of international practice reflected in law and protocol. In short, even when national cultures were incongruent, they developed, over long histories of contact, suitable mechanisms of accommodation.

With the break-up of the great colonial empires, an international system has emerged that is truly multicultural; a colorful mosaic of contrasting languages, religions, and ways of life. Relative conformity has given way to immense diversity. The external effects of this revolutionary broadening of international relations are apparent at every turn. International organizations which started out as forums for the traditional "charmed circle" are now dominated by Third World nations proud of their special identities. Few opportunities are lost, indeed, to emphasize this distinctiveness. The international agenda has also altered in consequence. Alongside the familiar questions of the balance of power and international trade, new issues have arisen. There are calls for a new international economic order, entailing a more equitable redistribution of the world's resources, and for a new information order not controlled by Western interests. Global campaigns—most notably associated with the name of Bob Geldof—are launched to draw attention to the problems of world hunger and welfare; the art and thought of non-European civilizations command growing respect and attention in bodies such as UNESCO.

At a bilateral level, the range of international relationships has proliferated. A successful foreign policy must deal with a vast array of nations that are profoundly unfamiliar in their conduct and concerns. More than ever, the diplomats and officials who administer that policy must act as "cultural interpreters," displaying tact and understanding in the face of local customs and sensibilities. Extraordinary virtuosity is required of government ministers traveling with bewildering frequency in an age of "Concorde diplomacy" from one capital to the next.

It is within this context that the Egyptian-Israeli relationship must be viewed—and that is what gives the case its wider, contemporary significance. France and England had a thousand years of contiguous statehood to evolve a common language of diplomacy. Egypt and Israel have had only a few decades of independence. Moreover, the Jews who established the State of Israel and formed its political elite were largely cultural strangers to the Middle East, rarely even speaking Arabic. In many respects the Egyptian-Israeli conflict is a paradigm of a relationship that became hopelessly entangled in the snares of cross-cultural dissonance.

Egyptian and Israeli elites, I hope to demonstrate, have never been able to draw upon a common fund of assumptions about the nature of language, society, politics, violence, and negotiation. Hence the sort of instruments of conflict resolution available to Europeans or Arabs have simply not been available to them. Self-evidently, cultural congruence or diplomatic expertise cannot guarantee international harmony. Otherwise war would hardly be as common as it has been between European states or within the Arab world. Given the anarchic nature of the international system—the absence of any central authority and the resort to self-help—conflicting ambitions and ideologies and competition for territory or scarce resources will always make armed conflict a possibility. But whereas other states in dispute have built upon shared interests and resolved redundant disagreements, Egypt and Israel were long unable to do so.

At the heart of the Egyptian-Israeli conflict is a recurrent pattern of misunderstanding and failed communication. Taken in isolation, neither side is inherently "aggressive." No visitor to Egypt can fail to be deeply impressed by that people's basic tolerance. Nor can the traveler who continues on across the Sinai to Israel miss that tortured people's yearning for peace. The conflict was not a product of deliberate malice. Incomprehension, rather, was the result of a tragic incongruence that arose when two cultures, alien to each other, came into contact.

To facilitate the task of "cultural interpretation," foreign services have sometimes called upon the skills of the professional anthropologist. Indeed the emergence of the study of intercultural communication as a field in its own right owed something to the confrontation between the practical problems of diplomacy and the insight of the student of culture. Edward T. Hall, who was involved for years in the selection and training of Americans for work abroad in both government and business, understood that the interaction between separate cultures raised quite special problems of comprehension. It was not sufficient simply to try and understand the working of the target culture in isolation; one had to unravel the confusions that arose between that particular culture and some defined other culture. The peculiarities of the Japanese-American relationship need bear no resemblance to those presented by Sino-Soviet ties. Recently Glen Fisher, a former foreign service officer, has explored the impact of cultural "mindsets" on international relations.[10]

The term *intercultural communication* brings to mind the minor misunderstandings and embarrassments that greet the traveler to exotic parts. What kind of gift would be appropriate? Would it be insulting to the host were one to decline the sheep's eyeballs? What clothing should or should not be worn to visit the shrine? In fact, differences of custom, diet, and costume are relatively easily learned and overcome. But these are simply the external features distinguishing one way of life from another. The real difficulties occur at a more profound level—when unconscious expectations, ingrained norms of conduct and conditioned patterns of behavior come into conflict. Something is wrong, both sides intuitively feel, without being able to identify exactly what. Cultural differences, in other words, are more than skin deep. Human "hardware" comes in a range of shades and shapes but can perform more or less the same tasks. It is the remarkable range of available human "software," the set of cultural assumptions and rules governing the programming of the system, that accounts for mankind's remarkable diversity and the incompatibilities to which it gives rise.

Many characterizations of culture have been suggested by anthropologists.

The classic definition was proposed by Edward Tylor in 1871. "Culture or civilization," he wrote, "is that complex whole which includes knowledge, belief, art, morals, law, custom, and any other capabilities and habits acquired by man as a member of society."[11] There are three key insights here: that each culture is a unique complex of attributes subsuming every area of social life; that it is a quality not of the individual as such, but of the society of which he is a part; and that it is acquired by the individual from that society.

Subsequent writers have added their own particular gloss to this basic idea. The school of thought associated with the names of Margaret Meade and Ruth Benedict would seek out and emphasize the unifying and distinctive themes of a culture. "A culture, like an individual," Ruth Benedict argued in her classic *Patterns of Culture*, "is a more or less consistent pattern of thought and action. Within each culture there come into being characteristic purposes not necessarily shared by other types of society. . . . Taken up by a well-integrated culture, the most ill-assorted acts become characteristic of its peculiar goals, often by the most unlikely metamorphoses. The form that these acts take we can understand only by understanding first the emotional and intellectual mainsprings of that society."[12] The undoubted dangers of this approach have frequently been pointed out: of its entailing the imposition by the anthropologist of an artificial consistency—*gestalt*—on the facts; of its inapplicability to anything other than rather static, simple, and self-contained communities, and so on. Nevertheless, the idea of culture as a set of organizing themes or motifs running through the way of life of a society in all its expressions is a suggestive one.

A third approach worth mentioning here is that of Clyde Kluckhohn. He argues that: "Culture consists in patterned ways of thinking, feeling and reaction, acquired and transmitted mainly by symbols, constituting the distinctive achievements of human groups, including their embodiments in artifacts; the essential core of culture consists of traditional (i.e., historically derived and selected) ideas and especially their attached values." Thus for Kluckhohn culture is a property of information or, as he puts it elsewhere, a "group's knowledge stored up (in memories of men; in books and objects) for future use."[13] This formulation points to the central role played by symbols in culture. If culture is seen as the underlying grammar of a society, a complex fabric of themes and motifs which give meaning to social life (to combine Tylor and Benedict), symbols—including conventions of behavior, rituals, stylized artifacts, and language—make up its observable facade. Of culture it can truly be said: "through its symbols you shall know it." From this perspective symbols act as a sort of cultural transmission belt, passing on traditional ideas and their attached values from one generation to the next.

Within a given society at a certain point in time, communication, then, rests upon the reference to and manipulation of a shared symbolic system. Without access to this resource, social life, in the sense of the harmonious coordination of the separate activities of countless individuals, each possessed of his or her own independent will, would hardly be conceivable. The whole wondrous spectacle of civilization is, indeed, synonymous with the symbols and signs which link together its members—past and present—in an infinitely intricate tapestry of common endeavor. Conversely, the problem of intercultural communication can be seen to derive from the fact that by definition different cultures make use of different systems of symbols.

It is in the realm of language that this diversity is most apparent; the signs and sounds of one group may be simply unintelligible to another. The deeper problem, though, is that incomprehensibility arises not simply from unfamiliarity with strange marks, articulations, and gestures but because of an incompatibility of underlying conceptions. Even when the dictionary meanings of the words are disclosed, the beliefs and practices they refer to may be alien. Patterns of behavior viewed by one culture as fitting or desirable are viewed by others as utterly deviant. The irreplaceable contribution of anthropology has been precisely to reveal to us the extraordinary variety of approaches generated by mankind in its confrontation with biologically universal problems such as death, nourishment, natural danger, health, family organization, housing, production, decoration, and so on, in an endless list of human needs. It is but a short step from this obvious premise to the realization that communication across cultures and their associated systems of symbols raises special problems of comprehension.

It is not only in the international arena that modern necessities have thrust like together with unlike. Immigration, travel, population mobility, ease of communications and transnational business have all combined to create a multicultural environment. We can no longer spend our lives secluded in the comfortable and exclusive company of our own kind. Multiculturalism is the new reality—a state of affairs in which, whether we like it or not, we are obliged to live alongside and accommodate the strange and possibly disturbing habits of the members of other cultures.

In recent years a number of general introductions to the study of intercultural communication have been published.[14] A more specialized literature has also begun to appear which addresses some of the practical problems of communication faced in intercultural contexts, whether by physicians, psychiatrists, teachers, social workers, or managers of multinational companies. Each of these areas presents peculiar professional challenges for those working across the cultural divide. What incentives and teaching methods work best with pupils of Hispanic, Chinese, or Caribbean origin, transplanted to Britain or the United States, when each group has its own particular concept of authority, "body language," approach to individuality, and the need for demonstrativeness in relationships? How are student exchanges between the United States and, say, India to be organized in the light of experience that such programs may promote resentment and even contempt rather than good will and greater understanding? How are business contacts in Indonesia to be handled by a Western company, given local sanction of bribery? What sort of negotiating techniques work best in Japan with its stress on face—and dislike of argument? How is a practitioner of Western medicine to understand complaints of "heart distress" from an Iranian patient?[15]

A number of writers have also begun to apply the intercultural approach to certain problems of comprehension in international relations. Without ignoring or minimizing objective sources of dissension in an imperfect world, this school of thought attempts to clarify the semantic confusion arising from cross-cultural dissonance. Its emphasis is on communication widely defined to include explicit and implicit, verbal and nonverbal exchanges of information. Sometimes the deeper, "philosophical" incompatibilities of a relationship are explored. So far various issues have been enlighteningly dealt with from this perspective, including international law, power, intelligence assessment, and negotiation. No single technique of analysis prevails, but most analysts seem to display a healthy skepticism of the tendency they perceive among both policy-makers and observers to impose their own culture-bound values and categories on other societies.[16]

The Scope and Limits of the Intercultural Approach

To what extent, though, is it valid to generalize about cultures and culture gaps in such sweeping terms? Do not objective convergencies of national interest invariably outweigh subjective divergencies? Can cultural congruence help to overcome a conflict of interests? Is the intercultural approach, in fact, not unashamedly reductionist—an attempt to explain everything in terms of a single cause? Answers to these questions are necessary to show just what the intercultural approach to international relations can and cannot explain.

It is certainly true that many societies, such as those of Britain, Canada, the United States, and even the USSR, are becoming increasingly multicultural. Now clearly some societies are more homogeneous than others. Observers of Japan and Egypt are in no doubt that thousands of years of autonomous development and political and geographical unity have produced self-sufficient "island" nations characterized by highly distinctive and cohesive outlooks on the world. At the other extreme, a state such as India is marked by great communal diversity. However, the point is not whether the society in question possesses a uniform culture in any absolute sense. This is a misleading way of looking at things because only groups that have been hermetically sealed off from surrounding influences could fall into this category. Nor does it matter. We are not interested in providing a blanket explanation of foreign policy behavior as such—indeed a reductionist and fruitless exercise. Culture is only one of a whole range of influences on a given state's political conduct. Our concern is to examine the effect of cultural differences on the success and failure of communication within particular bilateral relationships. Moreover, international relations rarely engage total populations anyway, but only governments and perhaps legislatures—a much narrower and usually more uniform section of society. At issue, in other words, is not the degree of cultural homogeneity within a single target society but the *relative gap* between separate national elites interacting and communicating with each other.

To the extent that the "culture gap" between the latter is significantly greater than the degree of their internal diversity, the possibility of cross-cultural incompatibility may arise. Whether this should indeed prove to be the case in any particular instance is a matter to be demonstrated or refuted by empirical investigation. Thus, while it is doubtful that cross-cultural differences have had much impact on Canadian-American ties, a number of studies have shown their clear effect on Japanese-American and Sino-American relations. Israeli-Egyptian relations fall strikingly into the latter category of relationships between incompatible cultures. Whatever the degree of internal diversity of Israeli and Egyptian society—and, in fact, both can be seen to display rather consistent and characteristic cultural features—it is the gap between them that counts. And here the evidence leaves no room to doubt their mutual incongruity.

Another objection to be considered is that cultural differences between societies may hold for run-of-the-mill citizens but not apply to professional diplomats, individuals specially trained to communicate with foreign colleagues irrespective of their backgrounds. One might even argue that the diplomatic community in itself constitutes a sort of subculture whose members are more like each other than their own fellow countrymen. Addressing this problem, Glen Fisher, with years of experience in the foreign service, suggests three possible answers: First, he argues, it is simply not true that diplomats can sever themselves from the "mindsets" of their parent societies. No one can achieve complete impartiality. Nor would they last very long if they could. Second, he wisely observes that decision-makers are constrained by the general sense of what is sensible and acceptable. They cannot stray beyond "the public's tolerable limits of morality or national self-image." Finally, Fisher notes that foreign policy is of its essence a group activity, minimizing the impact of individual idiosyncrasy. Decisions are made, on the whole, by groups, ratified by groups, and implemented by groups. Foreign services, intelligence agencies, cabinets, legislatures, and embassies are all deeply engaged. Each reflects and is sustained by the presumptions, perceptions, conventions, and values of the surrounding culture. Cultural influences, in brief, are inescapable.[17]

We may add to Fisher's arguments a distinction between routine and controversial issues. A common-sense view would be that diplomatic expertise limits and mitigates the worst excesses of cross-cultural confusion. The more technical the issue at stake and the higher the relative salience in the interaction of diplomats as opposed to parliamentarians, political figures, or other "nonprofessionals," the less the effect of cross-cultural differences. Conversely, the more emotive, "political," and public the issue, the more likely are cross-cultural effects to be felt. In the particular case of Egypt and Israel, officials have rarely been left alone to deal with problems arising between the two countries in a spirit of dispassionate, professional objectivity. So far, at least, even trivial matters have drawn the attention, sooner or later, of the political and military echelons and have often been mercilessly exposed to the searchlight of public opinion. And even with the diplomats, the weight of evidence indicates, shared experience and expertise have usually been overshadowed by divergent habits and traditions.

Assuming, for the sake of argument, that there are nontrivial problems of cross-cultural communication between a pair of states, does this necessarily make any difference? It is unreasonable to suppose that cross-cultural differences are salient in all situations; the reverse is equally far-fetched. In what kind of circumstances, within what bounds, might cross-cultural differences be more or less significant?

One outer limit for the working of intercultural misunderstanding would surely be the mutual perception of overwhelming national interest. Where both sides equally perceive the absence of any alternative, it is only logical that they will make every effort within their power to overcome dissonance from whatever quarter. The Nazi-Soviet pact of 1939–41 and the later Anglo-American-Soviet alliance against Nazi Germany must fall into this category. The more one learns from diplomatic historians about the details of the functioning of these alliances, the more one is struck by the extent to which culture-bound factors did influence the Allies' understanding of one another (for example, Roosevelt's grasp of Soviet purposes). Nevertheless, for all that, the pacts continued in force just so long—and hardly a moment longer—as was inescapable. The moment they ceased to be vital, the old disagreements reasserted themselves.

At the other extreme, it is likely that where vital national interests come into conflict, no effort at cultural comprehension will make any difference. The gap is an objective and not a subjective one—a product of genuine and not merely apparent differences. On the contrary, it may well be that the rivals understand each other all too well. Anglo-German differences at the outbreak of the Second World War would fall into this category: Germany sought European hegemony; Britain opposed this. A further limiting case of *force majeure* might be a situation where the power discrepancy between two states is so great that the weaker has no choice but to comply with the will of the stronger.

But lying between these various outer limits, there is surely a wide belt of ground where interests are ambiguous or controversial and where whether accommodation is accomplished or missed depends on skillful diplomacy: the ability accurately to judge the other's course, communicate one's own interest, and arrive, after an exchange of views, at a mutually satisfactory adjustment. Here, in this stippled area of shades and nuances, success or failure rests on one's ability to overcome not only substantive obstacles but also subjective barriers to understanding, including cross-cultural incompatibility. When the basis for accommodation is neither self evident nor inescapable, inaccuracy or miscomprehension can conceal possible points of convergence. If this were not so, international relations would be utterly deterministic and diplomacy would not matter at all, propositions that fly in the face of the dedicated efforts of countless diplomats and statesmen. Yet another possibility is that cross-cultural obstacles may not ultimately prevent agreement, but may so delay and embitter the diplomatic process that subsequent progress is abandoned in exhaustion or disgust.

In the Arab-Israel dispute, one can discern precisely these three categories: two poles at which cross-cultural factors were hardly salient and a middle ground where they came into considerable play. At one pole was the convergence of Israeli and Hashemite (Transjordanian) interests in the division of Mandatory Palestine during the 1948 War. (In fact negotiations had been underway before the war for just this purpose, but were overtaken by events.) Neither side was strong enough to destroy the other. The existence of one state, indeed, buttressed the security of its neighbor. Most important, both stood to benefit from acquiring territory—at the expense of the Palestinians—that neither had previously been allocated in the November 1947 United Nations partition plan. As a consequence, King Abdullah got the West Bank of the Jordan; Israel, the Galilee and the Negev. Until 1967 this tacit understanding worked well. Although it broke down in the June War it was quickly replaced by another informal, though equally effective, accommodation. True, Israel was in physical occupation of the West Bank; however, the "open bridges" policy ensured considerable Jordanian influence over the local population and good manners in Israeli-Jordanian relations. All that was lacking was a formal settlement. And, as then Israeli Defense Minister Peres commented in 1976: "If we change the current situation for diplomatic haggling for another arrangement, we might lose what we already have in hand."[18] It is an open secret that trade in both directions across the Jordan river is many times that between Israel and Egypt, despite the 1979 peace treaty.

At the other end of the spectrum there has been the Israeli-Palestinian conflict over the land. As long as both sides laid exclusive claim to the same piece of real estate, it was impossible to arrive at an accommodation. Zionism was a truly revolutionary movement that entered the area from outside with the determination to change demographic and political realities by creating a Jewish state. Declining subservient status in their own homeland, the Arab inhabitants of Palestine determined to oppose this intrusion. Arab rejection of the November 1947 plan for the partition of Palestine into Jewish and Arab states did not arise from misunderstanding. Any compromise would entail their net loss. Jewish rejection after 1948 of a Palestinian state equally derived from a perception (whether right or wrong is irrelevant) of self-interest. What good, Israelis argued, would a state in Jenin, Nablus, and Hebron be for people formerly resident in Haifa, Jaffa, and Ramla? Would it not be irrepressibly irredentist? It was no failure of communication between Palestinians and Israelis that resulted in the near-hundred-year war for Palestine. On the contrary, both sides understood each other only too well—far better, probably, than well-meaning bystanders.

Israel's relationship with Egypt falls into the category neither of overwhelming shared interest nor of irreconcilable conflict. But for Egypt's occupation of the Gaza Strip, with its large Palestinian population, after 1948 the two countries might have continued in remote and blissful unawareness of each other. There was no need for them either to fight or to embrace. Their only claims were those of good-neighborliness. Here, as one might expect, cross-cultural factors have been salient—complicating, souring, and confusing.

A final question is how one is to detect the effect of cross-cultural factors rather than other, more familiar causes of misunderstanding. For this there is no substitute for careful observation and comparison—the uncovering of recurrent and consistent divergence between the intended and perceived meanings of the various types of communications, verbal and nonverbal, military and diplomatic, that passed between the protagonists. It is the appearance over time of a pattern of discrepancy, irrespective of the personality of individual participants or passing and incidental factors, that raises the possibility that some profound source of dissonance is at work. Where the error repeats itself, though the timing, circumstances, and the make-up of the two opposing leaderships change, it strongly suggests that the difficulty is an inherent property of the relationship.

Of course this is not yet conclusive proof that the gremlins of culture-blindness have been up to mischief. One still has to demonstrate that the gap in understanding was a result of discernible cultural incompatibilities. To do this requires the identification of salient cultural contrasts in Egyptian and Israeli societies. This requires the exercise of judgment and imagination—the skills of interpretation rather than enumeration—and any explanation must stand or fall by its plausibility alone. Events in the real world are not amenable to the kinds of controls and replications possible in the laboratory, and therefore one cannot achieve the level of proof attainable in the natural sciences.

Given these provisos, the intercultural approach, having proved itself elsewhere, can add a significant dimension to the better understanding of the Arab-Israeli dispute. This study may also prove suggestive for the investigation of other intractable international conflicts. The virtue of this particular line of inquiry is that it is nonobvious, casts fresh light on a familiar and important problem—that of miscommunication between states—and, in addition, may have some practical applications. Finally, it also addresses itself to the unfortunate tendency of observers of the international scene to parochialism—one sin the intercultural approach is not guilty of.[19] If anything, it leaves one with the uncomfortable suspicion that many of the assumptions and theories we take for granted—about negotiation and deterrence, for example—are simply the product of our own culture and hence inappropriate for understanding, let alone dealing with, other nations.

II

EGYPT AND ISRAEL
THE TWO CULTURES

To the outsider, Egypt and Israel seem to have more cultural features in common than in opposition. They are ancient "Semitic" peoples worshipping sister religions, Islam and Judaism. Their faiths share many common features: the one God reveals his word to his prophet as recounted in a sacred text—in the one case the Koran, in the other the five books of Moses. Both religions permeate every aspect of daily life, including diet, integrate the political and the religious, and envisage their full flowering in a form of theocracy. Exhaustive sacred legal codes, the Shari'a and the Torah, legislate on every aspect of life and society and are interpreted and applied by a scholarly elite which thereby acquires a role of spiritual and sometimes secular leadership. Both possess strongly messianic overtones. At the social level, the values of family and home are paramount.

For all these superficial points of similarity, a more searching analysis reveals a profound chasm between the two cultures. On the one hand there is Egypt: one of the world's oldest nation-states, a relatively homogeneous society, culturally self-sufficient, the swarming masses of its people deeply rooted in the life and work of the innumerable villages that cluster along the length of the Nile, its ethos subordinating the individual to the needs of the group. Many great empires have come and gone; the *fellah* has outlasted them all. On the other hand there is Israel: a nation made up of immigrants from many lands who, for centuries, maintained a distinct way of life as a more—and often less—tolerated urban minority among strangers, preoccupied by a sense of divine election and the prospect of return to the promised land, their ethos combining the encouragement of personal autonomy with a strong sense of community.

In many important respects, therefore, Egyptians and Israelis draw on contrasting traditions: of political and social organization, of occupation, of historical treatment at the hands of foreigners, of language. Even the two religions, though similar in content, perform opposing national functions. Whereas Judaism and Hebrew have perpetuated Jewish separateness and sense of nationhood, Islam and Arabic join Egypt first with the wider Arab nation and then with the vast community of the faithful, the *umma*. More-over, the crisis of modernity, that is, the discrediting and displacement of tra-ditional ways of life and thought by secular ideologies, has affected the two societies unevenly. Whereas it has influenced a certain layer of Egyptian soci-ety, without it there would have been no Zionist movement and therefore no Jewish state at all. Finally, reinforcing the cultural divide between Egypt and Israel are the totally different roles allotted by the two societies to the individual. Reflected in every facet of social life and human relationships, it is this factor, more than any other, that can be seen to encumber cross-cultural communication.

Egyptian Culture

The cradle of Egypt's collectivist culture is the village community. For over four thousand years of uninterrupted settlement, the vast majority of the Egyptian people have lived out their lives in the thousands of villages of the Nile Valley and Delta, eking out a livelihood from the brown silt. Today much has changed. Millions of Egyptians are still tied to the soil, but up to 40 per-cent of the population now lives in cities, and migration from countryside to town continues. Since the 1870s, society has undergone a transformation, with the emergence of working and middle classes. For many, modern educa-tion has eroded the traditional authority of elders and weakened the family. Egypt's political elite are often products of a Western education and are thor-oughly urbanized. That said, although the physical hold of the village may have weakened, Egyptian culture still retains the indelible mark of its origins. Sadat, like his successor Mubarak, was village born and bred; Nasser was one generation removed from the ancestral community. Thus there is no un-bridgeable cultural gap between ruler and ruled; both draw on a common fund of symbols and experiences. It is quite natural for Mubarak—as it was for Nasser and Sadat—having delivered a polished address on state policy, to slip into the *baladi* vernacular to make some down-to-earth comment or relate a popular anecdote.[1]

The culture of the village is prior to Islam and is shared by Egyptians of both Christian (Coptic) and Moslem persuasion. Indeed, Jacques Berque argues that the oldest of all rural traditions have been handed down through the Copts, those repositories of the language of ancient Egypt and the descendants of Egyptian Christians whose church long preceded in its antiquity the arrival of the prophet Mohamed and the Arab invasions. Berque describes the rich variety of local rituals and customs (some of which retained not only Christian but even pagan traces) preserved into at least the last third of the nineteenth century. Islam, with its "capacity for ac-cepting Nature," had no radical impact on a culture which "promoted the continuity of village life" and "fused successive and heterogeneous systems in a syncretic whole, where the group was both agent and beneficiary."[2]

The "law of assimilation" decrees that the many invaders throughout the course of history who have come out of the desert or from across the sea— whether Persians, Greeks, Romans, Arabs, or Turks—and settled along the Nile, have in time been completely absorbed into the indigenous population and its timeless culture. Not that conquest and occupation have left Egypt unscathed. From the bombardment of Alexandria in 1882 to the 4 February 1942 incident (when a Nahhas government was foisted on King Farouk by British tanks), the experience of British colonialism was painful and humiliating. It has left its scar. Many of the failings of Egyptian society and government are put down to the baneful effects of "colonial oppression." Egyptians have also been left with an acute sensitivity to any real or apparent encroachment on their sovereignty. Proud of the antiquity and grandeur of their civilization and its centrality in the Arab world, they regard Egypt as a great power by right and bitterly resent any insinuation of subordinate status.

The ineradicable natural heritage of the Egyptian people is a joint struggle for subsistence. Most of Egypt consists of desert with virtually negligible rainfall, inhabited by a few nomadic bedouin. Only along the banks of the River Nile is there sufficient watered, and therefore cultivable, land to sustain settled life in any numbers. Every year until the construction of the Aswan High Dam, the flooding of the Nile inundated the surrounding fields. The *fellah*, the peasant cultivator, then had a brief period in September and October, working together with his fellow villagers in an intensive collective endeavor, to channel and dam the life-giving waters, so that his crops might be irrigated. At harvest time as well the villagers would work together, moving in groups from one plot to another.[3] By himself the individual peasant was ineffectual; only within the solidarity of the group could his efforts make the soil productive.

This was the crucial ethic brought by President Sadat, for one, from the simple family dwelling in the village of Mit Abu el-Kom to the presidential palace in Cairo. After his death he was criticized for failing to distinguish between the open-handed, easy-going generosity of the village and the more rigorous ethic called for by affairs of state. But for Sadat the village was an ideal for the nation as a whole. At the beginning of his memoirs he looks back:

> The village had no more than 2 weeks every year as a "statutory" irrigation period, during which all land in the village had to be watered. It was obviously necessary to do it quickly and collectively. We worked together on one person's land for a whole day, then moved to another's, using any *tunbur* (Archimidean screw) that was available, regardless of who owned it. The main thing was to ensure that at the end of the "statutory" period all the land in the village was irrigated.
>
> That kind of collective work—with and for other men, with no profit or any kind of individual reward in prospect—made me feel that I belonged not

merely to my immediate family at home, or even to the big family of the village, but to something vaster and more significant: the land.[4]

Throughout his life the *fellah* is dependent on the group. Existence outside its nurturing and protective confines becomes inconceivable. First and foremost there is the family—not the nuclear family of father, mother, and children of Western culture, but an extended family of parents, unmarried children, married sons and their families, siblings, grandparents, aunts, uncles, and cousins. Sometimes dozens of people cluster together under the same roof or in adjacent houses. At a secondary level there is the clan, grouping together different families descended from a supposed common ancestor, and numbering hundreds of people. Within the village there may be several clans of this kind.

The villager's entire frame of reference is provided by the group. He is in continuous and intense interaction with his fellow kinsmen, working, socializing, engaged in family matters, and cooperating in a protective front against other clans. His interests are inextricably bound up with those of the group. Solidarity and conformity are inculcated from birth. "The compelling moral law," argues Hamed Ammar, is "that the individual, to be in line with the group, should express group sympathy; if the group is angry, he should be angry, if it is insulted, he must feel that he is insulted." From a historical perspective, conformity may also have been fostered by the need of militant Islam to impose unity on a recently conquered empire.[5]

Thus the development of personal initiative and autonomy, characteristic of child-rearing and education in the Western world, is neglected by Egyptian culture, as it is indeed throughout the Arab world. Arab writers, drawing presumably upon their own experience, are often critical of what they see as a suppression of the individual personality. Sania Hamady writes of a tradition of upbringing which declines to treat the child as "an independent human being with autonomous desires and aversions." Denied freedom of choice, children learn to do only what they are told. Self-reliance and personal initiative are not encouraged because they do not contribute to group needs. The Arab, Hamady comments bitterly, never attains "full individuation as a person" and always remains "a non-differentiated part of his family." Hisham Sharabi makes a similar indictment. He sees Arab children as discouraged by their upbringing from exercising independence of judgment. They are taught to accept unquestioningly the views of others. Yassin El-Sayed, a director of the Political and Strategic Studies Center in Cairo, sees the "Egyptian mind" as characterized by conventional rather than creative thinking. At the same time, the agricultural way of life which fosters this trait is also, he argues, responsible for the gentleness, patience, and perseverance in the face of hardship which are also typical of the Egyptian.[6]

Given the facts of geography and nature found in the Middle East in general and Egypt in particular, the dominance of group values, transmitted and reinforced by the restrictive child-rearing practices described above, can be seen to be perfectly adaptive to the needs of the environment. An individualist ethic of the American kind, with its emphasis on personal enterprise, fits a pioneering society set on conquering the limitless spaces of a new continent. It is totally unsuited for the life of a people obliged to live out its existence cheek by jowl, for generation after generation, within the narrow and static bounds of the rural community. The necessities of village life have, therefore, created a culture in which the individual is bound to the group by indissoluble ties of rights and obligations ingrained from earliest childhood. "Complete mutual interdependence," in Hamady's phrase, is the rule. One must help one's kinsmen, not only with mundane tasks in the home and fields, but in time of deeper need, such as illness, debt, or strife with outsiders. Business is conducted, as much as possible, within the family circle. Plans cannot be made without extensive consultation, and advice will be rendered even when not requested. Emotional, let alone physical, privacy is a remote pretension. A call for assistance from a kinsman constitutes a compelling moral obligation. Failure to fulfil a family duty or perform an expected favor incurs severe disapproval and moral sanction. Above all, reciprocity reigns. "Come now and give me a hand; I will do the same thing for you one day." Engaged in a never-ending traffic of past favors received and future services to be rendered, caught up in a complex system of duties and obligations to the group, the individual merges into the collective like a knot in a fishing net.[7]

Like other collectivist cultures, Egyptian society is also preoccupied with questions of shame. "In the village, where we were brought up," President Sadat recalled, "we were taught something called shame."[8] Since the group is paramount, group opinion is inescapable and decisive. Here is a society, one must remember, where everyone knows everyone else. Whether approval for one's actions is bestowed or withheld is of perennial concern. Indeed, the weapon of shaming is one of the group's major instruments of social control. Loss of face, to be shamed before one's peers, is an excruciating penalty which one seeks to avoid at all costs. Once again child-rearing practices condition the individual from an early age to acute awareness of the norm. Punishment is administered in public and intensified by deliberate belittlement or ridicule. The humiliation is worse than the pain of the admonition itself. The effect of the punishment, one may conclude, is not simply to discourage misbehavior as such but to inculcate an abiding aversion to being disgraced in front of the group. In effect the child is taught that the penalty for wrongdoing is public disgrace rather than a sense of personal remorse. He is conditioned, therefore, to escape humiliation as much as sin. Since shame results from being found out and ridiculed, it can be avoided as well by concealment as by rectitude. Observers have concluded that in the shame cultures of the Middle East, prohibitions against forbidden behavior tend not to be internalized, that is, associated with feelings of guilt. If nobody is watching, one feels no particular compulsion to avoid the proscribed behavior.[9]

The corollary of shame is face or honor, that is, one's reputation in the eyes of others. A pivotal concept throughout the Arab world, honor embraces various forms and may be associated with personal dignity, hospitality, the fathering of sons, and the sexual virtue of one's women. Given the tendency of the individual within the collectivist culture to measure all behavior from the perspective of the group, one's self-appraisal is inseparable from one's public reputation. Face is valued as highly as any material benefit because it touches on one's fundamental sense of personal esteem. Raphael Patai points out that although the concept of face is certainly not unknown to the West, it has nothing like the scope and intensity attached to it in the Arab world. Pervasive at every level of society, from that of the individual, the family, and the clan to the nation as a whole, face is a "powerful consideration in weighing one's acts and words."[10]

The preservation of honor, whether of one's own person or of the group, is something like a categorical imperative—an overriding social obligation. To avoid humiliation, one will go to great lengths. Appearances are rated on a par with substance, and if face can be saved by preserving appearances, it is to this, rather than tackling the real problem, that one will direct one's efforts. The main thing, Hamed Ammar writes of the Egyptian village where he grew up, is for the family reputation to be "covered"—*mastourah*—to ensure public approval and escape public censure. Even if a field is not really properly cultivated, special attention must be given to its outer borders: "Make your harvest look big," runs the popular saying, "otherwise your enemies will rejoice."[11]

Diminution of a man's honor is known as "blackening his face" and is an intolerable deprivation, striking at his very dignity as a human being. If a man's face has been "blackened" he will be implacable in his search for revenge. It is no coincidence that shame cultures are also revenge cultures. In his classic study of the Egyptian peasant, first published in 1938, Father Henri Ayrout found that 80 percent of crimes were committed for revenge. Alongside the portrait of idyllic village harmony painted by President Sadat, Ayrout adds another complementary picture of hostility smoldering beneath the surface. Antagonism is liable to spring up over any triviality; a *fellah* takes offense at some real or supposed slight and "suddenly life counts for nothing":

> A neighbor takes some of his harvest, or a duck or chicken; someone tampers with his irrigation water or fails to keep his buffalo off his field; his son is bullied by another boy, or his wife insulted by the wife of another man; a friend delays too long in returning a few borrowed piastres, or looks too long at his wife; then this same fellah who is so patient under the injustice and exactions of his masters shows himself irascible indeed. The occurrence may be trifling, but at the moment it strikes him as intolerable and stings him to revenge. He reacts violently and infects the others with the same passion. Human life at such a time counts for little.[12]

Personal revenge has its counterpart at the collective level in the blood feud. The division of society into separate clans, found throughout the Arab world, invariably produces the vendetta as its concomitant. Mutual assistance between kinsmen requires the jealous protection of family honor against the encroachments of other groups. Ayrout gives an example, taken from the Cairo press, of a dispute which started over a chicken, drew in the relatives of the two protagonists, and resulted in a clash with 2 men dead and 37 wounded. Hani Fakhouri, in another study of Egyptian village life, cites the case of a single blood feud which started in 1951 and did not end until 1966. By this time 295 members of two clans had been killed. The logic of the blood feud is utterly remorseless. Honor must be requited.[13]

Here, then, is the central paradox of village existence: on the one hand, the imperatives of mutual help imposed by rural realities—the annual inundation of the Nile, the harvest, the unending struggle for sustenance; on the other hand, the vindictive obligations of the vendetta. Given the peculiar logic of the shame culture, however, there is no contradiction involved. Cooperation and antagonism are the poles between which group life, in all its intimate proximity and intensity, ceaselessly rotates. Loyalty to one's kin is paramount; impartiality is the one emotion not vouchsafed to the *fellah*. Anonymity, an approach to human relations based on purely economic or instrumental values, is quite impossible within the closely knit group. All relations are personal relations, and all duties are hallowed by the full weight of immemorial tradition.

In the face-to-face society, for such is the Egyptian village, the unmediated confrontation of human beings is all-important. Great perceptivity with regard to nuances of speech and outward appearance is acquired. Communication, both verbal and nonverbal, as we shall see in chapter 4, performs a socially emollient and not simply informational function—just as in any family, prolonged and close acquaintance accentuates people's ability to "read each other's thoughts" and lessens the need for explicit communication. At the same time the shame ethic encourages acute sensitivity to the slightest aspersion on one's honor, that of the family or its womenfolk. "Shame not others that thou shalt not be shamed," might well be the maxim. Murders have been committed because a man was observed winking at a girl from another clan. No gesture, facial expression, or nicety of tone is redundant. All are carefully noted and weighed. E. T. Hall has called the collectivist societies of the East *high context cultures*, drawing attention to their propensity to subtlety and allusiveness. As important as the explicit content of a message for individuals from these backgrounds, he argues, is the context in which it occurs, surrounding nonverbal cues and indirect nuances. Communication is pregnant with tacit references, and indirection is much preferred.[14]

Privacy, so important in the individualist culture, with its stress on personal rights and individual autonomy, is neither appreciated nor feasible in the familial proximity of the collectivist culture. But not only one's living space and business affairs are the property of the group. The same right of intrusion applies equally to one's "private" feelings. The result is that the collectivist individual is always on show, never free from the attention of his audience. Hence the further paradox of life in the face-to-face community of the Egyptian village: a seeming lack of inhibition in the display of emotion together with careful control over one's true feelings. The two apparently contradictory tendencies derive from the same premises: that the villager's performance is acutely self-conscious, played out for its effect on the audience and not to gratify any personal whim. With no escape from the group, "sincerity" is one luxury not to be afforded. Where the situation demands it, the display of emotion—grief, joy, anger, pleasure—is not merely sanctioned, it is required. It is not sufficient to be privately moved; others must observe one conforming to those feelings that are seemly in the eyes of society. Failure to conform will be understood as an intended and unpardonable offense against convention.

Equally, the spontaneous expression of true feelings outside their socially sanctioned context is tightly regulated. Egyptians possess a very strong sense of propriety—a point that cannot be too highly emphasized. Within the family circle, reserve, not effusiveness, is the rule. A man and wife will not openly display affection in public. A guest must always be received with a smiling face, whatever one's mood, because any sign of unease will be taken personally by the visitor. To spare others' feelings, to avoid embarrassment at all costs, requires the rigorous censorship of gratuitous emotion. When nothing is redundant, an unguarded gesture is liable to be seized upon to the individual's detriment or may offend and thereby arouse shame. In either case an unintended solecism will exact a high price. In a society balanced on a knife edge between group harmony and suppressed violence, dissimulation is not a moral failing but a social imperative.

In order to avoid the pitfalls of spontaneity and preserve the tranquillity of communal life, Egyptian culture, in common with other Arab cultures, has developed an exquisite code of good manners. From infancy children are trained in the social graces. Almost always in the company of others, they quickly learn the virtues of sociability. Courtesy, amiability, charm—the gift of mixing with others, of reducing tension in social encounters, of setting people at their ease—become second nature. The art of accommodation covers both positive and negative qualities. On the positive side, one must learn to please and elicit approval. Politeness is next to godliness. Nor is flattery to be eschewed. Social distinctions based upon age, rank, or family position and other requirements of etiquette are strictly observed. On the negative side, every effort is made to avoid offense, even at the cost of concealment and what seems to the outsider to be bad faith. Within the shame culture it is the failure to smooth over unpleasantness or the betrayal of one's inner feelings and motives that is branded as hypocrisy. Rudeness, not "insincerity," is condemned. There is no conceivable virtue in bad manners. To protect everyone's feelings, differences must on no account be openly expressed; direct confrontation is to be evaded. Bluntness and undignified behavior are anathema.[15]

Every social situation has its own set of conventions and etiquette, thereby reducing to the minimum the risks of uncertainty otherwise inherent in human encounters. Hospitality, of course, the reception of a visitor, is very finely regulated. Bargaining, as we shall see in chapter 7, is also strictly governed by an implicit code of conduct. Yet another situation of this kind, exemplifying the various themes and constraints outlined above, is the meeting of rival village factions to settle some point of contention. John Adams, in a study of the strains and stresses set off in an Egyptian village by the 1952 revolution with its call for far-reaching social reform, found that debate, which quite easily could have degenerated into violent conflict, was kept tightly under control. A strict code of good manners ensured that decorum was maintained. However much they might disagree, the speakers kept their voices at a moderate pitch, maintained a friendly disposition, and avoided threatening gestures. At all times stereotyped expressions of esteem and concern were strictly adhered to, so that one could hardly tell who were friends and who were rivals. Adams assumes, like E. T. Hall, that subtleties of tone and context are sufficient to convey culturally defined meanings.[16]

The paradigm of authority in Egyptian society is the relationship of father and children. Within the family, the father commands absolute authority: His wishes and comfort are paramount. The injunction "to obey one's father," to submit to his will and display filial piety, is unquestioned. To buttress paternal authority, another code of decorum is rigidly adhered to: the father keeps a dignified distance from his children and avoids the display of excessive intimacy; a son may not contradict his father and must conform to the outward signs of respect—not smoking in his presence or sitting while he is standing.[17]

Acceptance of hierarchy, combined with an instinctive deference to authority, first learned in the home, is echoed at every level of Egyptian life, from the extended family, via the clan, then the village, and on up to the highest echelon of government. To this day Egyptian leaders have taken the analogy of the father's position in the family as their ethic of government. Anwar Sadat suggested in 1971 that the Egyptian constitution should adopt village values as its guiding spirit: "We know that when the village head of the family is tough, we all respect that family."[18] On the other side of the coin, government officials and ministers tend to be reluctant to intrude on the exclusive responsibility of the *Rais* (leader) and to shy away from open disagreement with his views. Former Foreign Minister Mohamed Ibrahim Kamel's description of the relations between Sadat and his senior advisers is highly reminiscent of the distant and respectful relationship between the Egyptian father and his sons. Most officials would either express their feigned support or keep silent. Kamel does not conceal his belief that this was hardly the best basis on which to conduct official business.[19]

The gap between governor and governed should not be taken to imply that Egypt is or was a class society in any strict sense. It never possessed a hereditary landed aristocracy, although throughout history conquerors consolidated their rule by allocating land to their followers. On the contrary, the village is traditionally a strongly egalitarian society, where the effective divisions are not between rich and poor but between different clans. A sense of equality is reinforced by the injunction of the Koran to brotherhood among Moslems.[20]

Islam has also served to buttress respect for authority in society. Its beliefs, in Von Grunebaum's phrase, are "permeated by a sense of the autocracy of the Lord," of the juxtaposition of divine supremacy and human weakness, so that submission to God is the very foundation of the faith. "O true believer," the Koran ordains, "obey God, and obey the Prophet and those who are in authority among you." The absoluteness of the ruler's executive power over his subjects was never challenged in Moslem society.[21] At the same time Egyptian historians have suggested that the appearance of a dominating, central government is inherent in the logic of what they call a "hydraulic society"— a society which depends for its sustenance and survival on an efficiently maintained and regulated irrigation system. As Ahmed Gomaa puts it: "The Nile and the central authority were, in fact, two faces of the same coin."[22]

Not surprisingly, given these various complementary influences, deference to authority has become deeply ingrained in Egyptian culture. Psychological tests have shown that Egyptians score significantly higher in tests of obedience and unquestioning respect for authority than do Americans. Moreover, such results are not associated with the sort of deviant "authoritarian" personality traits usually found with Western subjects, strongly suggesting that they are culturally normal in an Egyptian context.[23]

Israeli Culture

A strict point-by-point comparison between Egyptian and Israeli cultures is not feasible because their structures are not symmetrical; analogous components are found to perform quite different functions. Given the extraordinary continuity of human settlement in Egypt, it is safe to assume that Egyptian culture, rooted in village life, long predates in its essential aspects the arrival of Islam. In the case of modern Israel, a nation of immigrants brought together from a 1,900-year-long dispersion, a shared religious tradition and a common fate, rather than local custom linked to uninterrupted settlement, are at the root of Jewish national continuity. Onto this ancient stock were grafted two additional, modern elements: the ideology of Zionism and the national trauma of the Nazi exterminations. Nothing remotely resembling these latter experiences has befallen the lot of the Egyptian.

Israel looks at first sight like a shapeless hybrid about which all generalization is impossible: a human improvisation patched together from amidst the debris of the shattered empires of the twentieth century with immigrants from as many countries as had Jewish communities. Nevertheless, it is meaningful to speak of an Israeli culture in the singular. Its mutability is that of a living organism evolving consistently with its own inner logic and in dynamic inter-action with its environment. There are few static cultures today; the question is whether a culture is able to survive in changing circumstances and remain true to traditional themes and values. Despite geographical dislocation, conti-nuity can be shown to have been maintained. Nor does the existence of a great variety of ethnic and sectarian subcultures vitiate the principle. Diver-sity remains at the level of folklore rather than of basic ethos. Israel's main communities, indeed, display remarkable points of similarity, and even their differences are being blunted by intermarriage and vigorous policies of inte-gration. Finally, for most of the history of the state it is possible to speak of the *political culture* of a dominant elite in relation to the conduct of govern-ment and foreign policy.

Israel's founding fathers, those pioneers who reached the shores of Pales-tine before and just after the First World War, were instrumental in the estab-lishment of the state, and provided its leadership until very recently, were steeped in a common heritage—the culture of the Yiddish-speaking Jewish community of Eastern Europe known as the *shtetl*.[24] Their influence on the development of the institutions and practices of Israel in all areas was deci-sive. Even though they sought to shake off the dust of the despised diaspora, they could hardly transcend unconscious habits of thought and behavior con-ditioned by millennia. Moreover, the culture they shaped has acted as a tem-plate, a mold for later arrivals. For example, neither the electoral system nor the range of parties in Israel today, with a population of over 3,500,000 Jews, is substantially different from that of April 1920, when the first elections to the assembly of delegates of the 55,000-strong *Yishuv*—the Jewish commu-nity in Palestine—were held.[25]

Another reason it is possible to speak of a single Israeli culture is that both circumstances and deliberate policy have exerted considerable pressure on minority groups to conform to prevailing patterns. Powerful mechanisms of socialization were established to "absorb"—the prevailing term—new immi-grants. The first of these was an educational system which sought to inculcate Zionist values into every age group, from kindergarten to high school. For adults the *ulpan* network of language centers achieved remarkable success both in teaching modern Hebrew and in introducing newcomers to the norms of their new home. An entire system of symbols, institutions, and festivals was created or borrowed from traditional sources to act as focuses of national pride and loyalty. Among these, religious holidays, the commemoration of the Holocaust, and the presidency figure prominently.[26] The Israel Defense Forces have also acted as a melting pot. Compulsory military service for both men and women has performed a major integrative role for newcomers and Israeli-born. A strong emphasis is placed by the armed forces on education for citizenship. Reserve duty until the age of fifty-five maintains the link between the armed forces and the citizen throughout the latter's working life. In peacetime, military parades, commemorations, swearing-in and graduation ceremonies, open days and incessant media coverage expose the public to this most powerful of all symbols of sovereignty.

But most important in the consolidation of Israeli society has been the history of the state. In the forty-odd years since independence, Israeli citizens have shared more collective experiences and challenges, some traumatic, others triumphant, than other states face in generations. As a small country, in which any event of note will impinge directly on either one's own life or that of someone of one's acquaintance, every war, border incident, or reprisal raid has strengthened that sense of joint purpose and destiny which underpins any viable national community. Research confirms that although the political affiliation of Israeli voters is affected by country of origin, the values and attitudes of young people are not strongly associated with their ethnic backgrounds. It has also been found that while more Ashkenazi (East European) than Oriental students identified with the Jews who suffered in the Holocaust, the difference was small enough to warrant the conclusion that the Holocaust has indeed become a national rather than sectoral memory.[27]

If the village is the seedbed of Egyptian culture, that of Israeli culture is the small, often urban Jewish community of the diaspora. For much of the history of the dispersion, Jews lived in self-contained communities set apart from the wider society. Within these communities—and this is as equally true of the Oriental as of the European branches of Jewry—Jews possessed a substantial measure of autonomy. They spoke their own languages, usually an amalgam of the local tongue and Hebrew, worshipped according to the Jewish rite—which is remarkably unvarying throughout the world—and were free to organize their lives as they saw fit. External forces and a strong sense of uniqueness helped to maintain their separate identity. Obviously they were influenced by their surroundings: Jews living in Christian Eastern Europe with its strong traditions of anti-Semitism developed more introspective and defensive habits than Jews living among Moslems and enjoying a recognized and protected legal status.

The focus of communal life everwhere and the historically common denominator of all Jews was Rabbinical Judaism as expounded in the Mishnah and Talmud. There were no separate churches among Jews, only shades of custom. The major sources and commentators were honored irrespective of geographic or ethnic origin. At the root of all belief was the ancient faith of Israel and Judea. Following the catastrophic failure of the Judean Revolts of A.D. 70 and 132–35. against Imperial Rome, and the subsequent exile of a large proportion of the Jewish population, the rabbis found themselves faced with a crisis of epic proportions. The traditional way of life, centered upon the authority of the priesthood and the temple service, had been utterly disrupted by the fall of Jerusalem. Without the temple, the seat of the cult, the calendar could not be determined, sacrifice was prohibited—and so neither could guilt be exculpated nor ritual impurity be purged—and the duties of pilgrimage remained unfulfilled. What could be saved from the ruins?

The answer lay in the painstaking evolution of a substitute way of life. Generations of scholars replaced the ancient rites by an elaborate system of study, prayer, practice, and ritual. A fence was erected around the Torah, the primary law code. No sector of life was to be left outside the scope of religious injunction. Instead of priestly authority came the independent judgment of the individual rabbi. The synagogue replaced the temple. The ritual study of written texts, particularly the Talmud, was transformed into a sort of vicarious experience of national life. Now the Talmud itself is largely a voluminous summation of discussions, debates, rulings, and even stories and anecdotes on every imaginable area of social and religious conduct which was redacted between the third and sixth centuries A.D. Much of it is not relevant in any strictly utilitarian sense—which is precisely the point. Minute analysis of the service of a destroyed temple or of agricultural practices in a lost homeland could provide a surrogate for the real thing.

Life in the diaspora centered on the self-sufficient Jewish community, a refuge in the midst of an alien environment. Within the community, the physical but also metaphysical chaos which had engulfed the Jewish people at the destruction of the Temple, when God had "hidden his face," could be kept at bay. Only among one's coreligionists, living an invariant way of life according to the precepts of the Torah, could certainty and consolation be obtained. To be a solitary Jew was a contradiction in terms. To live a traditional life, one was dependent on the services of the rabbi, the ritual slaughterer, the circumciser. The holiest prayers could be said only in a quorum of ten men. Without the synagogue, house of study, school, and ritual bath one could hardly educate one's children, celebrate the festivals, or maintain ritual family purity as enjoined by the Law. What was it all for? To ensure the preservation of the faithful until the coming of the Messiah and the restoration of the Jewish people to their rightful inheritance. For the day would surely come when God would once again reveal his face and the Temple would be rebuilt as in "days of old." Judaism—the way of life of the Jewish community—was not a peripheral collection of folk customs or part-time interests but a portable ecology, a sort of latter-day Noah's ark within which to maintain national survival until the waters of historical adversity receded.

For the individual, the collectivity was a *community of fate*—one's destiny was inseparable from that of the group. The concept of collective responsibility is fundamental to the Jewish view of history and runs like a scarlet thread through the biblical account of the triumphs and tribulations of ancient Israel. On the one hand, the covenant of the patriarchs gives the "children of Israel" a special place in divine affections. On the other hand, the whole people is to bear the penalty for misdemeanor. All misfortune, from the destructions of the Temple, via the Expulsion from Spain in 1492 and Chmelnicki massacres in the Ukraine in 1648–49, were seen to bear out this thesis. From this premise the Jews derived a strong sense of shared national destiny, great communal solidarity and intolerance of dissent, and a peculiar philosophy which saw in suffering not a denial of Israel's mission but its affirmation.

As long as Jews retained their confessional identity, there was no evading their historical fate. In the first place Jews, whether Ashkenazi or Oriental, had no separate political status within the wider society. Responsibility for their actions, in both a moral and a legal sense, was borne by the Jewish community. If a Jew offended in some way against a Gentile, all Jews were held culpable. When the community came under attack or was subject to some fresh imposition, there was no escape for the individual. For redress or protection it was futile to run to the host authorities. One took one's chances with everyone else; the only prospect of succor lay within the group. Survival was community business because the individual could not survive outside its protective bosom, while a threat to the individual Jew inevitably implicated the community as a whole. The lesson of shared responsibility—not only for one's local community but for Jews everywhere—was reinforced from one generation to another and has been amply confirmed by recent history. The Talmudic maxim "all of Israel stand surety for one another" is as true today for the modern state of Israel as it was during the centuries of dispersion.[28]

The solidarity of the Jewish community was quite unlike that of the Egyptian village. For one thing, the *shtetl* or whatever was not a unit of production but a confessional fraternity. For their livelihood, Jews looked to their own resources. It was not economic necessity that bound Jews together but shared faith, religious duties that could be performed only as a group, and dreams of national—not personal—redemption. For another thing, the Jewish community was not divided along clan lines. Jews were not, therefore, pitted against each other in the defense of tribal interests and honor—that source of so much discord in the Arab world—but were united as a minority against an alien and often hostile majority. Between the nuclear family of parents, possibly grandparents, and children, there was no intervening focus of loyalty to distract the attention of Jews from their communal identity.[29]

The status of the individual Jew within the community was and is also quite different from that of the *fellah*. Most of the collectivist Oriental cultures, that of Egypt included, achieve group cohesion only at the expense of individual rights. The distinguishing feature of the Jewish ethos is the combination of a fierce communal affiliation with deep respect for the uniqueness of the individual and the promotion of his personal autonomy. This motif is reflected throughout the culture. Rabbi Hillel said: "If I am not for myself, who will be for me?" But he also said: "Do not separate yourself from the community."

The requirement of scriptural and Talmudic study has had a decisive impact on the character of Jewish culture in general and the status of the individual in particular. First and foremost it elevated literacy to the level of religious obligation. The initiation ceremony for the male Jew when he enters manhood—*bar mitzvah*—entails the public reading of a biblical text. Where illiteracy severely restricts the geographical, historical, and intellectual horizons of a culture, literacy enables the development of a chronological and therefore causal perspective, provides access to a world far beyond the individual's everyday experience, and permits acquisition of the tools of logic and science. It is also a great equalizer. When all can read, no one can lay claim to special privileges—a lesson confirmed in European culture by the Reformation. From the point of view of their national identity, literacy strengthened the Jews' sense of their special place in history and, of vital importance to national solidarity and religious uniformity, facilitated communication between far-flung diaspora communities. The medieval archive (*Geniza*) of the Great Synagogue in Cairo, discovered at the end of the nineteenth century, gives striking evidence of correspondence between Jewish communities from one end of the Mediterranean to the other. Within the fraternity, the archive shows, absolute trust was expected and given. Extensive trade and financial transactions based upon credit might be underpinned by nothing more substantial than a letter of recommendation sent by one Jew in Syria to a coreligionist in Egypt about a third Jew in Spain. Jewish communities became the intersections of far-flung commercial, scholarly, and social networks.

The style of Talmudic discourse—the principal focus of the Jewish intellectual tradition through the ages—was also formative. Although the overriding aim of the rabbis was to provide a single, authoritative exegesis of Jewish scripture and practice, Talmudic study itself is far from dogmatic, within the bounds, of course, of its basic philosophical premises. Variant opinions are meticulously cited. No institution or dynasty has a monopoly of authority, let alone truth. Innovative explanations are highly prized. Personal study and meditation, which literacy fosters anyway, are encouraged. Moreover, tradition enshrines the value of the individual. "To save a single soul out of Israel is to save an entire world."

Individualism is encouraged from an early age. Child-rearing is geared to fostering the infant's sense of personal esteem. Learning by rote soon gives way to individual problem-solving. Individual discrimination and responsibility—conscience, not shame—is the guide to moral conduct. Comparative research has produced some noteworthy findings. In a cross-national study, Israeli children from both town and kibbutz displayed a reaction to social pressure different from that of the children of all the other thirteen countries surveyed. In general, children conform to conventional moral standards in order to gain approval. Uniquely, Israeli children provided their most moral responses when neither parents nor friends were present. The authors interpreted the result as "reflecting the emphasis placed in Israeli society and socialization on the development of moral autonomy and independence of action on the part of children and youth." They also pointed out that the spirit of self-assertion in the face of pressure to conform is a well-known pattern of Israeli/Jewish behavior, known in Hebrew as *davka* (from the original Yiddish meaning "in spite of").[30] Another study comparing Arab and Jewish schoolchildren in Israel confirmed the distinctive tendency of Jewish society to emphasize at one and the same time both moral autonomy and the welfare of the group.[31]

To what extent has the Zionist movement altered traditional Jewish cultural traits? The short answer is, much less than it set out to. Zionism was a messianic movement that clothed the traditional, religious goal of a restoration of the Jewish people to their historic homeland in the garb of secular nationalism. Yet paradoxically it also saw itself as a reaction against traditional culture. Echoing, ironically, some of the arguments of the anti-Semites themselves, the Zionists claimed that generations of minority status had produced a nation of parasites, living on the fringes of society, unproductive, helpless, and impractical. Only in their own land could the Jews once again become productive and self-sufficient. But to transform the nature of the Jews, it was not sufficient simply to change the political and economic framework of their existence. They also had to abandon the habits of the ghetto—and this included religion, mentality, and occupation. What was needed, in brief, was a cultural revolution.

The most prominent prophet of this doctrine was A. D. Gordon. His aim was the creation of nothing less than a "new Jew." The way of national rebirth

> embraces every detail of our individual lives. Every one of us is required to refashion himself so that the Galut [Exilic] Jew within him becomes a truly emancipated Jew; so that the unnatural, defective, splintered person within him may be changed into a natural wholesome human being who is true to himself; so that his Galut life, which has been fashioned by alien and extraneous influences, hampering his natural growth and self-realization, may give way to one that allows him to develop freely, to his fullest stature in all dimensions.[32]

Gordon's views, which he did his best to put into practice in his personal life, turning to agricultural labor at the age of forty-seven, became a cultural blueprint for the *Yishuv*—the Jewish community in Palestine. They had a formative influence on the pioneers of the second and third waves of immigration—the founding fathers of the State of Israel—were incorporated into the ideology of the dominant Labor movement, and molded, via the schools and youth movements, the ideals of young people. David Ben Gurion, the first prime minister of Israel and a dominant figure, was himself deeply inspired by Gordon's ideas. He repeated the call for a transformation in "the personal lives of the members of the people. The very essence of Zionist thinking about the life of the Jewish people and on Hebrew history is basically revolutionary—it is a revolt against a tradition of many centuries."[33]

At a practical level, the Zionist movement was dramatically successful in establishing all the components of an autonomous national community. It built factories, settled the soil, organized representative institutions, mobilized for self-defense, introduced the Hebrew language, developed a national theater and literature. The spiritual challenge, however, proved more problematic. Most of the changes were external, often merely negative. Religious ritual and the *halakha*—the code of behavior which governed the life of the traditional Jew from his "rising up to his lying down"—were rejected. Classical texts, such as the Talmud, fell out of favor. Conventional morality was abandoned. "European" forms of politeness and formal dress were forsaken as bourgeois affectation. Names were Hebraised. Frequently, tough Hebrew terms replaced lyrical European names. For instance, Rosenfeld [field of roses] became Peled [steel]. Attitudes of profound contempt toward the diaspora and the diaspora Jew became widespread. When new immigrants arrived in the country, they were encouraged to turn their backs on traditional beliefs and ways. Whatever was consciously associated with the despised past was cast off, as a hot-air balloon casts off ballast, the better to soar off into the future.

But it was one thing to know what one did not want; quite another to create something to replace it with. The Bible, which was pre-Exilic, was acceptable. Archaeology became something of a national pastime. Yael Dayan believed that it attracted her father, Moshe Dayan, because it created a bond with ancient roots: "Skipping the Ukraine, jumping over the shtetl mentality of his Zhashkov grandparents, not touching the Yiddish-speaking Diaspora, flying over generations of devastated communities, bypassing Inquisitions and exiles."[34] A cult of simplicity was affected, requiring plain working clothes and a spartan way of life. Much promoted by Ben Gurion, it hardly outlasted his departure from office in 1963. More permanent was the cultivation of a gruff, straightforward style of speech and manner, which has become something of a national trademark. Today educated Israelis, able to view European civilization in a more objective light, tend to bemoan the discourtesy and untidiness rampant in Israeli life.[35] In his later life Ben Gurion came to much the same conclusion: "In our country, even personal manners are deficient. Many of our inhabitants, including Israeli youth, have not learned how to respect their fellow-citizens and treat them with politeness, tolerance and sympathy. Elementary decency is lacking among us, that decency which makes public life pleasant and creates a climate of comradeship and mutual affection."[36]

The informality of Israeli society, at the best a bluntness of expression combined with a neglect of the external forms of courtesy, at the worst an unconcealed disrespect for tradition and a certain insensitivity toward others, stands in marked contrast to the attention to form and elaborate civility of Egyptian life. Is it possible to maintain one set of values at home and quite another in the conduct of one's diplomacy? In the next two chapters we shall examine the effect of this particular cultural gap on relations between Israel and Egypt over the years.

At a deeper level it is hard to detect a substantial change in patterns of Jewish behavior. The unwritten norms of politics in Israel—cooptation rather than election, an absence of ministerial accountability, a neglect of sound financial practices, a resigned acceptance of legal irregularity, the evasion of sound administrative procedures, the neglect of planning, decision-making outside formal frameworks—are more reminiscent of communal "fixing" than the government of a sovereign state. Only in one area has there been a profound transformation: the willingness to use force as a political instrument.

With the defeat of the Bar Kochba Revolt in A.D. 135, at a cost of hundreds of thousands of dead and the loss of national autonomy, the stateless Jews were obliged to accept a doctrine of submission to the powerful. Incorporated into religious thought, soft words were felt to be more effective than swords for turning away wrath. The rabbis discuss the conditions under which one must accept martyrdom but assume the hopelessness of physical resistance. Even the mainstream of the Zionist movement initially regarded force with deep suspicion, basing its prewar policy on the principle of *havlaga* (self-restraint). Following the 1948 War and the establishment of the Israel Defense Forces, more assertive attitudes began to take root. The virtues of military activism, which were contrasted with supposed Jewish passivity and supineness in the diaspora—and especially during the Holocaust—were much applauded. The soldier-hero became a paragon for youth. Israel's military prowess has unquestionably contributed greatly to Jewish self-esteem. Some might argue that elements of psychological compensation for past humiliations at Gentile hands have also been involved. Whether the novelty of possessing an army—a commonplace adjunct, after all, of state sovereignty—will wear off in time is an open question.[37]

Otherwise a "new Jew" has not been created. Shlomo Avineri, one of the main ideologists of the Israeli Labor party, concludes a study of Zionist thought with the warning that Jewish life in Israel is in danger of "coagulating into the traditional historical molds of Jewish social and economic behavior."[38] David Vital, the author of a history of Zionism, believes that this has already happened. The State of Israel, which was supposed to be a "symbol of rebirth and modernity," has replaced the traditional communities of Eastern Europe as "a new reservoir of conservative thinking, as narrow, in some ways, as the old."[39] As a cultural revolution, Zionism has turned out to be more superficial and short-lived than its proponents hoped. In fact, the elements of continuity between the diaspora experience and the Zionist experiment should always have been apparent. The ideology of Zionism, with its stress on the soil, labor, self-defense, communal life, and democratic government, certainly seems to owe more to the socialism of Marx, the utopianism of Tolstoy, and the nihilism of Pisarev than to Rashi and the Rambam (two of Judaism's greatest thinkers). As we have seen, the Zionist pioneers professed little interest in conventional religion or the Jewish classics. Yet despite their iconoclasm, most of them came from Orthodox homes and were personally steeped in the culture of the *shtetl*. Furthermore, it is impossible to adopt

Hebrew as one's native tongue without *ipso facto* acquiring an immense wealth of traditional resonances and associations. Hardly a sentence or expression in Hebrew fails to evoke the Bible or prayerbook. It was inevitable, therefore, that Zionism would be permeated with religious motifs and symbols.

At the heart of the movement was immigration, in Hebrew, *aliyah*, ascension, connoting a transition from a place of lesser to a place of greater holiness. There was to be an *ingathering of exiles*, a term which, with its various synonyms, recurs throughout the prayerbook in messianic contexts. (That the State of Israel has taken this injunction in deadly seriousness is illustrated by the fact that it has absorbed immigrants from every continent, continues to maintain immigration offices in most Jewish communities, and only recently flew in the black Jews of Ethiopia. This latter exploit was, in the words of Labor Prime Minister Shimon Peres, the accomplishment of "a sacred mission.")

The other pivot of the Zionist movement has been the single-minded, century-long campaign to "redeem" the land itself. Both separately and in conjunction, the concepts of land and redemption have potent biblical associations. "Land of Israel" and sanctity are virtually coterminous in the Bible, and the following verse might well serve as the motto of modern Zionism: "And ye shall take possession of the land, and dwell therein; for unto you have I given the land to possess it."[40] The word for redemption—*geula*—came to refer in a very characteristic way not only to the legal repossession of property by its rightful owner but also to spiritual salvation. The redemption of land is a key motif of the Book of Leviticus. The early pioneers did reject the idea of waiting passively for deliverance. What they did not question was the nature of that deliverance. To fulfil it they purchased land from the Arabs, reclaimed swamp and desert, built settlements, and worked the soil. From the 1880s to the present day, "the redemption of the land" has been a very practical program. But it has also been seen as another "sacred mission," the very fulfillment of Jewish redemption. In putting the land to productive use, the Jew saw himself as restoring its promised, biblical fertility, while rehabilitating his own productive character.[41]

The final formative influence on Israeli culture was the experience of persecution culminating in the catastrophe of the Nazi exterminations. The very founding memories of the race are of persecution and oppression. "Esau hates Jacob," the rabbis tell us, Esau symbolizing the Gentile, Jacob, or Israel, the eponymous father of the nation. The *haggadah*, the text read at the Passover feast, that most ancient of national celebrations, commemorating the exodus from Egypt, is a standing reminder that "in every generation they rise up to destroy us."[42] The motif of imminent disaster at the hands of a motiveless enemy recurs again and again, for instance, in the Book of Esther, which is read out at the festival of Purim. True, it is the Persian Jewish community that is threatened with extermination by the wicked Haman. But Jews everywhere, unwilling to abandon their separate identity and relegated to a permanent minority status, could identify with the legend. All, irrespective of their country of domicile or origin, had been faced at some time with persecution: the Sephardim had their Inquisition and *autos da fé*, the Ashkenazim their Chmelnicki massacres, the Yemenite Jews their seventeenth-century Mawza expulsion, and so on. The Zionist movement itself appeared against a background of Russian pogroms and disappointment at the apparent bankruptcy of nineteenth-century liberalism demonstrated by the Dreyfus case.

For all this the Nazi exterminations were still of a totally different order from anything that went before, since their ultimate objective was the extirpation of the entire people. To remind the reader, according to the testimony of SS Sturmbannfuehrer Dr. Wilhelm Hoettl given at the Nuremberg war crime trials: "Approximately four million Jews had been killed in the various extermination camps while an additional two million met death in other ways, the major part of which were shot by operational squads of the Security Police during the campaign against Russia."[43] This was out of a world Jewish population of about eighteen million.

Israel is what is known in the psychological literature as a *postdisaster community*. Communities which have undergone natural disasters—such as earthquakes, volcanic eruptions, and flooding—resulting in great suffering and loss of life, develop certain characteristic features. At first there are the defense mechanisms of denial, repression, and flight. Then comes the consuming fear of a repetition of the trauma, however unlikely this may be in objective terms. A great sense of solidarity is shared by the survivors. And there is the anger and hostility toward outsiders.[44]

Given the obvious differences between natural disaster and the deathcamps of Auschwitz and Treblinka, which were run, after all, by human beings and not impersonal forces, Israeli society has displayed analogous reactions. From 1948 to 1961, 463,000 Jews arrived in Israel from countries that had been occupied by the Nazis during the Second World War, about half the total immigration. They joined 650,000 Jews already resident in Israel in 1948, many of whom lost family in the Holocaust. Yet during these years the issue of the Holocaust was hardly dealt with at all by the educational system and tended to be repressed in daily life. Rather than treat the subject in an explicit way, the state preferred to commemorate it at a ritual level in the form of memorial and ceremony. Yet even then a national day of mourning was not introduced until 1959. The incongruous name chosen, the Day of Holocaust and Courage, reflected a sense of shame that Jews had gone "like sheep to the slaughter," as well as anguish. The annihilations were to be coupled together in the collective memory with ghetto revolts, especially the Warsaw ghetto uprising. Since the capture and trial of Adolf Eichmann in 1961, there has been a greater willingness, both collective and individual, to confront the concrete issues raised by the Holocaust.[45]

As for the emotional reaction to what happened, it is impossible to understand Israeli attitudes and conduct without taking the Holocaust into account. For many Israelis the Holocaust not only is an existential event but has become a symbol encapsulating the meaning of Jewish history and conditioning expectations of the future. Jewish-Gentile antagonism is reaffirmed as part of the natural order of things, thwarting early Zionist hopes that the State of Israel would free the Gentile of his anti-Semitism and the Jew of his persecution complex. Thus the condition of Israel as a beleaguered outpost, surrounded by enemies, is seen as a metaphor for the entire Jewish experience. The political fact of separateness is transformed into a positive virtue, and Balaam's biblical blessing of "a people that shall dwell alone and shall not be reckoned among the nations" is elevated into a universal value.[46]

The Holocaust has also become a prism through which ongoing events are filtered and perceptions organized. This has nothing to do with whether one actually went through the events in person. A number of studies have found that the Holocaust is deeply embedded in the consciousness of young people, irrespective of ethnic background. They see the world as "a hazardous place, where men are basically evil and dangerous" and view Arab intentions in a pessimistic light. A repetition of genocide, this time inflicted by the Arabs on Israel, is viewed as a real possibility.[47] Time does not erode these attitudes, and Israel remains a society living under the shadow of impending apocalypse.

The political implications of this angst are far-reaching. In times of crisis and tension, repressed memories and fears are liable to break through the thin veneer of self-confidence.[48] In May 1967, on the eve of the Six Day War, images of a new Holocaust were pervasive. Indeed, Israeli behavior is incomprehensible if this factor is ignored. In October 1973, as the Egyptian army established its bridgehead on the east bank of the Suez Canal, even Moshe Dayan, hero of three wars, was overwhelmed with deep despair and openly talked of the "destruction of the Third Temple" (i.e., the modern state of Israel).

Israeli leaders display an exceptionally low threshold of threat perception. The worst is always expected, and a tendency to hysteria on security issues is sometimes concealed with difficulty. What was the United States—which after months of careful exploration and preparation had become convinced in 1955 of the real possibility of a peaceful settlement of the Arab-Israel dispute—to make of Golda Meir's shrill dismissal of the sincerity of Egyptian intentions? Nasser, she insisted, "had declared war on international Jewry. His real aim was the destruction of Israel. . . ." When a senior American official reported to Ben Gurion his impression that Nasser was "definitely interested in a settlement," he was greeted with the Israeli prime minister's frank admission that "we are deadly afraid." To the implied criticism of Israel's policy of massive retaliation for cross-border infiltration, the envoy was greeted with an "almost hysterical" tirade. "Israel," he was told, "was already out-gunned, and out-manned, and if war started, nothing could prevent Tel Aviv and Haifa from being destroyed within half an hour."[49]

Recollections of the Holocaust imbue Israeli leaders with an oppressive sense of responsibility for the "surviving remnant" of their people—a grim awareness that there is simply no margin for error. Meir Rosenne, an ambassador to the United States and participant at Camp David, admitted that he had "always felt the greatness of the responsibility on my shoulders. When you come to speak in the name of the state of Israel, you also speak in the name of those who didn't manage to see the Jewish state and also those who will come after you." He also significantly added in the same interview: "I never dreamed at the age of ten, at a time of anti-Jewish pogroms in my home town of Yasi, Romania, that I was to be the Israeli ambassador to the United States."[50] Not surprisingly, the propensity of the Israeli leadership to take political risks or display negotiating flexibility is minimal.

Claude Lanzmann is also surely correct to link the Holocaust with the prominence of the army in the Israeli ethos. "The fact that Jews today have the capacity to exercise state violence must be connected to the fact that naked Jewish women waited defencelessly for their turn to enter the gas chamber."[51] Israel has demonstrably shown little willingness in its foreign and defense policy to turn the other cheek or refrain from the use of force. A high priority in the national scale of values is accorded to the defense of civilian lives, especially in border settlements, and the rescue of Jews in peril. "All is permissible," whether this entails a commando raid on Entebbe, the bombing of PLO headquarters in Beirut or Tunis, or the demolition of Iraq's Osirak nuclear reactor. Arguments to the principle of territorial sovereignty do not weigh particularly heavily.

All this is utterly remote from the Egyptian experience. Western statesmen, however impatient they may become with Israeli complexes, have at least some kind of historical knowledge of the Jewish experience. But what possible meaning could ghetto, concentration camp, and gas chamber have for a people living since time immemorial in serene tranquillity on the banks of the Nile? Matters have not been helped by the Israeli attitude that the world owes them a debt for past wrongs. As Arabs frequently point out, why should they suffer for the iniquities of the Nazis and their accomplices?

The picture that emerges from the juxtaposition of Egyptian and Israeli cultures is almost of two peoples inhabiting different planets. At no point do their assumptions about the individual, society, and the world seem to converge. Over the course of a history of contact, adjacent nations often evolve mechanisms, if not of coexistence then of mutual sufferance and conflict containment. But even this saving grace is denied Israel and Egypt, given the relatively recent date of modern Jewish resettlement in the region. There has simply been insufficient time for a "common language" to evolve between them. In the following chapters we shall trace in detail the problems that cultural incompatibility has posed across the board of their relations.

III

ARABIC VERSUS HEBREW

Does one's language influence the way one thinks? Can it shape and limit one's perception of the world? Yes, argued Sapir and Whorf, in a famous thesis. Language not only reports experience, it also defines experience.[1] No, retort most modern linguists. If a language lacks a word or concept, then it can be easily borrowed or invented as the need arises. Presumably they would also argue that language differences, for instance between Hebrew and Arabic, have a neutral effect on communication. Nothing that could be expressed in one language could not be reproduced, by a competent interpreter, in the other.

A different conclusion is reached by David Laitin. He set out to compare the behavior of Somali speakers of English in certain realistic situations in which they were required to use Somali and others in which English was called for. One of his observations was that in bargaining contexts a confrontational, angular style of give-and-take marked the English dialogues, in clear contrast to the diplomatic, tactful tone of the Somali language exchanges. Somali style was more allegorical and indirect and employed a questioning tone, suggesting an interest in finding a mutually acceptable solution to a given problem, not one in which one side gained an advantage. Laitin conjectures that the indirectness of Somali, its dislike of confrontation, is connected with the requirements of communal existence. Allegorical speech, for which the language is well known, permits testing the water without an explicit commitment that could entail loss of face. In small communities, he points out, "nasty encounters" have to be avoided, otherwise joint living would become very difficult.[2]

Laitin's argument is suggestive in two ways. First, the contrast between the relative abrasiveness of English and the emollience of Somali reflects a general distinction of language usage in individualist as opposed to collectivist cultures and can also be shown to hold for Hebrew in comparison to Arabic. Second, it suggests a satisfactory resolution of the debate over the validity of the Sapir-Whorfe hypothesis: namely, that it is not so much wrong to speak of language determining perception as it is misleading. A living language has no existence independent of culture. It is not the loom of culture but its data bank. As such, it serves the needs, past and present, of a given community.

As those needs change, language evolves to accommodate them. The Somali propensity for allegory may or may not influence the way its speakers think (how would one investigate this?). It certainly fulfills certain tendencies and requirements of the culture.

Language, then, is the collective memory, the archive, of a culture. On its spacious shelves are stored records of all the traditions, beliefs, assumptions, customs, habits, mannerisms, activities, and artifacts of a given linguistic community accumulated over the course of its history. Not all of them are in good condition. Some gather dust and fall into disuse. On the other hand, new entries are being made all of the time. Right of admission is usually acquired by birth, although sometimes lending rights can be obtained later in life. The archive is not the property of any single individual or group, but the shared heritage of a civilization, handed down from generation to generation. Indeed, it is one of the major means by which a society preserves and passes its culture on down through the ages. To the extent that a given culture looks at time, space, causality, marriage, and so on in a particular way, so will it be conveyed by its language.

From these initial premises it follows that one of the major areas in which the dissonance between incompatible cultures is likely to emerge is that of language. Where opposing cultures draw upon such contrasting assumptions as do Egypt and Israel, language cannot remain outside the contest. On the contrary, the attempt to transfer ideas from one milieu to another will be fraught with difficulty—not only because equivalent dictionary entries cannot always be found but also because, as we saw with Somali and English, language may be fulfilling different cultural functions in each case. If this should be so, far-reaching implications can be expected for the conduct of diplomacy: Foreign policy "signals" transmitted in the form of declarations or speeches made in one language or given on a domestic platform will necessarily be "encoded" in a form intelligible at home—but not necessarily abroad. Diplomatic exchanges may be equally fraught with misunderstanding, *even if a neutral third language is being used*. Few nonnative speakers are able to surmount completely the linguistic habits and assumptions of their mother tongue.

"High Context" versus "Low Context"

A useful way of looking at the problems of communication that arise between speakers of Arabic and Hebrew is suggested by E. T. Hall's distinction between *high* and *low context* cultures. In the former, "what is not said is sometimes more important than what is said." In the latter, "words represent truth and power."[3] Roughly speaking, high context cultures reflect a collectivist ethos, are sensitive to questions of "face" and shame, and value tradition highly. Low context cultures tend to be individualist, conscience-oriented, and "modern." Within each cultural system intelligible, coherent, and self-consistent conventions of language usage obtain. However, interactions across the boundaries of these two categories are particularly prone to confusion. Bearing in mind the simplifications and stark contrasts inherent in this model, it can be seen accurately to fit crucial aspects of Egyptian-Israeli relations.

As we have seen in chapter 2, Egypt clearly falls into the high context category. Within this kind of culture, speakers prefer to convey their ideas by implication rather than by explicit statement. Living in a face-to-face society and therefore able to draw on the kind of prior knowledge and shared experience not accessible to strangers, they can rely to a great extent on the intuition of their interlocutors. Information inherent in the setting and situation of a conversation and the relationship of the speakers can be taken as given. Shades of meaning can be hinted at indirectly or nonverbally. This does not mean that the high context culture is taciturn; words may be rejoiced in for their own sake. But important things touching on the lives of one's fellows are approached with the utmost caution and broached with even greater delicacy. Indeed, given the intense and enforced intimacy of the collectivist culture, discretion and allusiveness are more than a virtue—they are a necessity.

Language in the high context/collectivist culture cannot be thought of simply as a vehicle for transmitting "hard" facts. It is no less a *social instrument*, a device for promoting social ends. Conditioned to view themselves always through the eyes of the group, high context speakers know that everything will be scrutinized and taken personally. They learn to be acutely sensitive to the effect of their words. Every nuance must be weighed with care, for nothing will be missed. Within the group a hurtful remark will be taken to heart and never forgotten. Between the lines of a straightforward dialogue on a seemingly mundane issue, speaker and audience are busily insinuating information on those loaded matters of social standing, personal relationships, and emotional disposition which really concern them. Thus conversation tends to be made up, at one and the same time, of repetitive and loquacious flourishes—emollient expressions of esteem and courtesy—and a substantive element which is dense with meaning.

Directness and especially contradiction are much disliked. It is wrenchingly difficult in this kind of culture to deliver a statement that may cause distress, let alone offend. Great pains will be taken to avoid having to say no. Why cause unhappiness by painful precision when one can please so easily by inaccuracy? Circumlocution, ambiguity, and metaphor help to cushion against the dangers of candor. Timing is also important. Better to evade and delay than risk a premature initiative. Since a refusal or a rebuff will cause such embarrassment, a request will be preceded by much probing and endless small talk. Round and round the conversation will go until the supplicant can be sure of satisfaction.

To the outsider, the high context individual may appear insincere and congenitally suspicious, but this is to judge these traits from a culture-bound perspective. What may seem to be insincerity and even dishonesty is part of the veneer of elaborate courtesy and evasion essential to preserve social harmony. It may also be a tacitly accepted way of acquiring social advantage. Similarly, suspiciousness is not a deviant characteristic but a justified receptivity to hidden meanings, an alertness to subtle hints known from experience to be potentially present in the tone, occasion, or phrasing of a conversation.

Paradoxically, in view of the refinement and politeness of face-to-face interaction, public discourse may be immoderate and vituperative. Cursing in the streets and markets of Cairo achieves a remarkable level of obscenity, and the radio and press hum at times with scurrility. Arabic is rich in invective. In fact, the contradiction is more apparent than real. In both cases language is being used for effect, not to convey information. *"Ahu kalam,"* the Egyptian will say; "these are merely words." There is nothing really personal meant or perceived in the hyperbole. Arabic, as we shall see, is the heir of a great oral tradition of rhetoric which stands in particular contrast to the Jewish tradition of textual analysis.

Low context cultures reserve a quite different role for language. Very little meaning is implicit in the context of an articulation. What has to be said is stated explicitly. There is no virtue in indirection. Allusiveness is likely to be overlooked anyway. Bluntness is equated with honesty. Language is used instrumentally rather than socially, and therefore emphasis is on accuracy and not lubrication.

Although Hall uses the United States as the paradigm of the low context culture, what he has to say applies with even added force to Israel. Israel is a society with relatively meager semiotic resources. Its urban and human landscape is twentieth-century modern; many of its citizens are immigrant transplants. The Israeli scene is bereft of that intricate arabesque of signs and symbols that mark Egypt's high context environment. Israelis are not in a taut state of alert to subtle features of appearance, decor, and gesture. They do not need to be, for nothing hangs on such receptivity. The intimate intensity of the face-to-face community, with its stress on collective conformity over individual autonomy, is absent. Community is highly valued, but at a national rather than "clan" level.

In the early years of the state, people were indeed sensitive to distinguishing marks of ethnic origin such as accent, mannerism, and dress. At that time Israel was a kaleidoscope of newcomers from over eighty different countries speaking many different tongues. However, for neither the state nor the individual was there any benefit to be derived from perpetuating separate communal identities and the semantic subcultures that went with them. Quite the reverse—if anything, this would have been maladaptive. Integration was the order of the day and paid for at a high price. In the process of acquiring a common language and mutually comprehensible codes of nonverbal behavior, entire linguistic and paralinguistic ecologies were wiped out. Besides which, the dominant receptor culture of the pioneers had never had much time for "folklore" anyway and had nailed to its mast an abandonment of traditional forms in favor of an ethic of blunt simplicity and equality. What emerged from the melting pot was a *communicatory* lower common denominator, stark to the point of impoverishment. (This does not mean that ethnic pride has not survived as a matter of fact, as evidenced by voter behavior in recent elections.)

Hebrew as it is spoken in Israel today is not a language of shade and nuance. Literary Hebrew does have an extensive vocabulary, and there is no hesitancy about adopting foreign words and neologisms. But the language of street and parliament alike is terse and rather threadbare. Little use is found for the contrived formulas and verbal embellishments so characteristic of Arabic. Verbal redundance is therefore comparatively low. Contradiction is not felt to be offensive. Insinuation is lost on the Israeli. Subtlety or allusiveness in speech, if it is grasped at all, is not particularly admired. Since "face" plays much less important a role in the culture, one is less sensitive to what others say. Hints and roundabout expressions are simply unnecessary. If you have something to say, you come right out with it.

Public debate in Israel does become impassioned. Israel's parliament, the Knesset, is not noted for its decorum. The expression "synagogue politics," used by Jews with self-deprecating irony, refers to a Jewish tradition of polemics, familiar from the *shtetl* (where the synagogue hall was the scene of communal deliberation), which carried over to the politics of the *Yishuv* and then the state. It also carries the sense of an inability to distinguish trivial parish pump issues from those of more fateful moment. However, the intensity of argument derives from genuine disagreement and a sincere commitment of principle. Form simply follows substance. The language of public discourse, although there are variant traditions, remains on the whole factual. And since it is still seen primarily as a vehicle for conveying information, not affect, content is taken deeply seriously. No Israeli debater would say of his presentation, "these are merely words." Invective and eulogy would never be dismissed as empty rhetoric. There is little of the vitriolic hyperbole of Arabic. Hebrew, in fact, makes use of very few terms of abuse, those in currency often being borrowed from Arabic or Russian.

The picture presented here is stark and generalized. At issue is the behavioral norm, and atypical extremes are excluded. Clearly were one to focus on each culture in its own right, one would wish to insert many reservations and glosses. Of course there are exceptions to the rule. Mubarak's soldierly bluntness grates on the sensibilities of other Arab leaders. The Begin school of rhetoric is as different from Eshkol's low-key style of presentation as Mubarak's managerial style is from Nasser's flamboyance. But when the two opposing traditions are locked in contention in the diplomatic arena, individual traits tend to be subsumed by aggregate features of the group. For purposes of cross-cultural analysis, therefore, the need for presenting the full range of possibilities in each case is obviated. It is the relative contrasts be-

tween the two cultures and the implications these possess for mutual perceptions and expectations that interest us, not their internal variations. In the
following section we shall examine the effect of three particularly salient
antinomies—incompatibilities—on Egyptian-Israeli relations: the propensity
to high or low "social desirability"; the preference for indirectness or directness; and the proclivity for overstatement or understatement.

High versus Low "Social Desirability"

In my overview of the differences between low and high context cultures,
I hinted that the high context individual's characteristic dislike of disappoint-
ing and displeasing his interlocutor may result in promises' being given that
cannot be kept and of statements' being made whose accuracy is in doubt.
Where language is used primarily as a social instrument, the telling of truth
is less important than maintaining harmonious personal relations. In the low
context culture the reverse is the case. It is clear that this difference in priorities is ripe with potential cross-cultural misunderstanding. To the member of
a low context culture, the high context speaker risks being seen as dishonest
and insincere. Equally, when the roles are reversed, the low context speaker
may be perceived as pedantic and offensive.

The Arabic tendency to imprecision has frequently been remarked upon.
Sania Hamady quotes approvingly the view that truth-telling is not a categorical imperative in Arab society but a means to an end, to be disregarded when
inconvenient.[4] In a study of a Lebanese village, Michael Gilsenan describes
a community preoccupied with appearances in which "showing off" is pervasive and lying—*kizb*—endemic. *Kizb* has three functions: to trick others in
order to acquire a fleeting dominance; as part of an aesthetic of baroque in-
vention; and to disguise the gap that has opened up in a highly hierarchical,
status-conscious society, between the humiliation of real status and the status
society requires.[5]

As for the difference between Arab and Israeli approaches to the truth
ethic, one way of comparing the extent to which the two cultures submit
language to social rather than informational needs is provided by the *Social Desirability Scale*. This is an index derived from a set of questions,
carefully formulated in the subject's native language, designed to measure
his conformity to behavior and attitudes he knows to be approved of by
society. Hebrew and Arabic versions of this questionnaire were administered to Jewish and Arab high school students in Israel. How concerned
were the children to present themselves in a favorable light? In one item,
for instance, they were asked to mark as true or false the (improbable)
statement "When I make a mistake, I always admit I am wrong." Results
obtained indicated quite clearly that Arab subjects displayed a significantly
higher need for social approval than their Jewish counterparts.[6] This tallied

with an earlier study of Egyptian children which also revealed a strong tendency on their part to give "nice," that is, socially desirable, answers.[7]

What may be, in a social context, an understandable tendency can obviously be a source of serious confusion in the conduct of diplomacy. Many friends of the Arabs and even the Arabs themselves have acknowledged this. King Hussein of Jordan, deploring the absence of unity and consensus in the Arab world, believed this arose from "the lack of sincerity and honesty in some Arab leaders."[8] Glubb Pasha, for years the commander of the Arab Legion, wrote that President Nasser, although "delightfully frank and sincere in appearance . . . is nearly always telling lies," a judgment shared by many others at the time. Commenting on a completely mendacious Egyptian military communiqué, Glubb ruefully noted that he had "not found in the Middle East that truth can be relied upon to emerge." The Levantine Arabs and Egyptians, he observed, felt it necessary to maintain morale by telling lies. At all costs one had to avoid unpleasantness.[9]

Extraordinarily enough, Ismail Fahmy, President Sadat's foreign minister from 1974 to 1977, accuses his own boss of "storytelling," self-contradiction, and choosing his words to suit "the occasion and the audience." Not only did he tend to overdramatize and exaggerate, he would sometimes invent things that had not happened at all. Altogether, Fahmy claims, Sadat was not overly concerned about the truth. One's natural skepticism at this version is removed by the fact that Fahmy's successor, Mohamed Ibrahim Kamel, makes virtually the same charges. Sadat, in his experience, gave untrustworthy accounts, leaving out items that were "not to his liking." Nor could his promises be relied upon.[10]

There is no question that the "credibility gap" grievously harmed the prospects for peace between Egypt and Israel over the years. In the first place, Israeli decision-makers became convinced that the Egyptians were not serious people with whom one could do business on a realistic basis. Since they were perceived to be congenitally incapable of distinguishing between truth and falsehood, of fearlessly assessing either the balance of power or the advantages of a peaceful settlement, they could not, *a priori*, be considered partners for negotiation. Ben Gurion, speaking before the 1956 Suez War, claimed that he had at first been favorably impressed by Colonel Nasser. "But when I realized that he was a liar, not only did I begin to hate him but also to hold him in contempt."[11] More than anything else, the fantastic inaccuracy of the Egyptian media and the communiqués put out by the Egyptian military authorities contributed to this image of unreliability. The tragedy was a twofold one, because Israeli skepticism clearly also detracted from Egypt's deterrent credibility.

After the 1967 War, evidence that emerged of false reporting within the Egyptian army, and of a fictitious account of Egyptian successes in the war given at a critical point by Nasser to King Hussein, reinforced existing Israeli prejudices. General Yehoshafat Harkabi, a former head of military intelligence and a leading Israeli expert on the Arab world, argued that the Arabs in general and Egypt in particular had become detached from reality. An inflated self-image had interfered with the correct estimate of their strength and contributed to "the Arabs' inaccurate evaluation of their own military preparedness."[12] Defense Minister Dayan went even further in a speech given in October 1968. In his view the Arabs had wilfully steeped themselves in self-delusion as an escape from a grim reality. Logic, Dayan argued, indicated that defeat and occupation should push them toward a settlement. The reason for their recalcitrance lay in a mentality which cut them off from reality.[13]

With the benefit of hindsight, we can see that Dayan—ironically, known to Israelis as "more Arab than the Arabs," a backhanded compliment— had made the cardinal error of projecting his own rationality onto his opponents. From an Egyptian perspective, the prospect of direct negotiations with Israel from a posture of supplication was unbearably humiliating. It was not that Nasser was incapable of perceiving reality, a ludicrous suggestion, but rather that he viewed the cost and benefits of negotiating under existing circumstances differently from Dayan. A peace based on "territorial compromise" would not have assuaged the shame, merely compounded and perpetuated it. There was nothing at all illogical about Egypt's preferred strategy: to be willing for indirect negotiations through the good offices of the United Nations, provided assurances were obtained of Israel's complete withdrawal; failing that, via a war of attrition, to raise the cost for Israel of its continued presence on the Suez Canal, to maintain pressure on international opinion, to maintain the Egyptian army in a state of war-readiness.

A second obstacle to dialogue arose from the Egyptian habit of making conciliatory statements in private to Western diplomats and of saying something quite different in public. Incidentally, the Egyptians were themselves aware that this practice was a potent source of confusion and mistrust. In a letter sent by Nasser to President Kennedy in September 1962, the Egyptian leader acknowledged that "some Arab politicians were making harsh statements regarding Palestine publicly and then contacting the American Government to alleviate their harshness by saying that their statements were meant for local Arab consumption." Though he went on to promise to tell the truth as he felt it, old habits proved difficult to break.[14]

Some Israelis were prepared to accept that the public-private articulation gap could genuinely be explained away in terms of "Arab psychological necessities": that militant declarations were required for "public consumption" or to protect the Egyptians' flank against extremists in the Arab world. But genuine political dilemmas still remained. Even assuming that private statements were meant sincerely at the time, who could say that declaratory commitments to Palestine made in public would not, in the final analysis, prove inescapable? In 1948, for instance, Egypt had found its wider loyalty to the Arab cause to be more powerful than purely national considerations. Another powerful argument put forward by General Harkabi was that public declarations create public expectations. Policies are formulated by collectivities, and it was as collectivities that the Arabs would go forward to war or peace against Israel. Until they were prepared to announce to their own people what they were murmuring to foreign diplomats, little reliance could be placed upon the private statements of Arab leaders.[15] Harkabi might have added that Israeli public anticipations were as influenced by the declarations of Arab leaders as the Arab publics themselves. No Israeli government could realistically expect its own constituency to overlook these enunciations for the sake of private assurances that might—or might not—be true.

Until the 1967 War, Egyptian signals to Israel, usually passed on through the good offices of various intermediaries of one kind or another, invariably failed to meet that condition of publicity which might have demonstrated their veracity to Israelis, or at least been harder to explain away. After the 1967 War, the Egyptian government did indeed commit itself in public to positions that held out some possibility of progress. However, it then turned out that a credibility gap of a reverse kind had opened up: that Egyptian leaders were making public commitments which were watered down or refuted altogether in private. Since evidence of internal and inner-Arab consultations often fell into Israeli hands, the image of Arab "double talk" was merely reinforced.

One example of this was Egypt's position on United Nations Resolution 242 of 22 November 1967. This historic text, which for years afterward was the only mutually agreed basis for possible negotiations between Egypt and Israel, affirmed two pivotal principles. One was "withdrawal of Israeli armed forces from territories occupied in the recent conflict." The other was "termination of all claims or states of belligerency and respect for and acknowledgement of the sovereignty, territorial integrity and political independence of every State in the area and their right to live in peace within secure and recognized boundaries free from threats or acts of force." At first, the Egyptians had merely accepted the resolution by implication. They had been consulted in its formulation and, while unenthusiastic, had studiedly declined to reject it. A few months later, in April 1968, the Egyptian government spokesman announced Egypt's explicit acceptance and then Nasser himself acknowledged to army units, "We have agreed to implement the United Nations resolution."[16]

As far as many Israelis were concerned, Egyptian acceptance of 242 was an indirect and unsatisfactory substitute for a more explicit recognition of Israeli sovereignty. But it was surely better than nothing. Unfortunately, in the Middle East things are not always as straightforward as they seem. On the very day after the resolution was approved by the Security Council,

Nasser had informed a meeting of senior army commanders that it did not concern them. Israel would never voluntarily evacuate the occupied territories; "what had been taken by force can only be recovered by force." He concluded with a remark that would be bound to appear as a damning indictment of Egyptian duplicity if it ever found its way into an Israeli intelligence report: "So you don't need to pay any attention to anything I may say in public about a peaceful solution."[17] Was this cynical remark meant to cover his statement of 29 April 1968—or not?

Overstatement versus Understatement

Another linguistic incompatibility to have dogged Egyptian-Israeli relations over the years derives from the Arabic propensity for hyperbole (or, to put it another way, the Hebrew preference for relative understatement). Taken at their face value, the extreme utterances of Egyptian leaders have often complicated matters. Since the rhetorical tradition of a culture is also tied up with forensic assumptions held about the ways in which arguments are to be presented and opponents persuaded, the difference between Arabic and Hebrew has also affected the success of diplomatic contacts between Egypt and Israel.

Arabic particularly lends itself to an emphatic, ornate, and effusive manner of speech. Shouby pointed out long ago the language's aptitude for flamboyance. "Fantastic metaphors and similes are used in abundance, and long arrays of adjectives to modify the same word are quite frequent."[18] Exaggeration and overassertion are second nature for the native speaker.[19] A linguistic study of the rhetorical style of Arabic was recently carried out by Barbara Koch. She analyzed a number of texts, including two speeches delivered by President Nasser. Her conclusion was that their most salient feature was reiteration of both form and content. Words, synonyms, sounds, meanings, and arguments repeated themselves in rhythmic and hypnotic emphasis, sweeping the reader or listener along with persuasive momentum.[20]

Arabic hyperbole has been associated with the bardic, oral tradition of Arab poetry which, though pre-Islamic, achieved its finest expression in the Koran. Once enshrined within that most sacred text—the focus of religious worship and everyday recitation and quotation alike—this poetic eloquence came to stand as a paradigm for all speech. Arabic poetry, according to Clifford Geertz, was a sort of collective speech act which became the highest artistic expression of Islamic civilization. Now the Koran is more to the believer than a "testament," like the gospels, or a covenant, like the five books of Moses. Delivered by Gabriel to Mohammed, the words of the Koran are not statements at one remove about God but are seen as the very emanation of God himself. Thus the Koran can be compared in sanctity only to the Eucharist—the embodiment of the divine presence.[21]

The linguistic, let alone cultural, consequences of this belief are far-reaching. Arabic acquires a unique status as the language of God. To speak it is to harness a sacred force. If word and substance are identical in some metaphysical sense, then language ceases to be a mere symbolic representation of reality and becomes a form of reality in its own right. But most important from our point of view are the implications for Arabic rhetoric. Barbara Koch holds that the use of repetition as a technique of persuasion is far from coincidental. Since the truth is infallibly and definitively contained in the Koran's sacred verses, as acknowledged by all right-thinking men, argumentation does not have to prove anything, simply to disclose something already known. The idea that some fresh insight can be derived by logic or empirical investigation, she continues, is antithetical to the serene tradition of Islam that all that is worth knowing has already been revealed. Persuasion, in short, is by *presentation* rather than *proof*.[22] One might add that the educational corollary of this view was the practice of learning by rote customary in Koranic schools. By stressing the mechanical memorization of texts—without their necessarily being understood—this system was biased toward oral skills and helped to perpetuate the traditions of recitation and argument by "presentation" exemplified by Arabic rhetoric.[23]

In contrast to the Arabic speaker, the Israeli has no active rhetorical tradition upon which to draw (though the bardic stream in classical Hebrew is magnificently preserved in the Psalms and the book of Isaiah). If Arabic might be thought of as displaying strongly "oral" traits (without confusing this, of course, with illiteracy), modern Hebrew is stamped by the Jewish "literary" heritage of biblical and legal study and scholarship which, as we have seen, was central to diaspora life. As with Arabic, this tradition, perpetuated and reinforced through the ages by the system of religious education, has important contemporary implications both for language use in Israel—it is conducive to restraint rather than hyperbole—and for the typically scholastic style of forensic debate.

To understand the Jewish style of discourse and argument, it is necessary to start with the visual appearance of a page—any will do—of the Talmud. A surprise awaits someone accustomed only to Western literature. In the center of the page is located a small block of print surrounded on all four sides by a large selection of commentaries presented in a variety of typefaces. This central text, an elucidation in Aramaic and Hebrew of the earlier Mishnah, is never studied in isolation. Indeed, by itself it is terse and cryptic to the point of opacity for the average reader. In order to begin to interpret this text, the student must refer, back and forth, phrase by phrase—even word by word—to the great commentators. Talmudic study therefore takes the form of a constant give-and-take, query and response, exegesis and interpolation, between the reader, the original rabbinic contributors to the Talmud, and subsequent classic commentators.[24]

The implications of this tradition are manifold. A text is never taken as definitive but is simply a basis for never-ending interpretation. There is no "final" meaning—God forbid that there should be, for then scholarship would grind to a halt—only a search for enlightenment continuing on down through the centuries. Of course some opinions are more valued than others, but in principle no one is barred from contributing to the debate. Thus the Islamic sense of a set of authoritative truths revealed once and for all is missing from Judaism.

The style of the Talmud has also had a profound effect on the Jewish use of language. The classical texts are terse and condensed to a high degree. They had to be for the technical reason that otherwise they could not fit onto the page alongside the other commentaries. Their quintessentially laconic tone set a pattern for both spoken and written discourse which has persisted, via the early writers of the Jewish Enlightenment of the late eighteenth and early nineteenth centuries and the Zionist intellectuals who revived the spoken tongue at the turn of the twentieth century, into modern Hebrew. Thus the rich and subtle suggestiveness found in Arab culture in the face-to-face interaction, in both its verbal and nonverbal aspects, is reserved by Jewish culture for literary texts.

The technique of analysis engendered by the Talmud is also utterly characteristic: the painstaking, meticulous exegesis of the written word. Profound ethical and legal issues may well be at stake, but in truth the Talmudist is just as interested and more often engaged in the precise elucidation of some abstruse term or unusual turn of phrase. If study is in itself a form of worship—according to tradition the highest form—then it does not matter in the least whether the subject under discussion is "objectively" relevant or not. The idea that Talmudic study encourages scholastic hair-splitting cannot be denied, though one should immediately add that it also requires the application of the highest powers of logical analysis.

The tradition of argumentation in Judaism flows directly from the legalistic style of analysis. By virtue of the dialectical method, the interrogatory interplay between reader, text, and commentaries, debate and analysis meld together into a single activity. Interestingly, the dialectic habit asserts itself even in the social organization of Talmudic study, most of which takes place either within a weekly study group—a favorite framework for the casual student—or within the full-time academy of learning, between the partners of a *havruta*—two men who are assigned to work together. In both cases the thread of analysis is carried forward by each participant in turn while the others probe, question, and refute his arguments. Oratorical skills are quite useless and totally inappropriate in this context. In the face of challenges by other keen legal minds, verbal flamboyance is out of place. Persuasion must rely not on rhetoric, the power and especially the sound of the spoken word, but on skillful reasoning, the appeal to the fine semantic distinction and the logical argument. To the intellect trained in the dissection of Talmudic texts, only a watertight case, semantically sound and legally impeccable, will be taken seriously.

The effect on intercultural communication of the overstatement-understatement dichotomy was investigated in the 1950s at the American University of Beirut by E. T. Prothro. He asked two groups of Arab students, a bilingual one working in English and the other in Arabic, to assign various descriptive statements to a scale graded in terms of favorableness and unfavorableness. The judgments of the Arab students were then compared with the previously known judgments of American students. The results of the experiment were striking. Irrespective of whether they were working in English or Arabic, strongly favorable and strongly unfavorable statements were judged by Arabs to be more neutral than they were by Americans.[25]

Since its inception, the Egypt-Israel dispute has been accompanied on the Egyptian side by a constant drumbeat of invective and vituperation coming out of Cairo, both in the media and from the leadership itself. As early as 1950 former Egyptian Prime Minister Ismail Sidky acknowledged that it was "time to stop high-sounding phrases and hollow boasting in Egypt which always have brought injury in their train."[26] After the 1967 War it was widely recognized just how much damage innacuracy and exaggeration had done to the Egyptian cause. However, despite pious statements, Egypt clearly found it inordinately difficult to maintain a posture of verbal restraint. Some of Sadat's characterizations of Israel, before and after the 1973 War, were especially sinister in that they drew on both Koranic and European anti-Semitic motifs.[27] It is almost as though Arab leaders are unable to resist the temptation to hyperbole that the language places at their disposal. One is reminded of the anecdote Anthony Nutting relays of Nasser's insisting on speaking English during the Free Officers' coup of 1952, because "Arabic was not a suitable language to express the need for calm."[28]

Arab audiences have a healthy skepticism for the declarations of their leaders and the extravagances of the media—or, to put it another way, they are able, like Prothro's Lebanese students, to discount the inflationary element in the rhetoric. Even Sadat condemned the Arab propensity, in his own words, to "bluster and empty slogans"—not that this prevented his indulging in them on occasion.[29] Not by chance Sadat's historical statement of 9 November 1977 to the Egyptian People's Assembly, in which he declared his willingness to debate with Israel in "their very home," the Knesset, was dismissed as mere verbiage by listening Arabs. According to Ismail Fahmy, neither officials, delegates, nor ordinary Egyptians interpreted the statement literally, assuming it to be "just rhetoric." Arab League Secretary-General Mahmoud Riad took the words to be "an exaggerated form of challenge."[30] Significantly—and fortunately—the Israeli government was inclined to take Sadat's declaration at face value.

On the whole, though, Egyptian rhetoric had a consistently deleterious and incendiary effect on relations with Israel. It harmed Egyptian credibility, weakened the hand of Israeli moderates, and hardened Israeli public opinion. Moshe Sharett (Israeli foreign minister 1948–56, prime minister 1953–55 during Ben Gurion's temporary retirement), who was the leader of the "dovish" camp in Israel until forced out of office in 1956 for his views, drew the attention of Colonel Nasser through intermediaries to the harmful influence of hostile propaganda. He pointed out to American presidential envoy Robert Anderson (who shuttled inconclusively between Cairo and Jerusalem in January-February 1956) that denunciations of Israel were an obstacle to peace. "Nasser must stop showering fire and brimstone on Israel in his speeches. If this policy of fanning the flames of hatred continues, it will be impossible to break the vicious circle."[31]

General Harkabi, in his influential analysis of *Arab Attitudes to Israel*, warned against explaining away abuse of Israel as "Oriental exuberance."[32] One could not take Egypt seriously as an adversary while totally dismissing the articulations of its leaders. In May 1967 Nasser's various incandescent declarations of intent certainly contributed to the escalation that preceded the Six Day War (see chapter 5). One of the contributory causes of the breakdown of the bilateral stage of talks between Egypt and Israel in the period November 1977-January 1978 was an unbridled campaign of vilification conducted in the Cairo press against Israeli Prime Minister Begin, including caricatures depicting him as Shylock. Such onslaughts, in Ezer Weizman's view, harmed "prospects of peace" and "sprinkled salt on Israel's open wounds of mistrust."[33] The personal insults which are such a feature of inter-Arab rivalry rarely leave any lasting scars. Israelis find it harder to retain their equanimity. Regrettably, not even the 1979 peace treaty has put a stop to anti-Israel and also anti-Semitic articles and caricatures in the Egyptian press, which have continued on and off up to the time of writing. Israel's numerous critics of the 1979 peace treaty—who include Prime Minister Yitzhak Shamir among their number—can only be hardened in their attitudes.

On occasion relative Israeli understatement has also misled Egyptian decision-makers. The most momentous example of such misperception took place on the eve of the 1967 War (see again chapter 5). However, its effect was also felt at a critical juncture in Egyptian-Israeli relations in the 1950s. Contacts with Nasser were initiated by Sharett at the end of 1954 with a view to saving the lives of a group of Israeli agents on trial in Cairo and possibly also achieving progress in other areas. Two simultaneous channels of communication were used: one drew upon the good offices of Maurice Orbach, a British Member of Parliament and a member of the World Jewish Congress, who met directly with Colonel Nasser and other members of the Revolutionary Command Council in Cairo. The other involved meetings between Israeli and Egyptian envoys in Paris. Through both channels Sharett conveyed the following message to the Egyptian leader concerning the Cairo trial: "I cannot emphasize too strongly the gravity of the issue which is there in the balance.

I fervently hope that no death sentences will be passed, as demanded by the prosecution. They would inevitably produce a violent crisis, kindle afresh the flames of bitterness and strife and defeat our efforts to curb passions and to lead our people into ways of peace."[34]

Sharett, very much the poised, judicious diplomat, meant this phrase as a restrained but nonetheless explicit warning of retaliation. In his view, therefore, Nasser should have been forewarned about the reprisal raid launched against Gaza on 28 February 1955, just after the execution of two of the Israeli agents. However, it later transpired that Nasser had not taken Sharett's understated formula in this way at all. While complaining bitterly to Robert Anderson about the Gaza raid, after which "really serious deterioration started" between Egypt and Israel, Colonel Nasser commented on his inauspicious past experience of "direct contact" with Israel. Even when a channel of communication had existed, at the time of the Cairo trial, "he had been misled." On hearing this from Anderson, Sharett expressed himself mystified: "In my written approach there was a threat that if the death penalty was carried out, it would arouse shock and indignation. . . . What grounds did [Nasser] have for assuming that we would not react?"[35]

Directness versus Indirectness

Egyptians' high context preference for indirectness, the allusive reference rather than the blunt overture, and their dislike of confrontation and contradiction have been discussed at length. The exquisite courtesy which is such a marked feature of Egyptian society, as of Arab society in general, can be seen as a highly effective mechanism to cushion against unwelcome friction in one's personal relations. There is little doubt that this tradition of civility has greatly benefited the conduct of Egyptian diplomacy. Henry Kissinger had his own theory about this: in his view the natural dignity, courtesy, and conciliatory manner of the "educated Egyptian" had helped him achieve a margin of maneuver during millennia of foreign intrusion.[36]

The gap between high context pliability and the low context proclivity for straightforwardness and dislike of "deviousness" is clear enough. However, both European and American diplomats, with their own professional codes of tact and courtesy, learn to accommodate without strain to Egyptian sensitivities. If anything, the grace and politeness that mark the Egyptian official greatly facilitate the business of diplomacy. It is the misfortune of Israeli foreign relations that these are precisely the traits that come least easily to the Israeli envoy. Diplomats from third countries who have worked with both Arabs and Israelis often contrast the civility of the former with the roughness of the latter.[37]

In a recent cross-cultural study comparing Israelis and Americans, the authors confirmed, with the use of a questionnaire survey, the popular impres-

sion of Israeli discourtesy. They found that Israeli subjects tended to be less
sensitive to the rights of others and to see aggressive behavior as more justified than did Americans. Furthermore, the Israelis were quicker-tempered
and showed their anger more vigorously. Another conclusion, with interesting implications for intercultural communication and diplomacy, was that Israelis actually tend to distrust easygoing "niceness" as concealing some
deeper purpose.[38] Since cross-cultural studies comparing Americans with
Arabs indicate precisely the reverse result—namely, that Americans are
much less concerned about manners than are Arabs—it must follow that
Arabs and Israelis are at virtually opposite ends of the spectrum of civility.
We should therefore expect this factor to weigh heavily on Egyptian-Israeli
relations.[39]

It is not surprising to find, consequently, that clumsy Israeli handling has
been a recurrent source of unnecessary friction in contacts with Egypt. The
sign of a skillful diplomacy is its ability to preserve the outward forms of
courtesy—and therefore the possibility of future progress—even when a substantive conflict of interests precludes present agreement. An approach that
exacerbates differences and actually obscures points of convergence must be
seriously out of kilter.

The Israeli use of language also possesses, in an involuntary tendency to
brusqueness, a characteristic that is incongruent with the elliptical linguistic
habits of Arabic speakers and serves to reinforce, unintentionally, the impression of discourtesy. Hebrew, as it is spoken today, has none of the periphrasis which permits the rough edge of unpleasant facts to be smoothed
off. Under the influence of that cult of simplicity which was such a feature
of Labor Zionism, Israelis have been taught to avoid beating about the bush.
On the contrary, forthrightness is seen as an admirable quality and equated
with sincerity. For instance, although the Hebrew dictionary does present a
variety of polite forms of request, Israelis use the bare imperative, without
the addition of emollient expressions, with far greater frequency than the English, let alone Arabic, speaker.

Professor E. A. Levenston demonstrated this feature of Modern Hebrew
speech in a neat experiment. A questionnaire was given to two groups: one,
in English, to native English speakers, the other, in Hebrew, to native Israelis. Subjects were required to correct a glaring error they knew to have
been made by an imaginary interlocutor—mistaken directions to a well-
known landmark. English speakers, disliking blunt contradiction, inserted
apologies, explanations, and conditional forms of speech into their correc-
tions. Sixty percent of them, in fact, used qualifying phrases such as "I seem
to remember that . . ." or "Maybe I'm wrong, but . . ." and so on. In marked
contrast, Hebrew speakers preferred to answer the same questionnaire by
correcting any errors without standing on ceremony. Only 12 percent of these
subjects qualified their responses in any way.[40]

Abruptness has become something of a hallmark of Israeli foreign relations. Gideon Rafael, former director-general of the Israeli Foreign Ministry, accepts that his government "was more impressed by blunt talk and un-enigmatic action sparing it the burden of guessing." Diplomatic ambiguity and periphrasis were unlikely to have much effect. Much also tended to be lost in the translation. Israel's "style of life," Rafael wryly concludes, was bet-ter served by "plain talking."[41] This should not give the impression that diplo-mats such as Moshe Sharett and Abba Eban were not professionals to their fingerprints. The point is, rather, that the decision-making elite as a whole tended to lack sensitivity.

From the earliest days of the Zionist movement, Jewish leaders found it hard to deal with the Arabs, seeing them as "elusive, mysterious, and devi-ous." It has been suggested that Israel's relations with the Arab world might have been better served by Jewish envoys of Oriental origin, but these were and continue to be few and far between.[42] Eliahu Sasson, whose family was of Iraqi-Syrian origin and who played a distinguished role in the 1949 Rhodes armistice negotiations, is the exception to prove the rule. The fact that, in the absence of formal ties, contacts were often conducted by army officers (for instance, in the mixed armistice commissions set up in 1949 to supervise the various armistice agreements) or by the political echelon, did not help matters.

Relations with Egypt have been consistently hindered by Israeli abrasive-ness and lack of tact. During contacts between Egyptian and Israeli officials in Paris held at the time of the Cairo trial, in tandem with the Orbach mission mentioned above, we find Gideon Rafael, no less, who headed the Israeli team, accused of "treating the Egyptian envoy with offensive severity" and of having "antagonized his interlocutors on the other side."[43] At about the same time the Egyptian representative on the Israel-Egypt Mixed Armistice Commission complained how "hard it was to hold a conversation" with the Israeli military delegates, who were "inflexible and harshly-spoken."[44]

But it was at the abortive bilateral stage of the "peace process" of November 1977–January 1978—before the conciliatory skills of American mediation had come into play—that the clash of Egyptian and Israeli styles was felt most severely. Within hours of President Sadat's historic arrival in Israel, on the evening of 19 November 1977, with nerves at a high pitch of anticipation, Israeli diplomacy made its first tactless and maladroit overture. On the drive up to Jerusalem from Lod airport, Israeli Foreign Minister Moshe Dayan and his Egyptian counterpart Acting Foreign Minister Boutros-Ghali had the opportunity to get acquainted. Social niceties, however, were never Dayan's forte. Without trying to soften the blow in any way, Dayan brusquely informed Boutros-Ghali, with astonishing insensitivity, that since there was no chance of Jordan or the Palestinians' joining in the nego-tiations—as Sadat hoped at that point, anxious to avoid isolation in the Arab world—"Egypt had to be ready to sign a peace treaty with us even if she were not joined by others."[45]

Boutros-Ghali was profoundly shocked by Dayan's ill-timed proposal of a separate peace, as was Sadat when it was reported to him. At issue was not the idea itself, which was based on an objective analysis of the situation. Dayan was entitled to argue that none of the Arab states had any intention of joining Sadat in his daring initiative. It was the unsubtle directness of the approach that was utterly repellent to the Egyptian minister. This first conversation with an Israeli leader rankled in Boutros-Ghali's mind for years afterward.[46] For Sadat to come to Israel after all the years of enmity was a painful step indeed. The fear of failure and humiliation could never have been far from Egyptian thoughts. Yet here was an Israeli leader flaunting a brutal and arrogant disregard for Egyptian sensibilities—hardly an auspicious start to the relationship. Such a far-reaching proposal should have been put forward only after lengthy psychological preparation. The realization by Egypt that it was out on a limb, cut off from the Arab "family," could come only after much heart-searching.

Dayan's blunder was by no means exceptional. After the withdrawal of an Egyptian delegation from Jerusalem in January 1978, there were no direct talks between Israel and Egypt until a meeting at Leeds Castle in England in June 1978 under United States auspices. This surely gave Dayan sufficient time to reflect on the shortcomings of his diplomacy. Yet once again his blunt advocacy of the Israeli position almost resulted in a second Egyptian walkout. This time Dayan, impatient with the Egyptian position on issues such as the return of refugees, the status of Jerusalem, and the West Bank, decided, in his own words, "to get a clear answer from the Egyptians." Accordingly he abruptly informed them that if they rejected the Israeli proposal as the basis for a settlement, it would be withdrawn. He adds: "The Egyptians were embarrassed and did not hasten to respond." The senior Egyptian delegate at Leeds Castle, Foreign Minister Kamel, confirms that Dayan's plain speaking cast a "brooding tension" over the talks.[47] Deadlock continued.

In the aftermath of this failure, the Israelis and Egyptians did not meet again until the Camp David conference held under American auspices in September. Dayan became virtually *persona non grata* with the Egyptians for his blunt disregard of their feelings. Sadat felt quite unable to deal with the man, and it was with some reluctance that he agreed to meet him at all at Camp David. His forebodings proved justified; the meeting between the two men brought the conference to the brink of failure. Opening his remarks, the Israeli ominously informed the Egyptian president that he would "be blunt with him." Dayan then proceeded to restate Israel's refusal to withdraw from either the settlements or the airfields constructed in the Sinai since 1967. When Sadat pointed out that he could not conclude a peace treaty under those circumstances, Dayan told him that in that case, "We shall continue to occupy Sinai and pump oil." On the following day, 15 September 1978, Sadat ordered a helicopter to fly him out of Camp David and was dissuaded only by a personal appeal from President Carter. Mohamed Kamel is convinced that Sadat was genuinely at the end of his tether as a result of his conversation with Dayan and was not simply acting tactically.[48]

Others emulated Dayan's crude behavior. Prime Minister Begin, an infinitely more polished and cultured man, also fell into the trap on occasion of believing that the Egyptians could somehow be browbeaten into compliance.[49] But the tactic of shouting and table-banging, which is an integral part of political life in Israel, and sometimes makes its appearance in Israel's diplomatic behavior, was worse than ineffective against the Egyptians. Diplomats with experience in the Arab world are in no doubt that a loss of temper or display of annoyance is a serious mistake when one is dealing with Arabs.[50] Avoidance of confrontation is a precondition of successful business of any kind. Once an Arab is angered and his pride aroused, he becomes immovable. Eliahu Sasson recalled being warned of this danger years ago by friendly Arab leaders: "You Jews must be careful of this and always take it into account in speaking with us Arabs."[51]

Unfortunately, many Israelis have disregarded this advice. During the "peace process" negotiations with Egypt, they often demonstrated their obliviousness to Egyptian sensitivities. At the ill-fated official dinner of 17 January 1978, after which the Egyptian delegation to the "political committee," set up to continue the talks, was withdrawn from Jerusalem, Begin mortified the Egyptian foreign minister with a patronizing and hectoring address. Wondering whether to repay Begin's "rudeness" in kind, Kamel contented himself with a dignified reply. But he did not shake the Israeli prime minister's hand, or raise a toast to peace. This was not the way to negotiate a peace treaty. The whole unpleasant episode was indicative of a profound disjunction between Egyptian and Israeli sensibilities.[52]

While all this was going on in Jerusalem, parallel talks were being conducted in Cairo within the framework of a "military committee." The head of the Israeli delegation, Defense Minister Ezer Weizman, was one of the few Israelis to appreciate Egyptian susceptibilities. (Precisely because of his popularity with President Sadat and his willingness to see the Egyptian point of view, he became virtually excluded from the highest level of decision-making in Israel.) Weizman, who had served with the Royal Air Force in Egypt during the Second World War, did his best to brief his fellow Israelis on their Egyptian hosts. He therefore watched askance as his chief of military intelligence, General Shlomo Gazit, made one blunder after another. Gazit was unable to resist patronizingly correcting factual errors made by his Egyptian counterpart General Shaukat. He also offensively accused the Egyptian officers of haggling like the merchants in the market of Khan-al-Khalil. Sadly, Weizman comments, "Gazit did not even notice the impact his words were having. . . ."[53]

Diplomacy is defined in Sir Ernest Satow's classic guide to diplomatic practice as "the application of intelligence and tact to the conduct of official relations between the governments of independent states."[54] By this definition there was clearly something seriously flawed in the Israeli approach. There is no suggestion here that a lack of Israeli tact in the period immediately following Sadat's historic journey was the only cause of rupture. But neither was the dislocation simply a product of substantive disagreement; Sadat was well aware of the differences between the two countries before setting out on his mission in November 1977. Both sides did have reason to hope, though, that a dialogue had been set in motion which would ultimately lead to a resolution of the dispute. For this process to succeed, all the diplomatic skills—including intelligence and tact—available to the protagonists would have to come into play. Seen in this light, Israeli clumsiness contributed to the failure to exploit what might have been a one-and-only opportunity. By mid-January 1978, barely two months after launching his initiative, Sadat had concluded that the experience of dealing with the Israelis at first hand was simply too painful to continue. Had President Carter not been on hand to step into the breach as mediator, the damage done by Israeli clumsiness on the one side and Egyptian hypersensitivity on the other might have been irreparable.

IV

ISRAELIS AND EGYPTIANS
FACE TO FACE

For the member of a high context culture, as we have seen, "what is not said is sometimes more important than what is said." The nonverbal cues accompanying a conversation are of more interest and surely are more informative than any stylized exchange of verbal flourishes. Where speech is delivered for largely social effect, the degree of semantic redundancy must be high. "Body language" is likely to be seen as a more reliable guide to one's partner's innermost thoughts. Words can always be manipulated; not so one's involuntary behavior. Acts, it is felt, do indeed speak louder than words. (Whether or not this is really true is beside the point; in fact the high context individual necessarily becomes skilled at dissimulating his true feelings.)

Nothing is redundant in the familial intimacy of the collectivist culture. It is not just that acute alertness and discrimination are essential if the tranquil personal relationships essential to communal life are to be maintained and its ever-threatening frictions and rivalries avoided. There is also a great compulsion to seek out one's fellow's humanity, to draw aside the veil of polite formulas in order to disclose the "real person" behind the mask. Clues about one's interlocutor are soaked up from the tone of his voice, his facial expression, gestures, and dress. Setting and props are scanned for further information on the modalities of the situation. An acute receptivity—a sort of "sixth sense"—is cultivated for nuances and meanings tucked away in the lining of social intercourse. "Frontality," to borrow Rivka Yadlin's excellent term for the nature of relationships in Egyptian society, that is, the unmediated, sensual human qualities of the face-to-face encounter, is of the essence.[1]

In comparison, the member of a low context, individualist culture such as that of Israel is free to a much greater extent of social pressures and obligations—the inescapable and all-embracing duties that make up the bonds of the extended family. If one falls out with the group, one picks oneself up and goes elsewhere—a facility reinforced by a long history of migration, enforced and voluntary. At the same time, as I have stressed, the ethos that resulted from trying to compress a motley mass of immigrants into the antitraditionalist mold of Zionist ideology left little scope for "frontality."

The Israeli is concerned mostly with the overt, instrumental content of the social encounter. Those nonverbal quarter-tones and unusual harmonies to which the Egyptian's ear is so finely attuned mean very little to him.

Israel's anomalous position in the Middle East, a Jewish island in an Islamic sea, is nowhere felt more sharply than in the area of nonverbal behavior. The gestures and mannerisms of Israelis set them apart; their instincts are not those of their Moslem neighbors. The Egyptian, meeting with other Arabs, is a member of the "family," a brother; he is comfortably at home. He effortlessly shares with them that sensitivity to personal relationships, to the unspoken texture of the face-to-face encounter, so typical of cultures which take the extended family as their social paradigm. He and they draw upon a common nonverbal vocabulary, whether of "body language," the way one sits with an interlocutor, how a meeting is to be handled, the courtesies appropriate to various situations, or the exact weight to be attributed to a hundred little symbolic acts and rituals. In the Israeli-Egyptian cross-cultural encounter, such tacit rapport cannot be taken for granted.

The Importance of Being Personal

Discord is apparent first of all in the area of personal relations, where Egyptian "personalism" jars against the Israeli's relatively more impersonal political instincts. "Personalism" is a preference for conducting business face to face rather than by correspondence or through an anonymous bureaucracy and prevails in commercial and other dealings throughout the Middle East. Like so much else it springs from the habits inculcated by the close-knit group in its members. It is associated with that outlook that defines relationships in affective and familial, not instrumental and monetary terms. Trust is a rare commodity, not easily granted, and there is an instinctive reluctance to rely on impersonal institutions or, indeed, anyone outside the circle of one's personal acquaintance. The fiduciary relationship, the very basis of Western society and public service, whereby certain kinds of personal obligation are undertaken on the basis of an abstract concept of social duty, is unfamiliar to the collectivist culture. One's lawyer is seen not as a paid expert, bound by strict legal and ethical obligations, but as a friend—preferably of one's own kin—to whom one turns for advice on legal matters.

At the political level, personalism has its counterpart in *paternalistic* leadership, that is, a style of government in which power is concentrated in the hands of a single, dominant figure surrounded by an inner circle of advisers and ministers owing him their personal loyalty. Taking the patriarchal family as its paradigm, the system reflects traditional assumptions about the nature of authority. Indeed, in the classic Moslem texts, sovereignty, the right to enforce one's political will on a certain population, was viewed as a personal attribute of the ruler rather than of some legal abstraction such as the state.[2]

The Western system of a separation of powers has proved fragile under Arab conditions. As with most assumptions that are woven into the very warp and weft of a culture, the identification of the leader with the all-powerful father has demonstrated great resilience.

Important decisions in the *paternalistic* regime are always referred to the top, and there is little willingness by lower echelons to risk responsibility. Whether and with whom the ruler chooses to consult is a matter of his own personal whim. Egyptian leaders have been no exception to this general rule. Government under Nasser in the early sixties, American ambassadors of that period recall, was very much a virtuoso performance. Important speeches on foreign policy were written for Nasser by his confidant Mohamed Heikal without always being properly cleared with the foreign ministry.[3] As for Sadat, his most crucial diplomatic decisions were taken single-handedly. Fahmy has Sadat saying of his fateful decision to go to Jerusalem: "I will not discuss it with anybody, I don't care for anybody's opinion." And he charges that at Camp David in September 1978, Sadat "simply ignored the opinions of his colleagues," a judgment confirmed by both Foreign Minister Kamel and President Carter. The latter contrasts the Egyptian president's aloof self-reliance with Begin's dependence on his aides (and, one might add, his parliamentary constituency).[4]

The Arab combination of personalism and *paternalistic* leadership has far-reaching implications for outside powers involved in the Middle East. Reliance on routine channels of communication and the established bureaucracy is a recipe for frustration. Successful diplomacy depends, to an unusual extent, on cultivating a friendly and trusting relationship with the resident leadership. Now Third World countries, many of which display similar features of government, have little difficulty in accommodating this state of affairs. But the industrialized countries, with their sophisticated bureaucracies, complex and possibly diffuse patterns of political organization, and principle of delegated authority, are at a conceptual disadvantage. This applies to the United States, Western Europe—and also Israel. Reciprocally, Arab governments may find confusing the Western system of government, and especially its lack of a single, clear-cut source of authority able to make definitive decisions.

Against this background, developments that would otherwise appear inexplicable begin to make better sense. Sadat's conduct of foreign affairs was strongly marked by the effects of personal likes and dislikes. Ismail Fahmy and Mohamed Kamel's claim that Sadat's policy toward the USSR was influenced by personal grudge seems fantastic, were Sadat himself not to confirm that he had declined to receive Podgorny in June 1973 because he had never forgiven the Soviet president for "derogatory remarks about the Arabs."[5]

Most observers agree that Kissinger's grasp of the importance of the personal touch in dealing with the Arabs was of real assistance to the United States in supplanting the Soviet Union as Egypt's superpower patron in the

1970s and negotiating the interim agreements of 1974 and 1975. Sadat complimented Kissinger as being the first American official with whom Egyptians
had been able to work in two decades.[6] Among Kissinger's qualities were infinite patience, friendliness, a grasp of the Arab sense of propriety, and a willingness to lavish personal attention on his interlocutors. He was particularly
skilled at mobilizing the vocabulary of nonverbal intimacy—embracing, holding hands, sitting close, maintaining eye contact—so important to the Arab
and usually so embarrassing for the Westerner. Ismail Fahmy, no fan of
Kissinger, gives him due credit for his social talents. At only their second
meeting, Kissinger was regaling the Egyptian foreign minister with personal
stories and addressing him by his first name—just as if they were long-time
friends.[7]

On the whole, Israeli leaders have just not appreciated the need to establish
warm personal relations with Egyptians as a prior condition to conducting
business. Personal friendship and human warmth do not loom large in Israeli
domestic politics. Moreover, many of the most prominent figures among the
political/security elite that has dominated Israeli policy-making toward
Egypt, such as Dayan, Eitan, Gur, Rabin, Shamir, Sharon, and others, would
have found it genuinely difficult to emerge from the shell of dour insensitivity
with which they encased their professional careers and which is essential for
political survival under Israeli conditions. They have also tended to be disci-
ples of Ben Gurion's rather stark approach to international relations, with
its preponderant emphasis on power considerations and dismissal of the
human factor, personal trust—or, one sometimes feels, diplomacy at all—in
affairs of state. Statesmanship, in this view, was about the accurate calcula-
tion of impersonal forces and most certainly not about the cultivation of personal relationships.

There have been exceptions to this trend. Eliahu Sasson, who had grown
up in Damascus and was the Jewish Agency's and then the Israeli foreign
ministry's expert on Arab affairs, had supported the Syrian national movement as a young man, and never concealed his affection for Arabs, understood full well that "although Arab loyalty is impossible to obtain by conceding and subduing, it is obtainable by showing good faith and desire." He
succeeded so well at Rhodes in 1949 that the Egyptians insisted that he cosign
the armistice agreement on behalf of Israel together with the chief of staff
and the director-general of the foreign ministry. "This was not in accordance
with Israeli requirements," Sasson later explained. "It was in accordance with
Egyptian requirements. Over and above the formal faith which exists in all
bargaining, I represented faith in a man they knew."[8]

During the "peace process," Ezer Weizman's warm, outgoing personality
also struck a responsive chord with Egyptians and especially President Sadat,
who seems to have held him in genuine affection. Prime Minister Kamal Has-
san Ali complimented Weizman to his face on his understanding of "the Arab
way of thinking." From the beginning the Israeli defense minister was con-

vinced that his government was placing insufficient stress on direct contact with the Egyptian leadership. Convinced that personal diplomacy should be given more of a chance, he set out to fill the gap.[9] The Israeli defense minister's humor, patience, and talent as raconteur all served him well. And like Kissinger he intuitively appreciated the importance of displaying affection in the Arab style in his meetings with Egyptian friends. Hermann Eilts, U.S. ambassador to Egypt in 1973–79, believes that Weizman, who achieved a unique access to the Egyptian leadership, kept the embers of the peace talks glowing during the frostiest period of the Israeli-Egyptian relationship.[10]

Protocol

Alongside more familiar verbal means of expression, leaders have at their disposal a whole repertoire of symbolic resources for conveying political messages, including exemplary action, ceremonial enactment, dramatic gesture, and diplomatic signaling. These expedients do not replace language but possess certain qualities which can enhance the message of a speech or letter: the ability to seize the attention of an audience, to stir its emotions, and to startle it into conviction. Where words might fail to pierce the armor of incredulity or inattention, the nonverbal signal can be less easily dismissed. However, like all forms of communication, the symbolic gesture assumes that actor and spectator are broadcasting on the same wavelength—that is, share certain basic premises and indeed are equally receptive to nonverbal information.

In many cases this assumption is justified. Military signaling—including the movement and display of armed forces to deter or coerce an opponent—is very much a *lingua franca* of international politics. Diplomacy can also draw on a universally understood lexicon of moves. The withdrawal of an ambassador, an official visit, the absence from a state funeral, and so on are all diplomatic gestures conveying, within a particular context, a clear message whose meaning of approval or disapproval, warmth or frigidity has been established by convention. However, not all cultures place equivalent value on, or impute identical meaning to, symbolic acts of state. In Communist countries, for example, with their traditions of party infallibility and strictly limited access to the leadership, it is considered a diplomatic accolade of the very first order for a foreign visitor to be granted an audience with the first secretary. The principle of endorsement by proximity is much less salient in the West.

For the Arabs, protocol—the etiquette of diplomatic contact—has acquired disproportionate prominence. All Arab cultures, that of Egypt included, have a highly developed sense of propriety. Conformity to conventional norms, doing that which is expected of one, is inculcated from birth. With their distaste for personal unpleasantness and concern to maintain face, "good form" performs an essential role in avoiding surprises and maintaining social harmony. An elaborate code of conduct has accordingly evolved to cover every conceivable variation of relationship and social situation. Due rank and relative precedence must be strictly observed. The small politenesses—who goes first, who enjoys priority of service or treatment, who is or is not acknowledged socially—are immensely important. Greeting and parting have their own invariant rituals. The familial or social ties of interlocutors are meticulously reflected in formulae that precede and conclude a conversation. Hospitality, for which the Arabs are rightly renowned, is merely the best-known example of this general phenomenon. Visiting, bargaining, meeting, seating, all have their special etiquettes. Everyone has his due place, and everything is regulated by the appropriate rules.

Cross-cultural research confirms this fascination for manners and protocol. One open-ended study compared the spontaneous concerns of American and Egyptian students. American children's lack of concern for the social graces was found to contrast markedly with Egyptian children's interest in the matter.[11] another survey of Saudi-American business relations showed that Saudi managers were far more inclined than their American counterparts to see appropriate language and social ritual as obstacles to communication between the two sides.[12]

Given their domestic absorption in such issues, it is not surprising that questions of protocol and precedence are highly emphasized in Arab foreign relations. Of course, all governments wish to see their representatives paid the respect due to them and will invariably react fiercely to any form of discrimination felt to cast the slightest aspersion on their status or honor. Arab states have no monopoly of sensitivity in this respect. What they do possess—in common with other Third World societies but in contrast to the Anglo-American tradition to which Israel also belongs—is a preoccupation with protocol *for its own sake*. After all, protocol is supposed to be a means to the end of unhindered diplomatic contact and not an end in itself. Not so for the Arab diplomat. Time and again matters of form and rank have been seen to be no less important—and sometimes even more important—than matters of substance.

An entire symbolic choreography, redolent with status-consciousness, directs the steps of Arab governments. On one occasion King Abdullah of Jordan was on a visit to King Farouk of Egypt. Violating the traditional Arab code of hospitality, whereby the guest always has priority, Farouk took coffee first and in a bigger and better cup than that of his fellow monarch. Abdullah, understanding that this was intended to imply Farouk's superiority, never forgot the slight.[13] On another occasion Soviet Foreign Minister Gromyko, about to depart for a trip to Egypt, received a cable urging him to stop off en route in Damascus "to discuss urgent questions which needed special attention." When he arrived in the Syrian capital he discovered there was nothing urgent to be discussed at all. His explanation for this strange incident was that the Syrians simply wanted to demonstrate that they had been visited first—thereby presumably establishing their own precedence over Egypt.[14]

Saudi Arabia for its part has acquired a great sense of its own importance and insists that the protocol governing the visits of its representatives abroad go beyond that laid down by established convention. On one occasion Her Majesty's Government was informed that Prince Fahd, then minister of the interior and deputy prime minister of Saudi Arabia, would call off a visit to Britain unless he was received at the airport by Prime Minister Wilson in person—in British eyes a tiresome and unnecessary addition to an already overcrowded schedule but clearly one of symbolic value to the Saudis insofar as they saw it reflecting on their dignity and prestige.[15]

On a visit to Washington in February 1974, not long after Egypt and the United States had renewed diplomatic relations in the wake of the October War, Egyptian Foreign Minister Fahmy similarly insisted that he be met at the airport by Secretary of State Kissinger, although normally he would have been received by the chief of protocol. Fahmy was traveling with Saudi Minister of State Saqqaf and staying at the same hotel, which immediately raised a "prickly issue" of precedence: Kissinger was prepared to make the gesture of going over to their hotel for talks (instead of their coming to the State Department as would any Western foreign minister), but in whose suite would they meet—that of Saqqaf, who was senior in terms of service, or Fahmy, who was senior in terms of rank? Below the surface, of course, the question was whether Egypt or Saudi Arabia was to be given preferential treatment. In the end Kissinger decided that the meeting would take place in Saqqaf's suite, sugaring the pill by afterward escorting Fahmy back to his own rooms. Nor did this curious diplomatic jockeying for position—somewhat reminiscent of a French farce but deeply serious to the participants—end there. Kissinger and Fahmy conducted an argument through the medium of their respective memoirs as to who then saw whom to whose car with what purpose. . . .[16]

Not surprisingly, protocol has also been extensively manipulated by Arab governments over the years to symbolize and signal their rejection of the legitimacy of the State of Israel. Their ostracism has taken many and varied forms, from a refusal to meet officially with Israeli representatives, or to maintain diplomatic relations in any shape or form with the Jewish state, to more trivial gestures. Abba Eban recalls that as Israel's ambassador to the United Nations he had been seated, by alphabetical chance, next to the Iraqi delegate. One ashtray was provided for both of them, but when Eban deposited a dead match in it, his Iraqi colleague called an attendant over to ask for a separate receptacle for his own use. He was presumably appalled, Eban reflects, at the thought that loyal Arab ash "might mingle promiscuously with the Zionist ash from an Israeli pipe."[17]

Anecdotes apart, the logic of Arab ostracism was plain enough. Protocol is not a privilege one bestows at will but a set of rules and conventions governing the treatment by one government of the representatives of another.

By determining in advance where an official of a certain rank is to be seated, one obviates unnecessary confusion and any possible sense of discrimination. Private citizens, whoever they are, are not entitled by right to treatment according to protocol. For this reason, whether or not protocol is in evidence has come to be accepted as an acknowledgment or denial of the official status of a guest and implicit recognition of the sovereignty of the state which he represents. The Arab reluctance to accord Israeli representatives any protocol privileges was not meant as a display of bad manners for its own sake but reflected a refusal to recognize the sovereignty of the State of Israel.

Throughout the complex diplomatic maneuvering that followed the 1973 Yom Kippur War, protocol was used by the Arab states to communicate with great precision the nuances of their respective positions toward Israel. In December 1973 a conference was convened at Geneva of the combatants in the recent war together with the two superpowers. At the insistence of the Arabs, the conference was held under the auspices of the United Nations, although that body performed no substantive role, in that way it could argue that it was avoiding any recognition of Israel going beyond that already implied by their common membership in the world body. However, the meeting was billed as a "peace conference," and the willingness of Egypt and Jordan to attend, without insisting on the presence of the Palestine Liberation Organization, was a signal of flexibility. (A most significant one, as it turned out, notwithstanding the effective replacement of this international framework for negotiations by American mediation in the shape of Dr. Kissinger's "shuttle diplomacy" shortly after.) Recognizing the connotations of its presence in the same room as Israel, Syria declined to attend the conference at all. Its absence was marked by an ostentatiously empty table. Egyptian Foreign Minister Fahmy, in turn, disturbed by the symbolism of his physical proximity to Israeli Foreign Minister Eban, at first insisted that Syria's empty table be demonstratively placed between the two of them. Eban vigorously rejected "a seating arrangement with a hint of Israeli ostracism, as if we were afflicted with leprosy." How could two countries make peace with each other when their delegates could not even sit together? In the end it was agreed that Eban would be seated between UN Secretary-General Waldheim and Soviet Foreign Minister Gromyko. But when the conference adjourned after two days, not a single handshake was exchanged by Arabs and Israelis.[18]

Fahmy's reluctance to concede any hint of recognition of Israel beyond that entailed by the exigencies of the recent war faithfully represented the attitude of the Egyptian diplomatic establishment, although not, as it turned out, the strategic conception of President Sadat. Until November 1977 the establishment view prevailed. For instance, after the second disengagement agreement of 1975 between Egypt and Israel—by which Israeli forces withdrew deeper into the Sinai and security arrangements were consolidated between the two armies—Sadat proposed to sign one of the documents in person on behalf of Egypt. Fahmy strongly objected, arguing that the occasion should not be given "undue political significance," but rather its "military character" should be underlined.[19]

Israel was very well aware of the thrust of these gambits. After all, it had been their target for thirty years. There was no cross-cultural misunderstanding on this point. Its own routine countermove was to call for direct negotiations leading to a formal treaty of peace and the establishment of full-fledged diplomatic relations between the two countries. Nor was Israel unaware of Egypt's sensitivity on issues of protocol. Thus, when Sadat offered to come to Jerusalem in November 1977, Prime Minister Begin was quick to assure him, in the official letter of invitation, that he would be received "with respect and cordiality." In the event, the Israeli government pulled out all the stops not only to greet Sadat with the honor due him as a visiting head of state, but also to fit the occasion out with every trapping of hospitality, dignity, and even warmth. It was in their interest to do so, of course. A penitence at Canossa by a contrite and humiliated Egyptian president would have been quite worthless and transitory. Sadat's prestige had to be shored up and the man given full credit. The world must be left in no doubt of the historic significance of the visit. Here was an Arab leader, after a generation of enmity, acknowledging Israel's sovereignty in the most graphic and dramatic way imaginable. In his Knesset speech Sadat acknowledged the momentous transformation symbolized by his presence in the "home," as he put it, of the people of Israel:

> We used to reject you, and we had our reasons and grievances. Yes, we used to reject meeting you anywhere. Yes, we used to describe you as "so-called Israel." Yes, conferences and international organizations used to bring us together. Our representatives have never and still do not exchange greetings and salaams. Yes, this is what happened, and it still goes on. For any talks, we used [to] make it conditional that a mediator met each side separately. Yes, this is how the talks on the first disengagement were conducted and this is also how the talks on the second disengagement were held. Our representatives met at the first Geneva conference without exchanging one direct word. Yes, this is what went on. But I say to you today and I say to the whole world that we accept that we should live with you in a lasting and just peace.[20]

During the long months of negotiation—and frequent frustration—that followed Sadat's Jerusalem trip, the Egyptian president continued to bestow or withhold protocol favors in order to make political points. At the end of December 1977, a high-level Israeli delegation, including Prime Minister Begin, Foreign Minister Dayan, and Weizman again, arrived in Egypt. Sadat chose to hint at his disappointment at Israel's failure to reward his initiative with some far-reaching concession. At the Abu Swair military airfield, the Israelis were received correctly—but no more. There was a red carpet and a guard of honor, and Vice-President Mubarak was in attendance. But President Sadat himself was absent, and there were no Israeli flags and no anthems. Dayan, while noting his own—typically Israeli—lack of interest in "pomp and ceremony," remarked on the "political implications" of these omissions and contrasted the occasion with Sadat's glittering welcome in Israel. Weizman was also disturbed by "the flouting of the most elementary rules of protocol and courtesy" (an exaggeration) and had no doubt that it was meant as a deliberate snub. He had expected some kind of gesture on Sadat's part, such as his presence on the airport apron to greet the party, and felt that the ceremonial neglect of the Israeli prime minister—his name was even omitted from the colorful slogans and abundant decorations in praise of the Egyptian president which adorned the streets of Ismailia—was an unfortunate move. Putting himself in Sadat's shoes, Weizman speculated that the *Rais* wished to avoid further antagonizing the Arab world, which had been outraged by his trip to Jerusalem.[21]

Despite their low context instinct for simplicity and straightforward dealing, the Israelis quickly grasped the political uses to which protocol was being put by President Sadat. They did not themselves tend to regulate hospitality in quite this fine-tuned way, but they did get the point. Paradoxically, it was mostly after the signing of the 1979 peace treaty, followed by the establishment of full diplomatic relations and the exchange of ambassadors, that protocol (widely defined to include signs of friendship and hospitality in general) had unintended and hence disruptive implications for Egyptian-Israeli relations. In normal circumstances the calibration of protocol is a rather discrete and precise way for a host government to convey its approval, disagreement, or whatever to a resident ambassador. Its purport is plain to the trained diplomat, yet it avoids the finality of public declarations or more far-reaching moves. Most important, it avoids the glare of publicity and the complicating involvement of public opinion. When the situation shifts, it is easy to signal one's changing attitude by restoring some mark of favor. Unfortunately, the conditions of public indifference and official objectivity necessary for the success of this strategy did not hold in the case of Israel.

In February 1980, Israel and Egypt exchanged ambassadors. Sa'ad Mortadeh, the Egyptian ambassador in Tel Aviv, found himself the instant darling of Israeli society. No social occasion was considered complete without his presence. In Cairo the picture was very different. Eliahu Ben-Elissar, the new Israeli ambassador, found himself systematically discriminated against. Socially he was a pariah. Neither he nor his wife was invited to official receptions, officials and even private citizens declined to meet him, and he and his staff found great difficulty in renting apartments in Cairo. Not only was he virtually excluded from Cairo society, but news of a rare invitation to an unofficial function would lead to its being boycotted by Egyptian guests. A reception held by *Time* magazine at the Hilton hotel for its new bureau chief, to which the ambassador had been invited (but which he ironically did not attend), was an embarrassing flop when hundreds of guests failed to appear. It quickly emerged that the protocol department of the Egyptian foreign ministry had actually circulated a document containing explicit instructions that contact with the Israeli embassy and its ambassador be kept to a minimum. In a restrained account of her year in the Egyptian capital, Mrs. Ben-Elissar wrote that her most painful moment was when it became clear that she and her husband were the victims of a "social boycott." She had warm words for the Egyptian people but hardly concealed her bitterness at the behavior of the protocol department, going so far as to mention its chief, Diwani, by name.[22] Presumably, though, neither she nor her husband was under any illusion about the real source of the campaign; protocol is the servant, not master, of policy.

Ben-Elissar's quarantine at the hands of the Egyptian authorities soon became public knowledge.[23] A special term was coined in Israel at this time (1980–82) to describe relations with Egypt—the "cold peace." Admittedly, issues of protocol were simply the external sign of unresolved difficulties in Israeli-Egyptian relations. All the while the autonomy negotiations on the future of the Palestinians in the West Bank were dragging on inconclusively—to the evident displeasure of the Egyptian government, which remained isolated in the Arab world. Protocol was being manipulated by the Egyptians, as they had always manipulated it, to express their dissatisfaction at Israeli policy. Another way they found to signal their discontent was in the halting implementation—if that—of manifold "normalization" agreements in the fields of trade, tourism, and culture.[24] But it was the treatment meted out by the Egyptian authorities to Israeli delegations and representatives that seemed best to symbolize the yawning chasm that still separated the two peoples. Ben-Elissar was simply one tangible example of the lack of human warmth in the stumbling and anticlimactic relationship with Egypt. That "our man" in Cairo should be socially ostracized was deeply resented. What did peace mean if not friendship and cooperation between human beings? If peace implied merely an absence of war, why should Israel make further concessions to the Egyptian point of view?

For years Israeli leaders had talked of their desire for "true peace," *shalom emeth*, with their neighbors. The expression was drawn, like so much else in Modern Hebrew, from the Bible (Jeremiah 14:13) and was redolent with messianic associations. By it they meant much more than an end to belligerency and a minimal establishment of diplomatic relations. Following the conclusion of the Camp David accord, Begin broadcast a personal message to the people of Israel, beginning with the popular refrain "We have brought peace unto you." Nothing could have been further from his mind or that of his listeners than the "cold peace" which seemed to be the Egyptian concept of international harmony. The Israeli prospect of peace bore the inspiration of the prophets and was of a Middle East marked by fraternity and development. "It will be a great day," Golda Meir once reflected in her simple way, "when Arab farmers will cross the Jordan not with planes or tanks, but with tractors and with their hands outstretched in friendship, as between farmer and farmer, as between human beings. A dream it may be, but I am sure that one day it will come true."[25]

This kind of anticipation about what peace would entail was intuitively held by many Israelis. The theme of peace runs through the Jewish scriptures like a seam of gold. Every day the observant Jew prays that the Lord will "grant peace unto Israel," and the sublime vision of Isaiah and Micah is an indelible part of the cultural heritage of every Jew.

> They shall beat their swords into plowshares,
> And their spears into pruninghooks;
> Nation shall not lift up sword against nation,
> Neither shall they learn war any more.
>   (Isaiah 2:4)

It is surely not by chance that mankind's most evocative images of human concord are taken from the Bible or that the statue to peace donated—by the Soviet Union—to the United Nations echoes the same motif.

However, it is doubtful whether the Egyptian government shared this dream or ever grasped the powerful and negative resonances set off by its restrictive approach to peace in general and "normalization" in particular. The Koran offers no majestic vision of peace among nations, and classic Islamic international law views treaties of peace with the infidel as temporary expedients—truces—on the road to the universal imposition of Islam.[26] At the philosophical level, there was no meeting of minds between Moslems and Jews about what peace might entail. Even President Sadat, for all his sweeping imagination, was quite unable to empathize with Jewish hopes. In an interview with *Newsweek* in 1971, he abruptly dismissed another homely remark of Mrs. Meir that peace would come when she could "drive her car from Tel-Aviv to Cairo to do some shopping." It was, he affirmed, "a pipe dream, based on the victory complex."[27] The "peace process" never succeeded in spanning this conceptual gulf.

Symbolic Politics

The Egyptian high context propensity to nonverbal communication is strikingly reflected not only in the manipulation of protocol but also in an extraordinary talent for the symbolic political gesture. From the 1955 nationalization of the Suez Canal, via the expulsion of the United Nations Emergency Force from the Sinai in 1967 and the Soviet military mission from Egypt in 1972, to the 1977 Jerusalem visit, both Nasser and Sadat showed themselves masters of the dramaturgical art. In a society in which illiteracy, at least at the village level, is still widespread, the political utility of a striking and tangible act is self-evident. Television, as the visual medium *par excellence*, has become, indeed, an important instrument in the political mobilization of the Egyptian masses.[28]

It was natural for Egyptian leaders to make symbolic moves in their communications with Israel. In the first place this was the approach that instinctively occurred to them in the light of their own alertness to nonverbal nuance. At the same time, given the hostility and mistrust that marked Egyptian-Israeli relations for so long, nonverbal signaling would seem to stand a better chance of demonstrating good faith and overcoming Israeli suspicions. Finally, it must always be easier in the high context culture to make one's point elliptically rather than directly. What was not realized was that a mode of expression that was translucent to the Egyptian was only dimly discernible to the Israeli. Here, indeed, was a dialogue of the deaf. That Egyptian signals were often not fully appreciated by Israeli governments—which also missed opportunities for communicating with Egyptians in a language they would have understood—was not, of course, the fault of either side. Miscomprehension was simply inherent in the logic of the cross-cultural encounter.

The background to my first example is the overthrow of the monarchy in Egypt by the Free Officers group under Colonel Gamal Abdel Nasser on 23 July 1952. Encouraged by the reformist credentials of the revolution, Israeli Prime Minister David Ben Gurion made an important speech to the Knesset on 18 August 1952 in which he denied that there was any objective conflict of interest between the two countries and suggested the possibility of their cooperation. Israel, he continued, was interested in a free, independent Egypt and had demonstrated its good will by declining to take advantage of the difficult situation in which Egypt found itself in its relations with Britain (on 16 October 1951 the Nahhas government had unilaterally abrogated the 1936 Anglo-Egyptian treaty under which Britain maintained its massive Suez military bases, setting off a drawn-out crisis in Anglo-Egyptian relations).[29] This trial balloon was then followed up with an official proposal passed on by the Israeli chargé d'affaires in Paris to his Egyptian counterpart for peace negotiations between their two governments.[30]

Nothing immediately came of this initiative, partly because of leaks on the Israeli side and the domestic preoccupations of the new Egyptian regime. However, feelers continued to be put out. At that winter's General Assembly of the United Nations, Ambassador Eban presented an Israeli "Blueprint for Peace." During January and February 1953 there were further highly promising signals: the Americans were informed by an official at the Egyptian embassy in Washington that "it was time for Egypt and Israel to end their dispute and make some arrangement so the two countries could live together in peace"; contact was established by Israel with "influential Egyptians close to [Prime Minister] Naguib" who appeared to accept the principle that the solution to the problem of the Palestine refugees lay in their resettlement in Arab states; and finally, Ralph Bunche, the United Nations assistant secretary-general, was also active at this time, carrying messages between Cairo and Jerusalem.[31]

The culmination of these various contacts came in May 1953 in the form of a letter to Israeli Foreign Minister Sharett written on the official notepaper of the Revolutionary Command Council and signed by Colonel Nasser, Premier Naguib's nominal deputy, but the real leader of the Free Officers movement. In it Nasser requested that Israel use its influence with the United States on behalf of Egypt (in order to obtain American support in the matter of the difficult and crucial negotiations then being conducted with Britain for the evacuation of its forces from Suez). Proof of concrete Israeli assistance would help to bring about a final settlement in Egyptian-Israeli relations, and Egypt would also exercise its influence in Arab circles in the same direction. Nasser reiterated his assurance that Egypt bore no hostile intentions toward Israel. In order to demonstrate good will, his government would seriously consider the question of the free passage of Israeli ships through the Suez Canal (which until then had not been permitted by Egypt).

Ben Gurion's reaction in a memorandum of 17 May 1953 was mistrustful and dismissive. Was Israel supposed to prove its good faith toward Egypt while the latter continued its attacks (i.e., infiltration by irregulars out of the Gaza Strip) against Israel? It should be made clear to the other side, he wrote, that Israel would mobilize its political influence in Washington on Egypt's behalf only if it received "a definite commitment" to the free passage of Israeli ships through the Suez Canal. And until peace was assured, Israel would continue to oppose the supply of American arms to Egypt.[32]

The Foreign Ministry view basically followed this line. Nasser's note was intended to lull Israel into a false sense of security lest it exploit his dispute with Britain. Israel should exploit Egyptian difficulties to put his intentions to the test. Rather than indulge in "a drawn-out game of empty promises," it should demand, without further ado, free passage through the Suez Canal and a secret meeting at a high level. A reply in this spirit was accordingly drafted and sent.[33]

In effect Israel had returned the ball to the Egyptian court by declining a prior gesture on its own part yet requiring one from Egypt. Why had Egypt to be "put to the test" in this precipitous manner? As far as Egypt was concerned, passage through the Suez Canal was to be denied to Israeli shipping in the absence of peaceful relations. Once there was peace, the benefits of peace would naturally follow—but at the conclusion, not the beginning, of the process. What had Israel to gain by this ultimative and impatient approach? Even if Nasser was only playing for time, was not a golden opportunity to improve relations as an investment in the future being passed up? Although an improved *modus vivendi* might not be as good as a full peace, it was surely better than a relationship of tension—and might develop into something more. What is clear is that at this fragile stage of the relationship, it was unrealistic—and humiliating—to call for "a definite commitment" from the fledgling Egyptian government, struggling to find its feet at home and abroad. As so often before and since, an Israeli diplomatic frontal attack was to jar Egypt's sensibilities. Good will could be built up only layer upon painstaking layer, preferably by actions on the ground rather than by binding formulas. Besides, what would be the value of such a commitment in the absence of good will?

Surely, though, Ben Gurion and the Foreign Ministry officials had missed the whole implicit point of Nasser's overture. In effect Nasser *had made a subtle gesture* of Egyptian good will by the mere fact of the letter. According to diplomatic convention, a letter bearing an official letterhead and a signature has the status of a formal *Note* of the kind used by one government to communicate its official position on a matter of appropriate gravity to another government. By it Nasser was both acknowledging Israeli sovereignty and providing a warranty of his own good faith—for, should it so wish, Israel could seriously embarrass him by publishing the contents of the communication. It was an elliptical, nonverbal way of signaling precisely that commitment that Ben Gurion wanted to be put into so many words. But no less significant, while all this high-level diplomacy was underway, Nasser was signaling his interest in an accommodation through at least two other complementary, nonverbal channels. The first of these was, crucially, via the disposition of Egyptian forces on the ground. In May 1953 the Egyptian garrison in Sinai was reduced to a very considerable extent, and concentrated in the Nile Delta. Egypt was then wide open to Israeli attack.[34] Clearly the move was connected to the Anglo-Egyptian negotiations. Even so, Egypt had, in the most tangible way possible, removed itself from the ranks of Israel's enemies. As was apparent to at least the British, circumstances were therefore highly auspicious for a magnanimous Israeli overture.

The second signal was transmitted at a more mundane but no less indicative level. During this period Egyptian and Israeli delegations were engaged in a technical negotiation within the framework of the Mixed Armistice Commission set up in 1949. On 24 July 1953 the two countries signed a Coastal Waters Agreement—the first political accord since the armistice—permitting nonmilitary vessels of either country in distress to take refuge in the territorial waters of the other. It is inconceivable that this treaty could have been signed without an Egyptian decision at the very highest level. As with all nonverbal messages, official denials could not alter the facts on the ground. A first *public* step had been taken on the path of normalization. The Lebanese press had no doubt that there had been a breach of the Arab countries' quarantine of the Jewish state. Taken together with the Nasser letter and the Egyptian military withdrawal, it all signified most expressively that Egypt and Israel had reached a turning point in their relationship. That Egypt's evident interest in an accommodation, however limited, was not taken advantage of at this point, was a real missed opportunity.[35]

My second example of nonverbal confusion is taken from the difficult period of the War of Attrition of 1969–70 and is known in Israel as the Goldmann Affair. The June 1967 War, it will be recalled, had left Israeli forces in control of the Sinai peninsula and installed on the east bank of the Suez Canal. The price of their withdrawal was to be nothing less than direct negotiations between Israel and its neighbors leading to a full-fledged peace treaty. But on 1 September 1967, the Khartoum conference of Arab heads of state resolved that there could be "no peace with Israel, no recognition of Israel, no negotiations with it." Israeli troops remained in place, and demands for territorial changes—"secure borders"—began to be heard from Jerusalem. Unwilling to allow the *status quo* to congeal into a new territorial settlement, President Nasser launched a "war of attrition" along the canal in March 1969, consisting mainly of artillery bombardments of Israeli positions. In January 1970, in an attempt to undermine Egyptian morale, Israel began launching aerial attacks deep into the Nile Delta. Heavy casualties were inflicted on Egyptian civilian and military targets. On 12 February 1970, seventy Egyptian workers were killed and many injured in an Israeli air raid on a scrap metal–processing factory at Abu Zabal. Large demonstrations were held on the streets of Cairo. President Nasser, who had just returned from a visit to the USSR in a desperate quest for emergency assistance, then announced on 14 February that he was seeking Soviet MiG-23 fighter planes and technological aid to meet the Israeli threat.[36]

On 18 February—the timing is important—an interview appeared in *The Times* of London with Golda Meir, the prime minister of Israel, in which she declared that she would take the risk of breaking up the National Unity government (set up in June 1967 and containing ministers from the hard-line Herut party) if she was convinced that an Arab state was seriously interested in peace. Nasser was favorably impressed by this statement.[37] Almost simultaneously, an interview was published in *Le Monde* in which, in the convoluted way we have seen to be characteristic, Nasser affirmed his own interest in a settlement. The only litigation separating Israel and Egypt, he said, was the problems of the Palestinian refugees and Israel's occupation of the Arab territories. United Nations Resolution 242 of 22 November 1967 provided a solution to both these issues. Had Israel agreed to apply a previous UN resolution of 1948 which gave the refugees "the right to choose between repatriation in Israel and compensation," "we would have established a definitive peace more than 20 years ago." However, he did not envisage direct negotiations with Israel or an actual peace treaty but an accommodation reached through the good offices of UN mediator Gunnar Jarring.[38]

In the light of this apparent coincidence of aspirations, the time must have seemed ripe for some kind of diplomatic initiative to break out of the stalemate in which both sides found themselves—a war neither could win and which might escalate out of control. In the meantime, horrendous losses were being inflicted on Egypt, but Soviet arms—including the latest SAM-3 anti-aircraft missiles—would soon arrive on the scene and promised to restore the balance of forces momentarily tipped in Israel's favor. The problem for Nasser was how to achieve movement without an explicit infringement of the "three no's" of the Khartoum conference. On 23 and 24 February 1970, according to Eric Rouleau, *Le Monde's* Middle East expert (and one of the intermediaries in the affair), Nasser met Yugoslav President Tito at Aswan. Tito had long been trying to bring about a meeting between the Egyptian leader and seventy-five-year-old Nahum Goldmann, for many years the president of the World Jewish Congress and the World Zionist Organization, and the architect of the 1952 reparations agreement with the Federal Republic of Germany. When Tito then raised the matter, Nasser informed him that he no longer had any objection to receiving the veteran Zionist diplomat.[39]

Nahum Goldmann was in Paris when he was contacted by an unofficial envoy of President Nasser, Ahmed Hamrush, one of the Free Officers who had taken part in the 1952 revolution. The terms of the prospective meeting would be as follows: Goldmann was invited in the capacity of a private individual and not as a representative of the State of Israel. He could travel on his Israeli passport, though he also held a Swiss one. On the Israeli side, two conditions would have to be met before Nasser made the final decision to go ahead: that Golda Meir consent to the visit in advance and agree that it be made public. Goldmann then flew to Israel to inform the Israeli prime minister. At a meeting on 24 March, Meir expressed her skepticism and informed him that she would have to bring the matter before the cabinet; when Goldmann tried to dissuade her, suspecting that the news would leak out and that ministers could never give their *formal* consent, she insisted. Asked to authorize the trip, the cabinet voted against.[40]

There the matter would have rested, with no one the wiser, had the Israeli government, in order to forestall press speculation on the episode, not decided to make a public announcement on 5 April explaining its decision to turn down the proposal: The government, the announcement ran, "would have responded to any sign of readiness on the part of the President of Egypt for a meeting to clarify problems vital to Egypt and Israel, if each side were free to choose its own representative. In reply therefore to Dr. Goldmann's request that the Government authorize his meeting with the Egyptian President, the Government decided in the negative." The Egyptian government immediately responded with a disclaimer that any invitation had been issued.

With the publication of the communiqué—at eleven o'clock at night—a political furor, of the kind beloved in Israel, was immediately unleashed. Had or had not the government been asked by Dr. Goldmann explicitly to *authorize* his trip? Was there any difference between an official envoy and an unofficial visitor traveling with the knowledge of his government? Had a chance for peace been missed, or was the whole affair a cunning trap conceived by President Nasser to gain a propaganda advantage? Had not the government shot itself in the foot by its peremptory rejection of the idea? And so on.

On 7 April a parliamentary debate was held. Speaking on behalf of the government, Foreign Minister Eban explained why Israel had turned down what on the face of it appeared a most promising opportunity to break the deadlock. Dr. Goldmann, he made plain, was not an acceptable spokesman for the Israeli point of view. Indeed, the main reason the latter had been picked out as the first Israeli to meet with President Nasser was that he was "noncomformist" in his views and believed that the policy of the Israeli government was mistaken (Goldmann had indeed written an article critical of Israeli foreign policy for the latest issue of *Foreign Affairs*). What could be the point of a meeting with an Arab leader but to impress him with the soundness of the Israeli enterprise and to impart to him a clearer understanding of Israel's positions and motives? Such a leader must be brought to understand why Israel insisted on a contractual peace, on direct negotiations and secure borders. For this purpose only Israel could choose who was going to represent it.

But was not the main thing that such a meeting take place at all? Eban shrugged off this objection. Entire bookcases were filled with descriptions of summit conferences that had done more harm than good because they were poorly prepared and had ill-defined objectives. Israel "had to turn its attention from form and outward appearance and concentrate on the substance and essence of the matter. International statesmanship in our generation does not concern itself much with etiquette and symbolism; it deals with the gravest and most substantive problems that man can face—the issues of war and peace, of national existence or destruction."[41]

If the thesis of this chapter is correct, then it is clear that Eban and his colleagues had, like Ben Gurion in 1953, quite missed the point of Nasser's invitation. Arab statesmanship most certainly does concern itself a very great deal with "etiquette and symbolism"! Of all the speakers in the debate only Eliahu Sasson, by then a Labor Member of the Knesset, really grasped the basic issue at stake. In a gentle, implied rebuke to the foreign minister, he argued that Israel was bogged down in the details of negotiations and maps and solutions, when the real question was how to break the deadlock. The first priority was to begin talking.[42]

For this was surely the fundamental message underlying Nasser's initiative. By inviting a world-famous Zionist leader to Cairo on an Israeli passport for a publicized exchange of views—the first such meeting ever—Nasser was clearly signaling his willingness to enter into contacts with Israel. Of course, the fact that Goldmann held pragmatic opinions on the shape of a final settlement was relevant. His choice did hint at Nasser's preferences for the basis of a future dialogue. But the burden of Nasser's message, beside which all else paled into insignificance, was that dialogue should commence. For Israel to reject the overture because Goldmann was "nonconformist" was an act of remarkable obtuseness. Nasser not only knew full well that Goldmann held no mandate to negotiate on Israel's behalf but had actually required that he arrive in an unofficial capacity in order to express his personal views. One must also suppose that the president of Egypt was not entirely ignorant of those positions Eban wished to see articulated so vigorously—Israel had certainly not kept them secret. In short, Goldmann could be intended only as a stepping-stone to Golda Meir—the lady who was in unquestioned charge in Israel.

The willingness to talk, then, was the main theme of the performance. Yet Nasser's subtle orchestration of subordinate motifs also deserves careful attention. One of the problems faced by Nasser was how to reconcile contact with Israel with the Khartoum rejection of negotiations. Goldmann's unique role as a Zionist leader of over fifty years' standing, together with his nongovernmental status, permitted just that. His reception, as *Le Monde* realized, would have marked "a breach in the wall." The other major problem was that familiar one of pride. Nasser would not have been Egyptian if he simply could have sat down with a five-star envoy of the Israeli government, because this would have constituted a humiliating acknowledgment of defeat, a signal of capitulation. Face had to be saved by an indirect, preliminary maneuver which would both prepare public opinion and ensure that any subsequent negotiations would be conducted on a realistic basis and not end in a disastrous failure that would bring the worst of both worlds down on Nasser's head.

At the same time, Nasser's insistence on publicity for the visit was a powerful guarantee of his own good faith—the meeting would be openly acknowledged, doubtless to the dismay of all those in the Arab world who still dreamed of eliminating the Jewish state. What did they care if Goldmann had published an article critical of his government in *Foreign Affairs*? Here would be implied recognition of the state of Israel and acceptance of the need for negotiations. True, Meir was being asked for a reciprocal gesture, namely, her consent in advance to the encounter. But clearly she also had to give some sign of willingness to enter a dialogue. Moreover, Nasser was not being entirely inconsiderate. Meir had told *The Times* on 18 February that she would take the risk of breaking up the National Unity government if she was convinced that an Arab state was seriously interested in peace. Goldmann's exploratory trip (and he was, after all, a statesman of immense experience; presumably he would be able to report back accurately) would enable Meir to appraise Nasser's intentions at her leisure before deciding whether or not it was worth shedding her Herut ministers.

Harold Saunders, the former United States assistant secretary for Near Eastern and South Asian affairs, and a veteran of the Egypt-Israel "peace process," argues that the act of negotiation between Jews and Arabs has been less intractable than overcoming prior obstacles to negotiation: "Persuading people to sit down at the table seemed even more difficult than reaching agreement once they were there."[43] Without minimizing the difficulties of negotiation—which I shall deal with in chapter 7—the two cases examined so far provide strong evidence to sustain his argument. As long as cross-

cultural disjunction prevents opponents from even exploiting such fleeting opportunities for dialogue as emerge, the outlook for the peaceful settlement
of disputes must remain dim.

It is, therefore, to Sadat's great credit that he eventually did succeed—with
the indispensable help of the United States—in finding ways of overcoming
the "psychological barrier" between the two sides. He must have wracked his
brain in the search for a way to convince Israelis of his good faith. What
was needed, in the jargon of superpower relations, was "confidence-building
measures." But the obstacles, as we have seen, were daunting: a generation
of hostility, profound mistrust, and the absence of a common language of discourse in both a literal and figurative sense. Partly the answer lay in
Kissinger's step-by-step approach. In the aftermath of the second interim
agreement of 1975, though, it was clear that this strategy had run its course.
The larger problems could no longer be evaded. The "confidence-building"
solution that Sadat, the devout Moslem, came up with was a resort to the
nonverbal idiom of religious symbolism. In this way he might hope to touch
upon a deeper, less skeptical chord in the Israeli make-up, create a common
bond, and elevate a vulgar transaction to the level of a sacred compact.

But what possible symbols could Sadat evoke that might resonate with an
Israeli audience? Between opponents of the same faith, an appeal can always
be made to familiar themes. One recalls De Gaulle and Adenauer worshipping in shared communion at Reims Cathedral and embracing with the kiss
of peace. Arabs have the solemn rituals of the *sulh*. However, between Jews
and Arabs there are no mechanisms of reconciliation ready to hand, and many
shared associations are unfortunate ones. The Koran hardly draws a sympathetic portrait of the Jews who declined to accept the election of the Prophet.
Nor does the Bible present the neighbors of the Hebrews in a favorable light.
Indeed, the two faiths seem joined by a symmetry of aversion rather than
of affection.

Sadat's dramaturgic inventions displayed both empathy and originality. On
20 June 1977, following his recent victory in the Israeli elections, Menahem
Begin presented his cabinet for parliamentary approval. In his inaugural address he called upon Arab leaders to meet with him with the object of arriving
at a true peace. On 19 July Egypt returned with full military honors the
recently discovered bodies of nineteen Israeli soldiers killed on the Sinai front
in the 1973 war. "Why did I do it?" asks Sadat rhetorically in his memoirs.
"For the sake of peace."[44] He had chosen a powerful symbol of reconciliation:
To bring a body to rest in consecrated ground is an important Jewish religious
injunction with highly emotive overtones for the State of Israel. In the past
Israel had made great efforts to secure the remains of its fallen and often
paid a heavy price for the privilege. This time Egypt demanded no counter
concession, for no profane barter was involved. Nevertheless, the gesture was
not entirely philanthropic. Like many symbolic acts it carried a hint of ambiguity. The solemn military ceremony subtly evoked a war which had restored

Egyptian honor and cost Israel dearly. It was a reminder for Israel that in a peace settlement no one would be doing anyone a favor.

As for Sadat's visit to Jerusalem in November, the occasion was replete with religious symbolism. Here Sadat's purpose was manifold. To watching Arabs it was essential to legitimize the trip as an act of piety, not submission—a sacred pilgrimage to a holy city. From Americans, riveted to television screens by the extraordinary episode, sympathy and admiration could be elicited by echoes of that other mission of a Prince of Peace. To Jews the journey must demonstrate unimpeachable dignity as well as respect for the host and a sincere desire for an end to war. Sadat's itinerary was resonant with these aims. The very first site to be visited was the El Aksa mosque, Islam's third-holiest shrine, to kneel in prayer on the occasion of the festival of Id al-Adha. The timing was impeccable: the festival, which commemorates Abraham's willingness to sacrifice Isaac, recalls the common ancestor of both Jews and Arabs. From here Sadat moved on to the other great Jerusalem mosque of El Sakhra, the magnificent Dome of the Rock. The next stage on his tour carried a message for Christians everwhere: along the Via Dolorosa—the way of the Cross—to the Holy Sepulcher, the traditional site of Jesus' tomb. Then on to Yad Vashem, Israel's shrine to victims of the Nazi Holocaust, with its Tabernacle of Remembrance containing the eternal flame. Sadat realized, as he later recalled, that this visit to a place "most precious to the Jews" would be criticized in Arab countries. "But I did it to emphasize that I really want peace and do not want wars between us. I do not want oceans of tears over millions of victims."[45] It was an inspired move.

As the mundane and painful task of negotiation itself got underway, Sadat continued to delve for symbols of partnership. At Ismailia in December 1977, he chose to open the summit conference in an extraordinary manner. As the Israeli delegation, headed by Prime Minister Begin, took their seats, the Egyptian president announced that he wished to swear in his new foreign minister, Mohamed Ibrahim Kamel. The Israelis got up to leave but were signaled to remain. There, in front of ministers and officials from the two countries, Sadat administered the oath to Kamel on the Koran. His intention, he informed his officials, was "to enhance the impression of cordiality and peace."[46] In the absence of some more appropriate inaugural prayer or ritual, the simple yet dignified ceremony also served to launch the proceedings on a solemn note. Kamel, moreover, the instrument of Sadat's peace strategy vis-à-vis Israel, was being consecrated for the joint endeavor, pledging himself to pursue it as a sacred trust. Of the various Israeli accounts of this episode, only that of Ezer Weizman reveals any glimmering of understanding. Sadat, he conjectures, "wanted to make us feel at home," to unite Israelis and Egyptians "into a kind of large extended family assembled to consider its joint future and the future of its children."[47] That politics might be lent a transcendental dimension was otherwise lost on the overwhelmingly secular Israeli leadership.

What was needed to sustain the momentum of negotiations in the aftermath of the Sadat visit to Jerusalem was some kind of reciprocal Israeli gesture that would consolidate the president's position and win over Arab hearts. Israel, however, was quite oblivious to the symbolic as opposed to the substantive needs of peacemaking with Egypt. To heal the psychic wounds required more than a pragmatic deal but the ritual purging away of bad blood. Without the necessary psychological and cultural catharsis provided by some imaginative and surmounting act of grace on the Israeli side, practical efforts to resolve the dispute would be gravely encumbered. Even an openhanded but generalized acknowledgment of Egyptian and Palestinian rights in the form of a declaration of principles would have been sufficient in the early stages of the negotiation (this was Sadat's objective at Ismailia). Another possibility, actually suggested, surprisingly enough, by Agriculture Minister Arik Sharon, would have been to hand back to the Egyptians an important enclave such as the Sinai coastal town of El Arish as a mark of magnanimity. Unfortunately, both these alternatives were rejected by the Israeli government. On the contrary, they immediately plunged into detailed bargaining over Sinai real estate, much to Sadat's dismay. Their only gesture was to insist that Israel retain part of the peninsula.

When Weizman met with Sadat in Salzburg in July 1978, after six months of deadlock, the Egyptian *Rais* did not conceal his disappointment at Israel's failure to acknowledge appropriately his Jerusalem visit. "If you had only made some gesture in response—if you had only withdrawn to the El Arish-Ras Mohamed line [bisecting the Sinai]! I was expecting something like that." Now, to revive the talks, he suggested some dramatic act on Israel's part. It was an amazing proposal: the return to Egypt, even before the signing of a peace treaty, of El Arish and Jabal Musa—the traditional site of Mount Sinai. El Arish would be declared a town of peace, a place where other Arab leaders could join the negotiations. On Jabal Musa Sadat would build a mosque, a synagogue, and a church, in symbolic unification of the three great monotheistic religions. What more expressive token of reconciliation could one imagine?[48]

In fact this was not the first time that Sadat had brought up this project. In the past Israel's response had been derisive. This occasion was no different. Within forty-eight hours of Weizman's reporting back to Begin, the idea had leaked to the press; once out in the open it died of the cold. Asked to comment, Begin was contemptuous. "One doesn't get something for nothing!" he affirmed. To Sadat he wrote: "You will certainly agree, Mr. President, that no state takes unilateral steps."[49] It was an unworthy and insensitive response—a ringing slap in the face for the Egyptian president. Instead of having his position in the Arab world restored, Sadat had been further and probably irreversibly weakened. It was hardly calculated to encourage the others.

Deeply angered, Sadat declined to accept Begin's letter. Its contents had already been revealed anyway, with studied discourtesy, to the news agencies. In retaliation Sadat then decided to expel the Israeli military mission from Egypt. Through thick and thin this delegation had been allowed to remain in Gianaclis, the sole tangible reminder of the new era ushered in by the Sadat visit, a channel of communication that could be called upon when necessary. It was also evidence of Israeli Defense Minister Weizman's special relationship with the Egyptian president. By breaking this final link, Sadat was signifying that the "peace process" had come to a dead end; any renewal of contacts with Israel would now have to come about through the medium of the United States embassy.[50]

V

WHEN DETERRENCE FAILS

Successful deterrence—the discouragement by one state of another's resort to military action—very clearly rests on unencumbered communication, both verbal and nonverbal. Warnings, whether declaratory speeches, diplomatic notes, or oral messages, must be understood as intended. Given the likely sensitivity of the issues at stake, the inherent stresses of crisis decision-making, and the distracting noises of competing sources of information, aptness is of the essence. If a caution is too shrill, it may be counterproductive, that is, have an escalatory rather than restraining influence; if it is too muted, it risks being ignored or overlooked. Ambiguity, and hence uncertainty on the opponent's part about just what is being prohibited, may be desirable; on the other hand, it may simply encourage him to "press his luck." To achieve the intended effect, precisely the right balance must be struck between a whole range of tones including pitch, explicitness, precision, and choice of appropriate channel. All this assumes more than a minimal consensus on the meaning and usage of words. Where two communities—Egypt and Israel—use language, as we have seen, in such very different ways, the scope for misunderstanding in highly fraught situations of conflict can be expected to be considerable.

Much the same goes for the nonverbal dimension of deterrence. Now it has become generally accepted in recent years that the demonstration of military force or its limited application can often be usefully seen as a type of communication—"signaling"—by which states attempt to influence each other. The message may be indeed deterrence or something else, such as persuasion ("compellence"), support, or encouragement; the point is that the object of the display is being provided with information which, the initiator hopes, will induce him to modify his actions. The bombing of a factory in reprisal for a guerrilla attack on an army base may transmit, in the given circumstances, the signal: "If you do not desist from your current conduct, I shall destroy your industry." To which the reply might be a stepped-up offensive, saying in effect: "No deal. We do not believe your public opinion is prepared to sustain the present level of casualties." Seen in this light, force may be less a way of bludgeoning an opponent into submission than an offer in a tacit negotiation.

84

If it is accepted that verbal communication across cultures can raise problems of misunderstanding, then it surely follows that military signaling may be equally subject to semantic pitfalls. At the very least it is not self-evident that a given act of violence meant as a warning or an assertion of defiance by one government should be perceived in the same way by another government drawing upon a different world outlook. And if the combatants are unable to read each other's signals as intended, there is clearly a risk of an initially limited, demonstrative use of force degenerating, willy-nilly, into an unplanned and futile free-for-all.

In the concrete case of Egyptian-Israeli relations, there is evidence that over the years strategic instability, arising from an inability to either predict or control the course of political crisis, has been fostered by precisely this kind of mutual incomprehension. At critical periods serious miscalculations, deriving from an imperfect grasp of the "mentality" of the opponent, can be detected on both sides. To begin to understand what went wrong, it is helpful to unravel the culture-bound assumptions—and misconceptions about the opponent's assumptions—which underpinned both parties' use of force.

My point of departure is the two societies' very different traditions and experience of domestic violence. One tradition, rooted in concepts of honor and clan solidarity, gives rise to the revenge killing and the blood feud. The other, a product of minority status and vulnerability, shies away from personal violence—but with the restoration of statehood has acquired new and assertive habits of military action. An idea of how the confrontation of these seemingly incompatible ethoses has affected—and continues to weigh on—the course of events, may be obtained from the recent tragic case of the Ras Burka killings.

The Ras Burka Affair

The killing by an Egyptian soldier—described by the Egyptian authorities as "demented"—of seven Israeli tourists, including four children, at Ras Burka in the Sinai in October 1985, greatly shocked Israeli public opinion. The facts of the matter were certainly horrific enough. The soldier had been known to his comrades to possess fanatical fundamentalist leanings and to be a danger to any Israelis in the vicinity, but no action had been taken. Nor had other Egyptian soldiers reacted when the "crazy man," as he was known, opened fire. They had simply looked on, fatalistically. Following the shooting, in cold blood, of the unarmed civilians, other Israelis present at the scene were forcibly prevented from tendering first aid. The victims lay out in the sun for five hours while the Egyptian army assessed the situation. Subsequent post mortems showed that five of the victims had died of loss of blood and could have been saved by prompt medical assistance.[1]

Almost as distressing in Israeli eyes was the later handling of political aspects of the affair by the Egyptian government. Far from expressing regret, President Mubarak, on television, described the massacre as "nothing at all; a man lost his mind, it can happen anywhere," accompanying this judgment with an eloquently dismissive sweep of his hand. Even at this stage a further deterioration in the atmosphere of Egyptian-Israeli relations could have been prevented had Mubarak heeded Minister Ezer Weizman's friendly advice to the Egyptian chargé d'affaires in Tel Aviv and transmitted a report on the matter to the Israeli government as soon as possible. In the event, months passed before the semblance of a "report" was forthcoming. Israeli prompting merely angered Mubarak. "Perhaps you have forgotten," he declared in a newspaper interview, "but an independent judicial system is at work in Egypt and I cannot, nor will I permit, anyone from getting in touch with the court and requesting details or a report on the incident. The only report to appear will be the court's judgement and reasoning."[2]

Eventually, after it had long been clear that Israeli opinion was not going to allow the affair simply to disappear and that continuing bitterness was acting as an obstacle to progress in such matters in hand as the Taba border negotiations, the Egyptian authorities finally handed over a file consisting of various newspaper clippings dealing with the massacre and court case. After this "report" had been handed back by the Israeli foreign ministry, together with a vigorous complaint, a further "report" was delivered, this one made up of the actual transcripts and judgment of the trial of the Egyptian soldier convicted of the massacre. Although expressing official dissatisfaction at Egypt's continuing evasion of what were seen to be key questions relating to the incident, it was by now clear that Israel could not realistically hope to receive anything more satisfactory.[3] It was not until the two sides agreed to resort to arbitration in the matter of Taba, in September 1986, that the Egyptian government accepted in principle its obligation to pay compensation to the families of the victims.

Tragic enough in itself, the Ras Burka affair would be of merely transitory interest were it not indicative of a much more general disjunction in Israeli and Egyptian perceptions of the meaning of violence. The effect, over the years, of this dissonance has been seriously to complicate the possibility of orderly relations. Indeed, on occasion, misunderstanding by one side of the logic of the other's attitudes has resulted in grave and unforeseen complications.

Violence in Egyptian and Israeli Societies

Egypt and Israel display significantly different propensities to domestic violence. Israel is marked by political stability, civic order, and a relatively low incidence of violence on the streets. Egyptian society is in many ways agreeably good-humored and tolerant. But it is also prone, like other Arab states, to spasms of unpredictable violence and bloodshed. King Hussein of Jordan has admitted that "Arab lands are not like other lands. Life is all too often held cheaply, and death often passes unheeded."[4] Political assassination has claimed the lives of numerous public figures in Egypt, including those of President Sadat and foreign dignitaries. On three occasions since the establishment of diplomatic relations, Israeli officials have been attacked, resulting in two dead and four injured. Rioting is not uncommon, and uprisings (*intifada*), of sufficient gravity to threaten the regime itself, have occurred on several occasions, such as in January 1952 (six months before the Free Officers' revolt that brought down King Farouk), in 1977 over increased bread prices, and most recently in February 1986 when security forces themselves rioted, with scores of deaths. The possibility of civic unrest is a constant concern of Egyptian governments.

The picture is quite different in Israel. Since the foundation of the state there has been one political assassination (that of UN mediator Count Folke Bernadotte, in September 1948, during the wholly exceptional circumstances of the War of Independence) and one case of serious civic disturbance (in Haifa in 1959), but without any loss of life. Political demonstration is, indeed, very much part of the Israeli political tradition—as in the United States and Western Europe—but it is intended to influence government and not to topple it. Whereas Arab political culture sanctions violence as a fact of life, the Israeli does not. (This has nothing to do, of course, with the formal or constitutional legitimacy of violence.)

Comparative crime statistics reinforce the impression of a markedly different incidence of violence in Egypt as compared to Israel. For the period 1960–1970 the Egyptian authorities give an average annual murder rate of 5.12 per 100,000. The figure for the same period in Israel is a global murder rate of 1.18 per 100,000. However, the murder rate for the Jewish sector of the population is actually much lower, around 0.6–0.7 per 100,000, and the overall rate is brought up only by the much higher incidence of murder in the non-Jewish section of the Israeli population. For the year 1966, Landau and Drapkin discovered that the rate of non-Jewish offenders in Israel (mostly Arabs and Druze) was 6.45 times higher than that of Jewish offenders.[5] Interestingly, this is virtually identical to the ratio of murder rates in Egypt compared to those of Israeli Jews. Notwithstanding discrepancies of definition and reporting, and the contrasting age and residence profiles of the two populations, the trend is therefore unambiguous.

The explanation for the difference is not hard to find. If we return to Egyptian crime statistics, a very clear and suggestive pattern of behavior can be observed. In 1,070 cases of murder in Egypt in 1969 where the assailant was apprehended, it was found that 20 percent of the murders were based on a desire to "wipe out shame" (*mahw al-'ar*), 30 percent on a desire to satisfy real or imaginary wrongs (*intiqam*), and 31 percent on a desire for blood revenge (*akhdh altha'r*). Thus in fully 81 percent of Egyptian homicides, personal or family vengeance was the motive for the offense. In cases of kidnapping, revenge was also a major factor.[6]

Revenge is the classic motive for murder of the group-oriented culture. Where honor is of the essence, the loss of honor, shame, is the severest sanction. To "have one's face blackened," to be humiliated, is received as an unbearable blow, far worse than material loss, since it strikes at the very heart of one's sense of personal worth. Not surprising, then, that the "whitening of one's face," namely, revenge, the restoration of honor, should be such a recurrent cultural theme in a shame culture such as that of Egypt.

The Jewish tradition reflects a quite different approach to violence. The two necessary conditions for the blood feud—clannishness (segmental lineage) and a preoccupation with honor—are absent. On the contrary, there is a positive revulsion against the use of force in one's personal relations. Three interlocking layers of explanation for this phenomenon can be adduced—at the national, communal, and personal levels. In the first place, the rabbis acquired a highly skeptical attitude to the efficacy of force as a political instrument as a result of the two failed Judean revolts of 70 and 132–35 C.E., and the no less costly Alexandrian revolt of 119 C.E. (all against Rome). So disastrous were these insurrections that the Jewish people lost their national autonomy and, what was even worse in their eyes, Jerusalem, the seat of the cult. Submission to the powerful was adopted as conscious policy; nonresistance was felt to be more conducive to survival. Scattered abroad into diaspora communities, the Jews inevitably concluded that violence against the majority would be counterproductive.

Vulnerable minority status also rendered disruptive internal violence a luxury that could be ill-afforded. Solidarity, a closing of ranks against the outsider, became the supreme ethic. Elaborate formal and informal mechanisms of conciliation were perfected. There is also the factor of Jewish separateness. Following the dispersion, an ethic of separateness was fostered in order to preserve Jewish identity in the face of what was seen as the threat of assimilation to the surrounding majority population. Disappearance by absorption was the usual fate of dispersed minorities. But to accept it would have meant abandoning the special mission the Jews conceived for themselves. How, then, was assimilation to be prevented? Not by the erection of physical defenses, an impractical and anyway futile solution. The answer lay in the setting up of ethical and behavioral barriers; this was the approach enjoined by all the sacred texts, from Joshua to Isaiah.

At this point Jewish and Gentile attitudes to violence became relevant. If there was one single, blatant asset possessed by the majority and not by the minority, it was access to the use of force. A long history of pogrom and persecution associated the Gentile ethos in the Jewish mind with ruthless brutality and contempt for human life. To the supposed Gentile principle of coercion, the Jewish reaction was to oppose the doctrine of nonviolence. Rationality and moderation were elevated to the level of existential qualities;

the Jewish vocation would be to assert the preeminence of the intellectual over the physical. Violence was accordingly ruled out, not only as an ineffectual expedient for an exposed minority but also as a positive affront to Jewish identity.[7]

(It is in this context that the low rate of alcoholism among Jews, demonstrated in many studies, is probably to be interpreted. Charles Snyder argues that sobriety was established as a norm in the traditional culture of the *shtetl* both because it was consonant with the wider moderation of the Jewish ethos and because it became a mark of dissociation from a culture in which drunkenness was endemic.[8] Since drunkenness in Eastern Europe was often associated with violence, it can be seen that temperance in drink was part of a wider cultural reaction against immoderation in general. To borrow Ruth Benedict's well-known distinction, the Jews opposed Apollonian restraint to what appeared as surrounding Dionysian excess.)

Since the establishment of the State of Israel, it is obvious that historical inhibitions on the exercise of violence as a political instrument have lost their validity. Sovereign states are not subject to the limitations of minority communities. Nor is pacifism a viable alternative for a society locked into a historical conflict. However, this is not the whole story. After centuries of persecution, culminating in the Nazi Holocaust, military power has acquired more than just a pragmatic role in Israeli policy. Nonresistance was demonstrably bankrupt. The perception that one-third of the Jewish people "had gone like sheep to the slaughter" became a cause of deep and lasting humiliation. Observing Israel's assertive security policies over the years, it is hard to avoid the conclusion that they have reflected an element of psychological compensation as well as pure expediency.[9]

Is there no contradiction between military pugnacity and a low domestic propensity for violence? Clearly not: the former is covered by reason of state, the latter by interpersonal habits and ethics. One is perceived as functional to national survival, the other as dysfunctional. The experience of statehood has not altered traditional Jewish attitudes toward personal violence. Surveys show that despite the fact that Israel has compulsory military service and the United States has not, Israelis still tend to be more fearful of physical harm than Americans.[10] Not only is there no necessary connection between domestic and external bellicosity, it is surely sensitivity on the subject of personal violence that helps to account for Israel's low threshold of tolerance for terrorism. For an embattled society feeling itself surrounded by enemies, diligence for the lives of its citizens reinforces rather than lessens the perceived need for an activist security policy.

Asked to explain why Israelis were killing and being killed in the 1982 invasion of the Lebanon, the then defense minister, Arik Sharon, evoked the classic image of the Jew as victim. "Because they slaughter you, murder, for years, strike at Jews abroad and at home, not at military targets, at civilian residents—at children, women and old people. Is that how one is to be killed?

And to use our natural rights and our duty to defend ourselves in defensive war, that way one must not be killed? Is one not to be killed here? But to be killed only as sheep led to the slaughter?"[11]

In the light of my argument so far, it will readily be seen why the tragic events at Ras Burka aroused such consternation in Israeli public opinion. Mubarak's remark that "it can happen anywhere" might well apply to Egypt; it did not concur with the Israeli reality. On the contrary, it brought home the dichotomy between Israeli and Egyptian attitudes to violence. Ras Burka became a symbol of callousness, a striking confirmation of historical stereotypes. It also encapsulated that conflict between competing assumptions that underlay the failure of Israeli-Egyptian deterrence for so long. That pattern of incomprehension is well exemplified by events that preceded the two major wars of 1956 and 1967. It is to these episodes we shall now turn.

The Gaza Raid of 28 February 1955

Under the terms of the Egyptian-Israeli General Armistice Agreement of February 1949, which concluded the 1948 War, hostile activity by regular and nonregular forces and the movement of civilians across the armistice lines were prohibited. It was little realized at the time that armed raiding into Israel by civilians would quickly become the most vexing problem between the two sides. However, the presence in the Gaza Strip of large numbers of Palestinian refugees, uprooted by recent hostilities, yet only a few miles from their previous homes and occupations, provided highly combustible material. At first infiltration was a virtually spontaneous phenomenon carried out for a variety of purposes: family visits, the repossession of goods, travel on to adjacent Arab countries, smuggling, theft, as well as some revenge killing of Jews. Soon the raids acquired a more organized aspect. Gangs of marauders would slip over the unmarked and virtually undefended lines to steal agricultural equipment from local Jewish settlements or, under the sponsorship of Palestinian nationalist groups left over from 1948, to carry out acts of sabotage. In the latter case their purpose was clear—to maintain resistance and prevent a freezing of the *status quo*.

Until the spring of 1955—and this is the decisive point—there is no documentary evidence of direct Egyptian government sponsorship of these raids. On the contrary, research into Egyptian archives captured by Israel in 1956 and 1967 points to consistent efforts by the local government authorities to block off Palestinian infiltration. For instance, the annual report of the governor of the Gaza Strip for 1953 records that "we have been keeping track of acts of infiltration and have blocked them. Close to fifty persons have been arrested and these incidents have just about come to an end." Following an Israeli reprisal raid in August 1953 on a Palestinian refugee camp, the local head of Egyptian military intelligence explained to his superiors that the Israeli action came in response to Bedouin infiltration and noted that a renewed order had been given to "reinforce guarding and patrolling in order to prevent infiltration" and capture those responsible. The same officer strongly opposed drafting Palestinian residents of the Gaza Strip into a new Civil Guard (established at the end of 1953 to strengthen Egyptian control over the refugee camps) on the grounds that they would collude in infiltration and initiate attacks themselves, with a resulting increase in tension. He was in no doubt that Israel would avenge any incident.[12]

There is strong evidence, therefore, that the responsible Egyptian officials were committed in principle to maintaining the armistice agreement with Israel and were aware of the consequences of infiltration. Two reservations, however, should be noted: First, the interrogation of captured infiltrators by Israeli Military Intelligence appears to have indicated that some at least were being sent for purposes of espionage. Whether this was their primary mission or a supplement to other activities cannot be determined.[13] The second complicating fact is that, intelligence-gathering apart, the Egyptians were not very successful at actually preventing breaches of the armistice agreement on the ground. With very limited forces at their disposal—at the beginning of the 1950s, one company to man ten frontier posts and patrol the whole length of the border—as yet rudimentary authority over the local Palestinian population, and the incomplete compliance of lower ranks, the Gaza authorities were quite unable to put a stop to the problem of infiltration.[14]

It is unlikely that the young officers, under Nasser's leadership, of the Revolutionary Command Council in Cairo, who had come to power as a result of the 1952 revolution, had the distant Gaza Strip very high on their list of priorities. Consolidation of power and domestic reform were their main concerns at this stage and certainly sufficed to occupy their time. They may also have been badly informed in the details of armistice problems. In a conversation with Richard Crossman at the end of 1955, Colonel Nasser basically confirmed this picture of relative indifference. Until 28 February 1955, he claimed, he had been too busy smashing the Moslem Brotherhood to take much interest in Israel. He "did not read about it in any detail."[15]

Why, then, the reader may wonder, did Israel not bring the matter more forcefully to the attention of the Egyptian authorities before it was too late? The simple answer is that it did—but without success. During the course of 1954, Israel protested vociferously and continuously about the deterioration in border security, particularly in the Gaza area. For instance, in a message of 9 April 1954, Prime Minister Sharett activated all available channels of communication with Egypt (including Egyptian contacts in New York, Washington, and Paris) to transmit a serious warning. "Continual acts of violence," he wrote, "such as robberies, murders, assaults and raids, have created a state of perilous lawlessness. This mounting tension along borders, seen against the background of an Egyptian policy of active hostility and belligerent practices, constitutes a matter of grave concern to the Government of Israel. The Government of Israel does not wish to find itself in the position where its only recourse were to devise its own remedies for a situation which can be brought under control by the joint efforts of both governments."[16] Increasingly severe military reprisals were the other medium through which Israel attempted to drive home its mounting anxiety. But it was all to no avail. Diplomatic expressions of "grave concern" and limited reprisals seemed to fall on deaf ears. Not for the last time, as we shall see, a Cairo more accustomed to the shriller tones of Arab rhetoric was to fail to give Israeli deterrent signals their due weight. Israel would henceforth feel itself obliged to consider measures that could be less easily ignored.

Whatever the explanation for Nasser and his colleagues' failure to invest greater attention and resources in the preservation of the armistice with Israel, their neglect was to have disastrous consequences. In Israel the conviction grew that for all Egyptian disclaimers and protestations of innocence for the incursions—transmitted, for example, through the Egyptian-Israeli Mixed Armistice Commission, set up to hear complaints about infringements of the armistice—Cairo was at the very least displaying "apathy" to events on its borders. Chief of Staff Dayan added to this contemporary judgment the view that the preventive measures taken in the Gaza Strip were "largely for the sake of appearances." Looking back, he described how "painful" Israel found terrorist activity. It seemed to him that "the Arab authorities never quite understood our feelings or their implications, never grasped why we were so deeply concerned and reacted so sharply when our people were murdered, houses attacked, or roads ruined by infiltrating terrorists."[17] Moshe Sharett, who was the leader of the dovish camp in Israel at the time, continually struggling to restrain the "hawks" under Dayan, arrived at much the same conclusion. As a last resort he actually drafted a letter to Prime Minister Nasser at the end of 1954 (never actually sent), appealing to him for greater understanding of the Israeli position: armed incursions from the Gaza Strip into Israeli territory "resulting in sabotage and murder and rendering life unsafe in a large area" might "seem minor to an outsider. To us they are a most serious matter, completely destructive of security and creating a situation which is quite intolerable."[18] Here we may recognize all the familiar ingredients of a dialogue of the deaf: messages ignored, growing frustration, collision.

Dayan and the general staff's solution to the Gaza problem was a big reprisal raid which would shake the Egyptian government out of its "apathy." Relatively small-scale reprisals had been carried out against targets in the Gaza Strip for some time by special units of the Israeli army. Following a spate of incidents in September 1954, Dayan concluded that these "piecemeal" retaliations were ineffective and had not impressed Cairo.[19] We may assume that it was at this point that planning began in earnest for the large-scale reprisal raid on Gaza of 28 February 1955, which was to be a fateful turning point in relations between Israel and Egypt in the prelude to the Suez War.

A variety of motives lay behind Israel's general policy of retaliation at this time. Some of these were of domestic rather than external provenance and were not directly connected with the strategic logic of Israel's confrontation with its Arab neighbors. For the army, reprisal raids were not least seen as a vital instrument for raising combat standards, which had reached a low point at the beginning of the 1950s.[20] They were also considered important for maintaining the morale of the Israeli public; many of the villages within striking distance of the Gaza Strip were settled by new immigrants who had been incompletely absorbed into the life of the country. This latter point was complicated by domestic political considerations, as Sharett admits at one point in his diary. Failure to react forcefully would have weakened the ruling Labor party in its electoral struggle with the right-wing Herut party of Menachem Begin.[21] Then there is the psychological compensatory factor. According to Aronson and Horowitz, the foremost Israeli experts on the subject, it was precisely Jewish persecution and defenselessness over the ages, culminating in the horrendous loss of life of the Nazi exterminations, that "increased the pressure to respond in double measure to every Arab provocation." They quote the distinguished Israeli novelist Amos Oz, who ironically described the resurrection of the State of Israel as "one single great reprisal for everything that has happened to the Jewish people."[22]

Without ignoring these implicit and somewhat imponderable considerations, the stated and restated logic of Israel's reprisal policy was impeccably strategic and political. Had it lacked this "rational" dimension, one must strongly doubt whether it would have been implemented. At the military level, retaliation had the straightforward and familiar aim of deterrence. As Dayan argued in a speech of August 1955, reprisals were necessary to show that marauding "did not pay," or, in other words, to provide Arab government with incentives to put a stop to it.[23] If the inhabitants of Israel could not live in peace, Dayan noted in his diary, Israel would prove to the Arabs that neither would they. When infiltration continued regardless of Israeli reprisals, Dayan claimed that the situation would be even worse were the policy to be abandoned. But for its dampening effect, a rising tide of Arab aggression, encouraged by Israeli passivity, would result first in the collapse of the southern settlements and then in national catastrophe. So the next step, as long as the general staff remained wedded to deterrence, was to increase the "incentive" for good behavior by raising the level of the punishment. Only if they realized, Dayan wrote, that they would not be left with one stone on top of the other, would the Arabs curtail the activities of the fedayeen. Until then terror would continue and Israeli casualties rise.[24] This was the irresistibly escalatory logic that led, via the Gaza raid, to the 1956 Sinai campaign.

As for the political rationale for the reprisal policy, this was well put in Dayan's August 1955 speech, in which he reasoned that the Arabs, seeing themselves helpless to counter Israeli military retaliation, would be forced to the realization that they had no choice but to make peace with Israel; in effect they were to be bombed to the conference table. Since Egypt had not declared war after the Gaza clash, Dayan argued, this proved that it could not defeat Israel. In the face of Israeli retaliation, it would prefer to accept the existence of Israel rather than to go on losing face.[25]

This, then, was the philosophy that produced the disastrous Gaza raid of 28 February 1955. Its assumptions turned out to be utterly misplaced. The Egyptians were not provided with incentives for clamping down on infiltration or for negotiating with Israel. Quite the reverse. In the first place, Egyptian efforts, however inefficient, to block raiding out of the Gaza Strip were replaced by the energetic encouragement of retaliatory incursions as part of a strategy of attrition. The fedayeen—"self-sacrifice" irregular forces—were officially established in April 1955, and the security situation along the armistice lines rapidly deteriorated to an intolerable point. The murder of Israeli citizens, the mining of roads and tracks, and the ambushing of army patrols became a regular occurrence. Israeli reprisals increased in frequency and ferocity.

Most ominous, whereas internal development had previously had priority for the Egyptian government, the exigencies of defense could now no longer be ignored. After Gaza, Nasser told Crossman in December 1955, "I could not sleep. I had nightmares. I had been caught with my pants down." Other members of the Free Officers' movement came to him and said: "We told you so. You refused to allocate enough for the arms budget, and concentrated on the social program, and now you see what has happened. We were caught defenseless." In April 1955 Nasser participated in the Bandung conference of Afro-Asian nations, and steps were taken by him, with Chou En-lai's skilled mediation, to acquire modern weapons from the Communist bloc. In September the Egyptian leader announced the historic cotton-for-arms deal with Czechoslovakia. "Now the situation is less perilous," he judged in his conversation with Crossman. "Now I think B.G. [Israeli prime minister David Ben-Gurion] will think twice before launching another attack. But please, Mr. Crossman, will you tell him something for me? Tell him this, tell him he cannot force me to make peace. He cannot force peace. That is what you must tell him."[26]

Finally, the Gaza raid put an end to promising, if exploratory, negotiations that had been underway since November 1954. There had been useful contacts between officials of the two sides in Paris and elsewhere, and the Anglo-Jewish member of parliament, Maurice Orbach, had acted as a mediator between Nasser and Sharett, carrying messages between them. These conversations had been initiated by Israel, in the first instance, to save the lives of a group of Israeli agents on trial in Cairo. But the outline of a wider agreement on some outstanding issues had begun to emerge. After Gaza it was to be that much more difficult to embark on substantive negotiations. Although Egyptian Foreign Minister Fawzi remained interested in pursuing various mediation efforts that were pushed by the United States and Britain in 1955 (including the secret "Alpha" and "Gamma" projects), Nasser had been deeply wounded. He told Elmore Jackson—an American Quaker who also tried his hand at mediation in the summer of 1955—that he had lost all confidence in his Israeli counterparts as a result of the February debacle.[27]

It is not hard to identify the miscalculations, on both sides, that lay behind the tragic train of events described above. On the Egyptian side there was an imaginative failure to grasp Israel's obsessive sensitivity to the loss of innocent life. The resources put at the disposal of the Egyptian authorities in Gaza to block infiltration were inadequate, and this unsatisfactory state of affairs dragged on for several years before the Gaza raid. Recurrent Israeli warnings and protests through the Mixed Armistice Commission, mutual friends, and direct contacts were ineffective.

Is it far-fetched to put down Egyptian equanimity in the face of Israel's appeals not only to inattention but also to a certain cultural myopia? We have noted the relative frequency of domestic violence in the Arab, as opposed to the Jewish, tradition. If the feud and the revenge killing are familiar features of Egyptian life, they are alien and abhorrent to the Jew. Could the Egyptian leadership, in these circumstances, fully appreciate the weight attached by Israel to civilian casualties? One must doubt it. Furthermore, the institution of irregular warfare, even under ostensibly peacetime conditions, which pervades the Arab world is equally unfamiliar to a Jewish ethos that sees in peace the almost metaphysical antithesis of war. In contrast, no observer of the Arab world can fail to be struck by the widespread peacetime practice of subversion, infiltration across borders, and sabotage. There is hardly a state in the region that has not been the victim of such clandestine, undeclared activity at some time. To put it bluntly, the odd car bomb, cross-border raid, or assassination plot is not something Arab governments get excited about. Humphrey Trevelyan, an old hand in the Arab world and British ambassador to Egypt in the 1955–56 period, would judge Nasser's attitude to subversive operations "in the light of a climate of opinion which considered subversion and conspiracy as a normal method of governmental operation and only condemned it [sic] when it was unsuccessful."[28]

Acceptance of clandestine warfare—directed, all too often, against civilian targets—is surely part and parcel of that more complacent attitude toward violence we have noted in Arab culture. Raiding and intertribal warfare were for long very much a way of life among nomadic groups such as the Bedouin, Kabyle, and Senoussi; it is only relatively recently that the practice was suppressed by strong central governments. The effect of this belligerent tradition must have been to blur, even in nonnomadic Arab societies, that bifurcation between war and peace taken for granted by classical international law. Moreover, tolerance for irregular warfare in international relations can be seen as a corollary at the state level to that acceptance of the revenge killing and the blood feud which we have found to be present at the societal level. A solicitous regard for the lives of one's neighbors' citizens is consistent only with an equally scrupulous concern for human life within one's own borders. Compassion is indivisible.

Against this background, it is doubtful whether the Egyptian government was imaginatively capable of grasping the pain and outrage in Israel caused by the Gaza raids across the armistice lines of the early 1950s. Had the full gravity of the situation in Israeli eyes been understood, it is hard to believe that more could not have been done to choke off infiltration altogether. Given the political will, as Egypt finally demonstrated after the 1956 War, it was certainly technically feasible.

On the Israeli side, there was no less serious a failure to appreciate Egyptian sensibilities. As long as Israeli reprisals maintained some kind of correspondence to the original crime, they were not necessarily seen as unreasonable by Egypt within the context of its own peculiar cultural assumptions. Whether they actually had a salutary effect is more debatable. But there could be no greater mistake than to suppose that the revenge ethic permits indiscriminate reprisal. On the contrary, the right of retaliation has always been carefully regulated by a sort of customary code precisely in order to avoid conflicts' getting out of hand. Central to the code are the conventions of proportionality, correspondence, and retribution. Proportionality requires that the retaliation fit the original provocation in degree. Excess is not only deprecated but positively counterproductive in simply justifying a further round of reprisals. Correspondence implies that the punishment resemble the crime in kind. Finally, the principle of retribution obliges the avenging party to obtain satisfaction from those who are related to the offender in some defined way. Thus, however offensive the taking of revenge might appear to outsiders, there is no question that in practice it is required to conform to quite precise principles of natural justice.[29]

The Gaza raid of 28 February 1955 did not conform to the unwritten code governing revenge in any way. The incident which provided the occasion for the retaliation occurred two days before, when a gang of marauders crossed over into Israel, broke into an office in Nes Ziona, and then killed a passing cyclist before escaping back across the border. There was no suggestion that the infiltrators were regular troops, although the circumstances of the break-in might point to an espionage mission.[30] It should be noted that there had been no other incidents for at least a month—except, that is, for the hanging of two out of eleven Israeli agents found guilty of espionage in the recent Cairo trial. Whatever the actual provocation, the Israeli response could be seen only as utterly inappropriate. In the first place, the target chosen hardly conformed to the principle of retributive justice; it was no more and no less than the Gaza garrison headquarters of the Egyptian army! There was no evidence to associate marauders, let alone the Cairo courts, with it. Furthermore, the number and identity of Egyptian casualties—thirty-eight dead and thirty-one wounded, mostly officers and men—bore absolutely no relation to any provocation. This was not retaliation—an eye for an eye—but gratuitous violence on a massive scale.

However, the Israeli attack was not just a retaliation for the Nes Ziona cyclist or the executed agents. Israeli motives were also, if not primarily, strategic. The raid was intended as both a calculated deterrent and a compellent step, and for this purpose proportionality was irrelevant. According to deterrent logic, the *more disproportionate* the punishment, the greater the probability of the victim's compliance. Egypt was in fact being encouraged, in conformity with Dayan's declared philosophy, to choke off future infilitration and to reconcile itself to Israel's existence.

Unfortunately, Egyptian rationality refused to conform to the Western, utilitarian, model designed by Israeli strategists. From an Egyptian perspective, the Israeli attack was as incomprehensible as it was unforgivable; a stinging humiliation which cried out for revenge. Israel's escalation of violence, Colonel Nasser explained a few months later, left him no choice but to respond. "His honor and that of his army was at stake."[31] By choosing a prominent military target, Israel had thrown down the gauntlet to the Egyptian army—still smarting from its defeats in 1948. Moreover, with their own personal prestige indissolubly linked to the honor of the military, there was no way that the officers who made up Egypt's Revolutionary Command Council could pass over the raid in silence.

The timing of the raid was unhappy in another way. Shortly before, Nasser had rejected Western overtures to adhere to the British-inspired Baghdad Pact against Communism. The Gaza strike presented Israel as an avenging cat's-paw of Western interests, confirming Egyptian prejudices. "Your leaders do not understand our mentality," was how one friendly Egyptian diplomat put it to his Israeli contact. "You frequently do things that give the impression that you are a tool of an alien policy in the Middle East."[32] The upshot of this train of Israeli miscalculations was to ensure that Egypt, far from being encouraged to moderation and accommodation, was effectively impelled toward vigorous resistance. No Egyptian government could allow itself to be humiliated like this or appear to be bending to such blatant pressure.[33]

May 1967: The Prelude to the Six Day War

Although President Nasser of Egypt was the prime mover in the three weeks preceding the June 1967 War, the tinder for the conflagration was first laid, not on Israel's border with Egypt but on that with Syria. In February 1966 a radical, pro-Soviet wing of the Baath party came to power in Damascus and quickly demonstrated its anti-Zionist fervor. Three serious issues disturbed Syrian-Israeli relations: a dispute over exploitation of the waters of the Jordan, disagreement over rights in the demilitarized zones set up by the

1949 armistice agreement, and infiltration into Israel by the Syrian-backed El Fatah organization. Tension built up as a spiral of incident, incursion, and reprisal menacingly recalled the events preceding the 1956 War. In July 1966 Israel attacked, with aircraft and artillery, the site of a Syrian project intended to divert water from Israel's National Water Carrier. A new element was added to the equation on 4 November of that year when Syria concluded a mutual defense pact with Egypt. Only nine days later, following an incident in which a patrol went over a mine south of Hebron, Israel launched a massive and unprecedented daytime reprisal raid, involving infantry, armor, and air support, against the Jordanian village of Es Samu. Then on 7 April 1967 an incident in the demilitarized zone on the Syrian-Egyptian border escalated into a full-scale clash. After tanks and artillery had exchanged fire, aircraft were introduced. By the end of the day, Syrian positions had been silenced, and six of their aircraft shot down.

Any Israeli hopes that the situation with Syria would improve after 7 April were quickly dashed. Infiltration increased rather than slackened. On the eve of Israel's Independence Day, 15 May, severe warnings were directed by Israeli leaders toward Damascus. In two speeches of 11 and 13 May, Prime Minister Eshkol noted that if incursions from Syria continued, Israel might "have to adopt measures no less drastic than those of April 7." Israel would "not recognize the limitations [the Arabs] endeavor to impose upon our acts of response." Even more pointed was a UPI dispatch from Jerusalem datelined 12 May which quoted "a high Israeli source" as saying that "Israel would take limited military action designed to topple the Damascus army regime if Syrian terrorists continue sabotage raids inside Israel."[34]

In Cairo and Damascus there was profound alarm. The Syrians became convinced that an Israeli attack was imminent and turned for help to their Egyptian ally. President Nasser, who had been supplied with information from Soviet sources that Israel was massing huge forces on its northern border, resolved to act decisively. From this point on the crisis escalated, step by step, to war.

The main public events of the three weeks or so preceding the actual outbreak of hostilities are quickly sketched in: On 15 May units of the Egyptian army were observed passing through Cairo on their way to cross the Suez Canal. The following day the Egyptian chief of staff informed the commander of UNEF that his troops were to be withdrawn from the Sinai immediately. On 18 May Egyptian forces took over UN positions at the strategically vital point of Sharm el-Sheikh, which controlled the Straits of Tiran and therefore the passage of ships from the Indian Ocean and the Red Sea into the Gulf of Aqaba and on to Israel's southern port of Eilat. With President Nasser's announcement of 22 May that the straits were now closed to ships flying the Israeli flag, the situation between Egypt and Israel had reverted to that existing before the 1956 war. At this point diplomacy tried to move into the breach. U Thant, the secretary-general of the United Nations, met with Nasser on 24 May but was unable to persuade him to reopen the straits. On 26 May Abba Eban, Israel's foreign minister, met with President Johnson at the White House to seek American support. A subsequent Anglo-American attempt to set up an international flotilla to break the blockade of Eilat attracted minimal support. With the perceived failure of peaceful diplomacy, Israel cleared the decks for war. On 1 June the Israeli cabinet was widened to include members of the opposition parties, and on 4 June the die was cast. The next morning Israel attacked.

These are the bare chronological details. But behind the seemingly inexorable descent into war lies a series of grave mutual failures of deterrence. The first of these was in the lengthy period of growing tension that preceded the May crisis when Israeli reprisals proved ineffective in restraining infiltration from Syria—or, indeed, in inserting a wedge between Syria and Egypt. The second failure occurred in the third week of May 1967. Since 1957 Israel had publicly and solemnly committed itself to regarding the closure of the Straits of Tiran as a *casus belli*. Yet despite repeated warnings, the Israeli government was unable to dissuade President Nasser from this momentous step—or, indeed, from dismantling, one by one, the gains Israel had made in the 1956 Sinai campaign. The third failure was that of the Egyptian leader and lay in his inability to conserve the fruits of the first week of the crisis by persuading Israel that his goals were limited and that no threat was intended to the existence of the Jewish state. It is axiomatic that a nation that perceives itself driven into a corner will stop at nothing in its fight for life.

To account for the utter breakdown in communication between Egypt and Israel, it is instructive to disentangle the various messages that passed between them, contrasting the intended with the perceived meanings. All too often these did not coincide. It is my contention that the discrepant calculations of the two sides can be accounted for in terms of certain fundamental cultural incompatibilities. The first of these derived from the very different salience and significance of honor in the two cultures. Just as Israel's reprisal policy before the Sinai campaign of 1956 had exacerbated rather than reduced tension with Egypt, so did a similar policy of "deterrence" pave the way for the May 1967 crisis. When justified retaliation turned into disproportionate humiliation, it not only failed to deter but positively invited escalation. Israel's responses were counterproductive in terms of their defined objectives because they were posited on the assumption that the Arab states shared the Israeli calculus of cost and benefit.

When Syria and Egypt signed a defense agreement on 4 November 1966, Israel found itself confronted with a classic strategic problem: a hostile coalition holding out the threatening prospect of a two-front war. Given recent incursions and exchanges of fire on the Syrian border, Israel could view this development, with some alarm, only as a marked deterioration in the balance of power between it and the Arab states.[35] A Syria fortified and emboldened by the recent treaty might become dangerously irresponsible and had to be taught a lesson. It is in this light that the Es Samu raid of 13 November 1966 has to be understood. The scale of the operation and the fact that it took place in daytime are extremely significant. On this occasion Jordan was no more than the surrogate victim. The real audience for this blatant display of power was Syria, which was where the infiltrators actually had their home base. The message of the near-invasion was a twofold one: that the Syrian government ran the risk of a real invasion which would topple it from power unless it reined in its client El Fatah guerrillas (Chief of Staff Rabin had said as much in an interview with the armed forces journal *Bamahaneh* on 12 September 1966), and that its new ally Egypt would not be able to help.

As the situation continued to worsen in the north, Israel concluded that the 13 November demonstration had not made any impression on the Syrians. In fact, by striking at Jordan, Israel had effectively acknowledged Syria's immunity as a client of the USSR. Thus it was felt that another demonstration was called for: Syria had to be shown with brutal clarity that its unrepentant militancy was endangering the very existence of the regime, and Egypt had to understand that Israel was not to be intimidated by the prospect of Egyptian intervention. The incident of 7 April 1967 was the result of a considered Israeli decision. 7 April was the anniversary of the Syrian Baath party; the confrontation was set off when a tractor was sent into the demilitarized zone to plow, an act which it was well known would draw Syrian fire; only after a cease-fire, conditional on a withdrawal of the tractor, had been declined after consultations within Israel at the highest level did the initially limited exchange escalate into a wider clash involving the use of aircraft.[36] Having shot down six Syrian MiGs, two of them on the outskirts of Damascus in full view of the festive populace, the victorious Israeli jets then swept over the Syrian capital, proving that it was completely exposed to Israeli air power.

Surely Syria would now take cognizance of its vulnerability and prevent further incursions against Israel from its territory? The last thing that occurred to Israeli planners was that further escalation would follow. "We were certain at the beginning of 1967, and this opinion was strengthened in April of that year when in air battle we brought down the 6 Syrian MiGs," Yitzhak Rabin later recalled, "that the air force had proved its strength so persuasively that one could not suppose that the Arab States would seriously contemplate challenging Israel."[37]

On the contrary. While Syria could accommodate itself to casualties resulting from an exchange of fire on the border, the loss of two of its aircraft in full view of the Damascus crowds and the shocking revelation that the government was unable to defend its capital from the Israeli air force were quite intolerable. At stake now was much more than the question of support for El Fatah or opposition to Israeli policy along the Jordan river. After 7 April the issue was the prestige of the regime in the eyes of its own people and the wider Arab world. Israel, unwittingly, had touched on the most sensitive component in the Arab make-up: one's standing in the community. In Syrian eyes compliance with Israel would accordingly imply an abdication of pride as well as of principle. Far from providing Syria with incentives to cooperate, Israel had ensured the intensification of the conflict.

After 7 April it was utterly predictable that incursions from Syria into Israel would increase rather than slacken. But locked into a particular and ethnocentric conception of deterrence, Israel simply concluded that it had not gone far enough—Syria remained unconvinced of Israeli resolution. As late as 22 May, one week into the crisis, Yitzhak Rabin argued that "if Syria had been given a harder blow we would have prevented the present situation."[38] The evidence of the first fortnight in May points to just such "a harder blow" as having been on Israel's agenda. The following assessment (like the UPI dispatch, the fruit of a briefing to military correspondents on 12 May) appeared in *The Jerusalem Post* of 14 May:

A major military clash with Syria now seems inevitable unless the sabotage campaign is called off forthwith. According to authoritative sources here, recent statements by Israeli leaders, including the Prime Minister and the Foreign Minister, are seen as in the nature of ultimatums. Military experts here believe that Israel is prepared to risk Egyptian intervention in its determination to put an end to Syrian aggression. The anticipated clash is not thought likely to assume the dimensions of a full campaign, but to be in the nature of a military expedition intended to take the wind out of the Syrians' sails once and for all.

A parallel account was published in *Ha'aretz*.

The other target of Israel's deterrence strategy, following the signing of the Syrian-Egyptian defense treaty on 4 November 1966, was Egypt. Israel's strategy was to insert a wedge between the partners. For some years President Nasser had maintained a policy of the utmost circumspection toward the Jewish state, insisting that the time was not yet ripe for a settling of accounts. At least fifty thousand of his troops were bogged down in the Yemen. Assuming that the last thing Nasser wanted at this juncture was war with Israel— least of all for the sake of a notoriously fickle and unstable Syria—it was "reasonable" to suppose that a demonstration of Israeli power would dampen the ardor of his commitment to the alliance. His passivity might also be expected to embitter relations between the alliance partners.

At first the strategy seemed to be working. After the Es Samu incident, President Nasser's adviser and confidant, Mohamed Heikal, made it clear that Egypt's obligations to Syria applied only to the conquest of Arab territory by Israel and not to localized raids or exchanges of fire.[39] But soon Nasser was sorely embarrassed by his inaction. The Jordanian radio and press scathingly criticized his failure to stand by Arab states attacked by Israel and taunted the Egyptian army with sheltering behind the skirts of the United

Nations Emergency Force (UNEF), set up in the Sinai and the Gaza Strip in 1957 as a buffer between Egypt and Israel. The commander-in-chief of the Egyptian army, Field Marshal Abdel Hakim Amer, was so disturbed by the propaganda campaign that he saw fit to send an urgent message to Nasser from Pakistan, where he was on a visit, suggesting that Egypt should put an end to the taunts by asking for the withdrawal of the UN force and reoccupying Sharm el-Sheikh. At the time Nasser was unconvinced. Israeli intelligence may somehow have got wind of this message, because according to the then chief of staff, Yitzhak Rabin, the view gained currency that in the circumstances of another raid like the one against Es Samu, Egypt might feel obliged to respond by moving its army into the Sinai.[40] Given Israel's strategic outlook, this assessment acted as an incentive and not a restraint to further action: If, despite continuing incursions from Syria, Israel failed to retaliate, this would be taken as an admission of weakness in the face of Syrian-Egyptian ties and an encouragement to Arab militancy. Nasser had to be made to understand that Israel was not to be intimidated by the prospect of Egyptian support for Syria and that any intervention would cost him dearly. Thus the second audience for the deterrent demonstration of 7 April was in Cairo.

As in the case of Syria, Israel's display of military superiority could not have been less calculated to deter. When an Egyptian military mission hastened to the Syrian capital to examine the situation, it was greeted with bitter recriminations. Es Samu was embarrassing enough; this was a deliberate "blackening" of Nasser's face by Israel in the eyes of the Arab community. To the Arab leader, the fraternal Arab states are what the family is to the individual: the source of his identity and reputation. The revelation of Nasser's impotence in full view of his peers was an excruciating humiliation which would not go unavenged. There would be no recurrence of 7 April.[41]

That the question of honor was in the forefront of Nasser's concerns in the May crisis was repeatedly confirmed by him. It was a leading motif in his conversation of 24 May with U Thant: After surveying the issues at stake, Nasser turned to

the great importance and need for the restoration of Arab dignity and honour. Ever since 1956 . . . Israel had embarked on a policy of affront and humiliation of the Arab villagers in retaliation for the activities of Al-Fatah. . . . And now Israel was embarked upon changing the existing regime in Syria. . . . The Syrians had now asked for Egyptian help under the Mutual Defence Pact signed in 1966. Nasser said that his country was committed to honour this pact and hence their decision to activate it by asking for UNEF's withdrawal and by sending the UAR's forces into the Sinai. The blocking of the Gulf of Aqaba was an inevitable consequence of such a military move. By these actions the UAR had fully restored the situation as it prevailed before the 1956 war and Arab honour had been vindicated.[42]

During the actual crisis of May 1967, a key factor in the breakdown of mutual deterrence is to be found in a familiar semantic confusion—the disparity between Arabic hyperbole and relative Israeli understatement. Speeches and broadcasts coming out of Cairo, by their sheer cumulative immoderation, convinced Israelis in all walks of life of the Arabs' genocidal intent and of the inevitability of war. Nasser's disclaimers and qualifications were not apparent to the Israeli ear. For its part, Israel's considered strategy of verbal and nonverbal restraint, to avoid fanning the flames, was quite lost on the Arab leadership.

Egyptian leaders have always insisted that their moves in the May crisis were not preparations for war but were simply meant to deter a possible attack on Syria. "Our deterrent action," Foreign Minister Mahmoud Riad told U Thant on 24 May, "would make Israel think twice before they attack now."[43] Certainly the first military moves of 15 May were blatantly demonstrative: the passage of troops through Cairo's busiest streets was covered by radio and television, and some units were sent on a detour to take them past the U.S. embassy. At this stage Israeli assessments were consonant with Egyptian intentions. The authoritative view of military intelligence given on the morning of 17 May was that Egypt wished to "deter Israel from the intention imputed to her, an attack on Syria; to influence the great powers to put pressure on us to avoid an attack in the north; to boost Egypt's prestige."[44]

Meanwhile, in diplomatic messages to third parties, Nasser gave assurances that Egypt would not be the first to attack. This was the gist of a letter sent to Indira Gandhi on 17 May and immediately made public, and of a communication to the American chargé d'affaires of the same day.[45] There is no evidence that these messages made any particular impression on the Israeli government one way or the other. Nevertheless, until 23 May and the closing of the Straits of Tiran, there was no basic change in Israeli estimates of Egyptian intentions. Despite growing anxiety as a result of the ejection of UNEF on 18 May, the Egyptian military build-up, and photo reconnaissance flights by MiG 21 jets, the consensus of military intelligence, foreign ministry, and secret service opinion remained that Egypt was still not bent on war.[46]

Had Egypt reined in at this point, there is a good chance that it would have retained the considerable gains of the previous week. But at an emergency session on 21 May of the Higher Executive Committee of the Arab Socialist Union, it was decided to close the Gulf of Aqaba to Israeli shipping. The participants were optimistic that Israel would reconcile itself to the *fait accompli*. For its part, Egypt would not take the military initiative. According to President Nasser, "it was clear to all of us that our role would be purely defensive; we should not attack unless there was an aggression against Syria; we merely had to be in a state of preparedness."[47] As long as Egypt avoided offensive action, it was felt that the risk of war could be contained within acceptable limits. Egyptian leaders were not convinced that Israel, given American opposition, would dare to take the offensive.

The effect of the closing of the Straits of Tiran on Israel was not at all that expected by Egypt. It was true that while in theory Israeli leaders had insisted and declared since 1957 that a blockade of Israel's southern port of Eilat would constitute a *casus belli*, in the actual circumstances of May 1967 there were divided views on how to act. One powerful school of thought declined to accept war as inevitable. But Egypt's intemperate communications strategy changed all that. The speeches and radio broadcasts coming out of Cairo laid the basis of a consensus in the Israeli cabinet where none had existed. As we have noted, the Egyptian leadership had decided against offensive action on 21 May and was hopeful about the possibility of "deterring the enemy," as Nasser put it in his 9 June resignation speech. However, instead of making the offer to Israel of a return to the pre-1956 *status quo* without war sound more palatable, Nasser made it sound to Israeli ears as though the closing of the straits were in itself a "declaration of war," in Eban's phrase. Had Nasser made it crystal clear that his aims were political, not military, the Israeli government would have found it difficult to go to war.

What Nasser actually said on 22 May was:

> The Jews threaten war. We tell them you are welcome, we are ready for war. Our armed forces and all our people are ready for war, but under no circumstances will we abandon any of our rights. This water is ours. War might be an opportunity for the Jews, for Israel and Rabin to test their forces against ours and to see that what they wrote about the 1956 battle and the occupation of Sinai was all a lot of nonsense.[48]

Strictly speaking, he did not actually make an explicit and unconditional threat of war. A careful reading of other parts of the speech shows that Nasser was at pains to point out the difficulties in the way of an Egyptian offensive: "Today US Senators, members of the House of Representatives, the press and the entire world speak in favour of Israel, of the Jews. . . . It is clear, therefore, that an alliance exists between the Western powers, chiefly represented by the United States and Britain, with Israel."

That this was indeed the impression Nasser wished to convey—and that Egyptians received—was confirmed by War Minister Shamseddin Badran at his trial for treason in February 1968. As he recalled it, the pilots at the Bir Gafgafa air base who were the audience for the speech were disappointed by Nasser's presentation, which "did not match up to [their] enthusiasm." They took it to mean that they were *not* going to get a chance to fight. In Badran's words: "The President was talking about politics and he wanted to make them understand the situation—he said such things as: if there should be no war, it need not be regretted, for there is the United States to consider."[49] But whatever Nasser's true intention, this was certainly not the way the speech was interpreted in Israel. Abba Eban, the most prominent "dove" in the cabinet, interpreted the declaration of a blockade as a calculated throwing down of the gauntlet. He concluded that the Egyptian leader would be satisfied with nothing less than war.[50]

The problem of interpretation emerged again on 26 May. In a speech made, significantly enough, to a delegation of the "Damascus Arab Workers' Conference," Nasser said the following: "The problem today is not just Israel, but also those behind it. If Israel embarks on aggression against Syria and Egypt, the battle against Israel will be a general one and not confined to one spot on the Syrian or Egyptian borders. The battle will be a general one and our basic objective will be to destroy Israel."[51] There were three points being made here: first, that Israel was not alone—a point repeatedly returned to in the same speech ("Today Israel is America"; "All the Western powers have adopted Israel's point of view"; "the whole of the West is with Israel"); again, with hindsight we can see that this was meant as an explanation of why Egypt was not going to attack Israel rather than a "declaration of war." Second, that war was conditional on Israel attacking first. Finally, that were Israel to attack, the Egyptian war aim would be to destroy Israel. The only one of these points to receive attention in Israel, understandably enough, was the third one. It was seen as providing further proof of Nasser's true intentions. To a culture unfamiliar with immoderation and exaggeration as a habitual style of discourse, Nasser's hyperbole drowned out accompanying nuances. Only an ear accustomed to a higher pitch of rhetorical intensity would be able to discriminate the message from the noise.

When President Nasser learned through the Americans that they had been informed by Israel that an Egyptian attack was imminent, he was astonished. He "could not understand where the Israelis got their story," according to Mohamed Heikal. "However, in order to make his position absolutely clear, he made speeches on May 27 and 29 in which he said: 'We are not going to fire the first shot. . . . We are not going to start an attack.' . . . He thought he had made his position plain and devoid of misunderstanding."[52] Clearly Nasser was utterly oblivious to the yawning cultural gap that ensured that his vituperative rhetoric was taken at its face value by Israel. His best efforts to clarify his intentions were quite inadequate to allay Israeli fears—and probably it was too late anyway. In a news conference for the world's media on 28 May (not "on May 27 and 29"), Nasser did indeed repeat several times that the initiative lay with Israel, but this was concealed by a thicket of threatening hyperbole.

Adding to the Israeli conviction that politicide was in the offing were the vitriolic radio broadcasts of surrounding Arab stations, and especially the Cairo-based "Voice of the Arabs." Not only did they dismay public opinion, they also affected the political/military leadership. It simply became impossible to ignore or discount the cacophony of martial songs, blood-curdling threats, cries of exultation, and calls for the total extermination of the Jews that filled the airwaves. One example from Cairo Radio of 25 May will set the tone: "The Arab nation is determined to wipe Israel off the face of the earth and restore to Palestine the Arab honor." Intelligence reports circulated several times daily to decision-makers contained samples of such material.[53]

Israel is certainly not the first non-Arab country to be unfavorably impressed by Arab rhetoric. U.S.-Egyptian relations have been harmed by this factor at various times. But what transformed Israeli concern at developments into profound alarm was the memory of the Nazi exterminations—in short, the "Holocaust syndrome." When Nasser and other Arab leaders talked of "destroying Israel," they were playing on Israel's most sensitive nerve. Israeli experts on the Arab world are well aware of the flamboyancy of Arab rhetoric. But not even they were immune from the sinister resonances set off by threats of extermination. Nasser's speech of 22 May announcing the closing of the Straits of Tiran convinced the people of Israel that the nation was faced by a mortal danger. Irrespective of community of origin or generation, Israelis were gripped by the visceral conviction that the catastrophe was about to repeat itself. At a meeting of the Cabinet Defense Committee on 23 May, the judicious Abba Eban felt "memories of the European slaughter" flowing into the room like turgid air. Meir Amit, head of the Mossad secret service, judged that war was now unavoidable. Looking back, many of the participants in the drama confirmed the feeling that the choice, in Yigal Allon's words, was now whether "to live or to perish."[54]

Of especial interest is the reaction of the general staff. On the morning of 25 May it was learned that the crack Egyptian Fourth Armored Division had crossed the Suez Canal into the Sinai. The conclusion of military intelligence was that Nasser was about to launch an immediate attack. Following a meeting between members of the general staff and Prime Minister Eshkol (who was also minister of defense) an urgent telegram was sent off to Foreign Minister Eban, who had just landed in Washington: In his conversation with President Johnson, the question of the blocked Straits of Tiran was no longer to be presented as the central issue; it was to be emphasized "that the Arab world was drawn up for a war of extermination against Israel."[55]

Nasser's failure to deter Israel was echoed in Israel's reciprocal failure to restrain Egypt. Yet Israel's communications strategy was the reverse of Egypt's. While Nasser's words and actions were redolent of anger and excess, Eshkol opted for "a soft answer that turneth away wrath." His speeches were studiedly unprovocative, and if the Egyptian army made its dispositions in a glare of publicity, Israeli countermoves were deliberately surreptitious. Israel may have been influenced in adopting this low-key approach by the escalatory effect of its earlier warnings to Syria. In fact the analogy was misleading. In the first case Egypt had not been intimidated by Israeli rhetoric but had been convinced by what seemed like a consistent pattern of indisputable evidence on the ground of the existence of an actual "plan." This evidence came from two sources: the factual and by no means bombastic statements of Israeli leaders and, most important, Soviet information about Israeli troop concentrations. (The ultimate source of this intelligence has never been cleared up.) After 15 May Israel had to persuade Egypt of the credibility of a contingent threat, which was quite a different thing. What is clear is that the assessment that a low-key approach would be sufficient to calm Arab fears and curb Arab exuberance proved to be seriously mistaken.

With the first rumbles of alarm emerging from Damascus and Cairo on 13 and 14 May, it was decided in the Israeli cabinet to try "to hold the fever down." In contrast to the situation in previous years, armored vehicles were to be kept out of the Independence Day parade, scheduled to be held in Jerusalem the next day, and the number of troops was to be limited. Ironically, the signal was totally misunderstood. Far from being interpreted as evidence of moderation, the reduced scale of the festivities was taken as proof that Israel had indeed concentrated most of its army on the frontier with Syria.[56] Meanwhile, the first Egyptian troops had entered the Sinai, and Israel was obliged to take certain minimal countermeasures. Only a single battalion kept watch in the Negev, facing the border with Egypt. It clearly had to be reinforced, but the cabinet decided to do so "without fanfare." This became Israel's basic approach: to mobilize as required by the situation but to avoid alarming the Egyptians. Thus on the night of 16–17 May the army was ordered to "refrain from ostentatious movements so as not to fan the flames." The logic of the strategy was spelled out on 18 May: "We felt ourselves obliged to act with great caution," Chief of Staff Rabin writes, "because a large scale mobilization, beyond essential needs, might result in an escalation of tension, and this we wished to avoid." Unfortunately, just as Nasser had interpreted the scaled-down march past of 15 May as evidence and not disproof of Israeli preparations to attack Syria, the absence of troop concentrations in the south was taken to demonstrate an offensive disposition in the north.[57]

As long as UNEF remained in place, the Egyptian maneuver basically conformed to a confrontation that had taken place between Egypt and Israel in February 1960. At that time Nasser had pulled out his forces after a decent interval. But with the withdrawal of UNEF on 18 May, the post-1957 *status quo* began to come apart. Now was the time for Israel to switch from reassurance to vigorous deterrence if the central achievement of the 1956 War, free passage through the straits, was to be preserved. It was decided to persevere with a strategy of restraint. The possibility of a public warning to Nasser about the consequences of his reestablishing a blockade of the Gulf of Aqaba—on the lines of a solemn declaration that Israel would be obliged to go to war in such circumstances—was weighed and rejected. Both Eshkol and Eban agreed that as long as shipping was allowed through the straits, there was "no reason to force [Nasser's] hand by rhetorical defiance."

Instead, a number of diplomatic initiatives were taken through third parties. Between 18 and 20 May the leading maritime powers were informed that "if the Straits of Tiran were closed, Israel would stop short of nothing to cancel the blockade." On 19 May Eshkol cabled General De Gaulle with the following message, the words of which were chosen with the utmost care: "Israel on her part will not initiate hostile acts, but she is firmly resolved to defend her territory and her international rights. Our decision is that if Egypt will not attack us, we will not take action against Egyptian forces at Sharm-el-Sheikh—until or unless they close the Straits of Tiran to free navigation by Israel." In notes to the British and French foreign ministers Eban affirmed that Israel's intention not to acquiesce in the blockade was "solid and unreserved. It is essential that President Nasser should not have any illusions." Finally, the Israeli ambassador in London was instructed to add orally: "Our decision is that unless attacked we shall not move against Egyptian forces unless or until they attempt to close the Straits to Israel-bound shipping. They have not yet done so."[58]

Israel tried to leave the door open for Nasser's retreat, in Abba Eban's phrase, until the very end. On 22 May Eshkol addressed the Egyptian leader from the rostrum of the Israeli parliament. His speech was cautiously worded after wide consultation. Any appearance of a public challenge was studiously avoided. Israel was still ready to "participate in an effort to reinforce stability and advance peace in the region." The tone of restraint was preserved even after Nasser's own bellicose address announcing the closing of the straits. Replying to the debate in parliament on the evening of 23 May, Eshkol forwent any breath of a threat of a possible resort to force. Israel wished "to reduce the tension." He called on "international organs to show effective responsibility for the preservation of peace."[59] But by then it was too late. The blockade was already in place.

The closing of the Straits of Tiran on 23 May marked the bankruptcy of Israel's deterrence strategy. Despite its long insistence that this act would constitute a *casus belli*, in the final analysis the Egyptian leadership remained skeptical of Israeli determination. Some uncertainty surrounds Nasser's personal appraisal. In a speech on 23 July 1967 he described himself as putting the possibility of war at 50 percent at the key meeting of 21 May 1967, at which the decision to close the straits was taken.[60] But we have already seen that at Bir Gafgafa the following day he spoke in terms that implied that he did not expect war. And we also have the first-hand testimony of Anthony Nutting, a former British minister, that only a few hours before the war broke out Nasser remained "convinced that the Israelis would not be prepared alone to fight a war on two fronts, if only for fear of the striking power of Egypt's Russian-equipped air force."[61]

At any rate, the crucial estimate of Egyptian military intelligence cited by Badran in his trial testimony was that given Egyptian superiority on the ground, "Israel was not about to commit suicide."[62] So much for the Israeli decision to mobilize "without fanfare." On 23 May Mahmoud Riad gave the opinion to Nasser that "an outbreak of hostilities was out of the question."

Badran and Field Marshal Amer concurred that "Israel, which had a clear picture of the deployment of our forces, would think twice before attacking."[63]

How is one to account for Egypt's fatal misjudgment? It must be partly explained in terms of overconfidence and the mistaken perception that Israel could not act independently of the United States. However, the onus must be on the deterrer to actively dissuade the challenger from his initiative. That the latter may overrate his chances of success is axiomatic. To mount a successful campaign of deterrence, Israel had, first and foremost, to transmit the unmistakable message that it would use force rather than see the straits closed. It was up to Israel to leave Egypt in no possible doubt of the danger of such a move. Even this might not deflect Nasser from his chosen course, but at least he would be unable to overlook the likely consequences of his actions. Such a message need not have been provocative or escalatory. In the event, no adequate warning was given, and a misleading impression was conveyed. Mohamed Heikal, for one, was of the opinion that the Israeli government's seeming hesitation played a role in Egypt's mistaken evaluations.[64] In the classical tradition of European diplomacy described by Harold Nicolson, precise but cautious understatement is of the essence. While preserving an atmosphere of calmness and courtesy, it is supposed to enable statesmen "to convey serious warnings to each other which will not be misunderstood."[65] Israeli diplomacy adopted this style under its first foreign minister, Moshe Sharett, and fully conformed to it during the May crisis. From this perspective the crucial messages sent by Israel on 19 May were impeccable: "if Egypt will not attack us, we will not take action against Egyptian forces at Sharm el-Sheikh—until or unless they close the Straits of Tiran"; "unless attacked we shall not move against Egyptian forces unless or until they attempt to close the Straits"; and so on. In content these formulations were unprovocative, conditional, and limited to the issue at hand; their tone was neutral and unemotive. However, such circumlocutions were utterly out of place in the impassioned context of a Middle East crisis with its clamorous hyperbole. Given those linguistic characteristics of overassertion and exaggeration noted above—which were such a marked feature of Arab behavior in the crisis—it is clear that only the most strident signals had any prospect of penetrating Nasser's consciousness and giving him pause at this time, if at all. As it was, the measured warnings and unobtrusive military dispositions preferred by Israel either failed to register with the Egyptians or were simply taken as proof of weakness.

A good case, therefore, can be made for the view that cross-cultural factors did indeed affect the course of events preceding the 1967 War. In essence, the crisis escalated out of control because of a breakdown of the communications process. Both Egypt and Israel failed to translate the deterrent messages that they wished to convey into terms comprehensible to the other side. The decisions taken may in themselves have been mistaken, but they were at least the result of careful consideration. Their fatal flaw lay in a fundamental cultural myopia, an ethnocentric distortion, and not in some procedural lapse. Put another way, the assumptions underlying policy and the signals used to implement it were limited by culture-bound considerations and did not take into account the opponent's predispositions. As a result of this pattern of conceptual and semantic bias, both Egypt and Israel deprived themselves of the means to modify each other's behavior. They were, figuratively speaking, broadcasting on channels the opponent could not tune into.

A series of serious errors of this kind can be discerned. First, the reprisals initiated by Israel in the aftermath of the Syrian-Egyptian treaty of 4 November 1966 were based on a projection of culturally inappropriate values onto the opponent. Despite the severity of the punishment inflicted, a deterrent affect was not achieved because the loss of face entailed by compliance with Israel was perceived in Arab eyes to be costlier than the prospect of military loss. For his part, Nasser was equally wrong-headed about Israeli values, displaying exceptional insensitivity to Israel's receptivity to threats in general and expressions evocative of the Holocaust experience in particular. Finally, the two opponents based their respective communications strategies in the crisis on assumptions that were inappropriate to the target culture. What one side perceived as overstatement, the other side saw as understatement, and vice versa. Where Nasser's speeches were registered in Israel as recklessly belligerent, Israeli articulations were totally unsuitable for Egyptian consumption. This symmetrical set of errors was repeated at the nonverbal level: Egyptian military movements were ostentatious, those of Israel inconspicuous. As a result, the message of deterrence that both sides sought to convey was hopelessly obscured.

VI

OBSTACLES TO NEGOTIATION

International negotiation can be defined as a structured dialogue of claim and counterclaim in which an attempt is made by the accredited representatives of states to reconcile opposing views and reach agreement on subjects of mutual concern. In an anarchic world without any accepted overarching authority able to resolve disputes and allocate resources between contending powers, negotiation remains the principal mechanism for the peaceful accommodation of contending interests.

Yet its benefits are rivaled only by its inherent difficulties. Diplomatic negotiation is a deeply serious business, and may engage core values and vital interests. Issues at stake are contentious by definition and are also often unclear, intricate, and emotive. At the best of times the process taxes human ingenuity to the utmost. Even the possession by the parties concerned of shared assumptions about the forms and techniques—implicit and explicit—of negotiation is self-evidently no guarantee of success. What, though, are the consequences when negotiators are not simply the representatives of separate nations, but also the products of different cultures and negotiating traditions? Before they even sit down to discuss substantive issues, they may find themselves bogged down in questions—such as the etiquette and procedures appropriate to negotiation or the ultimate object of the entire exercise—the answers to which seem so self-evident that one's opponent's contradictory version can be put down only to deliberate obstructiveness. The full effect of cross-cultural incompatibility is then felt: an inability to set out on the journey of mutual exploration, let alone reach a haven of safety, although both may wish to do so. Travelers in adjacent trains running for a time on parallel tracks, the parties are doomed to gesture incomprehensibly at each other through the glass until their ways part for divergent destinations.

For many years the main stumbling block to a resolution of the Egypt-Israel dispute was not so much the intractability of negotiation as the inability of the two sides to get to the negotiating table at all. At the root of this preliminary deadlock—the first, incidentally, of a whole series of deadlocks at every stage of the negotiating process—lay cultural preoccupations which were as mutually unintelligible as they were antithetical. On the Israeli side it was a profound sense of insecurity; on the Egyptian side an overriding concern with face.

Israel's Security Complex

Ezer Weizman's pithy summing up of Israeli fears is that "you can take the Jew out of the diaspora, but you cannot take the diaspora out of the Jew." In other words, the habits and attitudes of a vulnerable and persecuted minority, for whom every non-Jew was a potential enemy and a pogrom might lurk round every corner, are too deep-seated to be eradicated overnight. The "basic Jewish problem," Weizman believes, is "the idea that we are hated, that everyone's out to trick us." Zionism—the independence of the Jewish people in its own land—was supposed to solve the problem, but it has not yet done so. Israel still suffers from a "total mistrust in everything, bordering on the paranoid."[1]

Again and again after the first peace feelers were put out by various parties at the beginning of the 1950s, Israel took steps that seemed more likely to thwart negotiation than facilitate it. Leaks aborted promising initiatives. Reprisal raids interrupted mediation efforts. Opportunities for meetings were passed up. Ideological adversaries of the Jewish state—and, in the words of the Jewish joke, even paranoids have enemies—will see this as proof that powerful elements in Israel's political/security establishment were not really interested in a peaceful settlement until the 1973 disaster. But one does not need to resort to conspiracy theories to explain Israeli behavior. Those who know Israel well will recognize in the pattern of obstructiveness evidence of that complex of suspicion, pessimism, and terror of the unknown that is the heritage of a people for whom calamity has been more familiar than triumph. "We had suffered too many catastrophes in our history," Moshe Dayan told President Carter, "for us to ignore the possibility of their recurrence in the future."[2]

With such an outlook on the world, every proposal is interpreted as a hostile ruse, every initiative as a potential snare. More reassuring is the certainty of the beleaguered stronghold and the enmity of the world than the excruciating and perhaps disarming path of negotiations leading into the obscurity of an uncertain future. At least that way Israelis knew where they stood. Peace: what Israel both craved and dreaded.

Meir Amit, the head of Israel's Mossad security organization from 1963 to 1968, tells a characteristic story of his government's paralyzing mistrust. At a certain period (which he declines to specify), following contact with an important Egyptian in Europe, it was proposed that Amit travel to Cairo to meet with Nasser. Though he himself was ready and willing, the government turned down the idea on the grounds that a trap was being laid and he would be held hostage. To Amit it was clear that the Egyptians' word of honor could be unhesitatingly relied upon. "Those who opposed the trip," he comments, "did not know the Arab mentality."[3]

If there is an antidote to paranoia, it is not to be found in the turbulent and Machiavellian world of Middle East politics. Now an objective assessment of the Arabs' reliability in maintaining their commitments would reveal a mixed picture. Boutros-Ghali, for many years minister of state in the Egyptian foreign ministry, acknowledges in a study of the Arab League that member states are far from meticulous in paying their dues and that Arab defense pacts have all too often proved dead letters.[4] Nasser came to be thoroughly mistrusted by Western governments; Qadafi of Libya has inherited the latter's reputation for duplicity. In the Lebanese context, agreements—internal and external—are demonstrably worthless. On the other hand, Saudi Arabia, the Gulf Emirates, and the Hashemite Kingdom of Jordan have acquired sound reputations in the West for dependability. President Sadat also established excellent credentials. So generalizations are really impossible.

Israel's subjective judgment excluded fine distinctions, though. Faced by rivals whose language and legal customs were utterly confusing, Jews saw their suspicions, on the whole, confirmed and reinforced. Legal expectations that were a product more of the academy than of the chancellery would have no truck with the imperfections of Middle Eastern treaty observance. Pacts were to be kept—not only as a maxim of international law but as a categorical moral imperative. "The Arabs," it was quickly concluded, "are not to be trusted." Experiences that refuted this intuition were minimized, while those that seemed to bear it out stuck in the collective memory. Four key episodes in particular involving an apparent breach by Egypt of its commitments weighed heavily on Israeli leaders.

The first of these concerned a perceived Egyptian failure to comply with the terms of the 1949 armistice. Article II section 2 of the agreement prohibited warlike or hostile acts by both regular and *nonregular* forces of the signatories against each other and also forbade any crossing of the armistice line. But within a short time, acts of murder and sabotage carried out by infiltrators from the Egyptian-occupied Gaza Strip against Israeli settlements became a distressingly common occurrence. The fact that until the spring of 1955 most of the infiltrators were Palestinian refugees, smugglers, and thieves, and not agents of Egypt, was less important to Israel than the fact that the border was being violated and domestic morale seriously affected. As far as Israel was concerned, responsibility rested with the Egyptian authorities, irrespective of any difficulties they might have on the ground in enforcing the accord.[5]

A second disappointment lay in store for Israel as a result of contacts with Egypt in the affair of the Cairo trial (November 1954–January 1955). Using every channel of influence open to it, Israel swamped Egypt with requests for clemency for a group of Egyptian Jews accused of being Israeli agents and having engaged in sabotage (they were and had). In the end various assurances of one kind or another were received by Israel, the most important of which were the following: To the Anglo-Jewish Member of Parliament Maurice Orbach, Colonel Nasser stated on 18 December that he would "do his very best to see that no inflammatory sentences were passed, but it must be recognised that the defendants were in the pay of a foreign power, and were under the orders of the Israel Intelligence Service. Their crime was a grave one, and he [Nasser] was in an unenviable position." This statement was made at their third meeting, after Nasser had twice cautioned Orbach "that the trial was now before the court and he could not interfere."[6]

Other contacts took place in Paris between Israeli and Egyptian officials. To a written appeal from Prime Minister Sharett, Nasser replied with a message read out by a special envoy. In the paraphrase of Gideon Rafael: "The Egyptian government could not intervene in the proceedings of the Cairo trial which was being conducted with strict observance of fair procedure. The defendants were receiving all the legal aid they had requested. In the personal view of the envoy there would be no execution of death sentences."[7]

In the event, two of the accused were hanged, four received heavy prison sentences, and two were acquitted. Opinion in Israeli government and military circles was sickened at the executions—Israel had no death sentence—and outraged at what was seen as a breach of faith. Gideon Rafael of the foreign ministry, who had orchestrated the Israeli campaign, was outraged. He told the more philosophical Sharett that Nasser had "deceived us, deliberately cheated all those who approached him, led us all up the garden path."[8] But were the assurances morally binding? At a distance of more than thirty years, they sound far from unconditional: Nasser certainly proposed to do his best but equally hinted that his authority was not absolute. One of Rafael's colleagues on the Paris mission, Arab expert Shmuel Dibon, had, from the beginning, been far less sanguine than his boss. As he read it, Nasser's envoy had given "no definite commitments but extremely reserved promises."[9]

It was hard to know just what had gone wrong. In their more dispassionate moments, Rafael and Sharett realized that a double-cross was not the only possible explanation. Arab League politics, a split within the Revolutionary Command Council, and domestic considerations could all account for the unexpected sentences. Be that as it may, within a fortnight of the verdicts, one of the channels of communication with Nasser came to life again. Since the autumn of 1954, the American Central Intelligence Agency—quite separately from the Cairo trial contacts and also of the Anglo-American "Alpha" consultations—had been busy with project "Gamma," a scheme to set up a meeting between the Israeli and Egyptian prime ministers. On 10 February 1955 Sharett was informed via the Mossad liaison in Washington that the CIA was renewing its efforts. Nasser did not view the trial as affecting the planned meeting. He was sure that the Israeli government would understand that, in the circumstances, with all good will, he had been prevented from acting differently. In any case he wanted them to know that he viewed the hangings with disfavor and that they were carried out against his wishes. He was still willing for a meeting, and the ball was in Israel's court.

For the moment, Sharett concluded, Israel would have to send a negative reply. Nasser's behavior demonstrated one of two things. "Either he is a hypocrite or he is unable to keep his word. One way or the other he is not an acceptable bargaining partner as far as we are concerned."[10] And that, for the time being, was that. Sharett, not the strongest of prime ministers, was obliged to consent to the disastrous Gaza retaliation of 28 February 1955, lessening confidence even further. The good will needed to take risks was now lacking, and Sharett and Nasser's domestic room for maneuver had greatly narrowed. Mutual accusations of bad faith overshadowed continuing American efforts to bring the two sides together. When the CIA took up the challenge again in June 1955, it was told by Nasser that he had lost his confidence in Israel because of the Gaza incident. To Israel's claim that it had also lost confidence in him following the hangings, he retorted that he had never promised that there would be no death penalties but had said all along that everything depended on the court. . . .[11]

The Cairo trial was very much a watershed in the development of Israeli attitudes. After it Nasser's "duplicity" became virtually a received truth. Since, *a priori*, one could never trust the word of the Egyptian leader, there was no point in trying to reach an accommodation with him, except on terms, as we shall see, that he would find unacceptable. On the Egyptian side, there was an equal sense of grievance at Israel's policy of disproportionate retaliation. There were various other contacts and mediation attempts during the period of murderous escalation that preceded the 1956 Suez War, but they also foundered on the reefs of mutual mistrust and incomprehension.

The Suez War did solve Israel's problems in the short term. The Gulf of Aqaba was opened to Israeli shipping; the Gaza Strip was occupied and the fedayeen bases destroyed. No formal settlement, however, was to legitimize the new *status quo*. Ominously, even those few channels of communication that had existed before were now blocked. In a euphoric speech of 7 November 1956, David Ben Gurion denounced the 1949 armistice agreement with Egypt, thereby terminating the functioning of the Mixed Armistice Commission. He also, quixotically, called for direct negotiations. But the best is often the enemy of the good. The arrangement that eventually emerged was actually worse than that of 1949: no peace treaty, no armistice, indeed no agreement at all between Israel and Egypt, simply an understanding arrived at by Israel and the United States in the form of an address to the United Nations General Assembly given by Foreign Minister Golda Meir on 1 March 1957 expressing "certain hopes and expectations." Interference with Israeli shipping through the Gulf of Aqaba would entitle Israel to act under the self-defense provisions of the United Nations Charter. Were the situation in the Gaza Strip to deteriorate, Israel would defend its rights. Three days later,

Egyptian Foreign Minister Mahmoud Fawzi stated explicitly that his government would not be bound by any "hopes and expectations" uttered at the United Nations—a speech, incidentally, that was ignored entirely by the Israeli press.[12] By 7 March the newly created United Nations Emergency Force (UNEF) had taken over from the withdrawing Israeli army in the Gaza Strip, and within the week an Egyptian governor was reinstalled in Government House.

Ten years later, in the crisis of 1967, Israel found that it had fallen into a pit of its own digging. Forebodings of foul play in international relations have the uncanny habit of being self-fulfilling. If Egypt was neither formally nor morally bound by the 1957 settlement, how could one complain when it proceeded to ignore it? But the lesson derived by Israeli leaders from the events of May 1967 was not that the only viable settlement was one resting on mutual confidence. Their suspicions of Egypt were simply corroborated. Yigal Allon, deputy prime minister, forgetting Ben Gurion's speech of 7 November 1956 and that of Fawzi of 4 March 1957, accused Egypt of violating the armistice agreement. Interim arrangements had proved their worthlessness: "This time Israel must not content herself with less than a peace treaty accompanied by mutual and effective security arrangements"—a euphemism for territorial revision.[13]

The final Egyptian "breach of faith"—again more apparent than real—to enter the collective wisdom of the Israeli government was that of the ceasefire of 8 August 1970. On 19 June 1970, United States Secretary of State William Rogers had proposed a new initiative intended to put a halt to the dangerously escalating War of Attrition along the Suez Canal and to revive the mediation mission of UN special representative Gunnar Jarring, with a view to implementing UN Resolution 242 "in all its parts." An intensive American diplomatic effort eventually resulted in the acceptance by Egypt and Israel of a ninety-day truce. The crucial clause of the agreement read as follows:

> Both sides will refrain from changing the military *status quo* within the zones extending 50 kilometers to the east and to the west of the cease-fire line. Neither side will introduce or construct any new military installations in these zones. Activities within the zones will be limited to the maintenance of existing installations at their present sites and positions and to the rotation and supply of forces presently within the zones.

It was left unclear as to what was actually being prohibited. What was meant by the term "military *status quo*"? What constituted a "new military installation"? Further, who was to supervise the implementation of the agreement? On none of these points did the text provide any guidance. To fill the gap, a separate understanding was negotiated between Israel and the United States, ruling out any movement, construction, or installation of (antiaircraft) missiles in the area covered by the cease-fire, though it was not clear how Egypt was to be bound by it. To make matters worse, there were no aerial photographs taken of the area at the moment the cease-fire went into effect, nor was Egypt informed of the American-Israeli understanding until thirty-six hours later.[14]

Within hours of the entry into force of the truce, there was an extensive movement of Soviet SAM-2 and SAM-3 missiles into the standstill zone, which was immediately detected by Israel. Instead of heralding a renewal of negotiations, the cease-fire became the occasion for an outburst of angry accusations from the Israeli government and press. Once again, it was alleged, Egypt had demonstrated its treachery and the uselessness of trying to reach agreements with it. Weeks were wasted in mutual recriminations between the parties. By the time Israel had convinced a reluctant and disappointed United States of the facts of the redeployment, the Rogers Initiative was a dead letter. On 6 September 1970 Israel announced that it could not participate in the Jarring talks until the Egyptian missiles had been removed.

Technically speaking, Egypt had merely exploited the gaping loopholes of the cease-fire accord to improve its position on the ground. However, even if the missiles did not violate the letter of the agreement, they hardly conformed to its spirit. That Nasser was prepared for a political rather than military resolution of the conflict had long been clear. His positive response to Rogers's proposals bore out his willingness to "establish a just and permanent peace based on recognition by all sides of the sovereignty and integrity of the territory and independence of every state." (Former Egyptian Prime Minister Mustafa Khalil has recently confirmed that this was, indeed, Nasser's intent.)[15] His desire to restore some kind of military equilibrium along the Suez Canal did not necessarily contradict that overall strategy. In fact, evidence of deepening Soviet involvement had been a powerful incentive to Israel to accept the initiative in the first place. On 30 July, the very day before it gave its consent to the truce, Israeli aircraft had shot down four Soviet jets with their Russian pilots some thirty kilometers west of the canal. The prospect of a full-scale confrontation with the USSR could not have been welcome. (Defense Minister Dayan, like his mentor Ben Gurion before him, had always been acutely sensitive to the dangers of confrontation with the Soviet Union. This may also explain why the text of the cease-fire, for all its glaring deficiencies, was accepted by Dayan with very little attention to the fine print.)[16]

For all this, the Rogers proposals provided a valuable opportunity for talks which at least deserved a trial. In accepting them as a basis for negotiations, Golda Meir was obliged to sacrifice the unity of her national coalition government, intact since the 1967 War. For Herut ministers Landau and Begin, any reference to "withdrawal" was anathema, and they resigned from the cabinet. Nasser himself was strongly attacked by Iraq, Syria, and the PLO for consenting to the cease-fire. But the sacrifices made by both sides were squandered: By moving the missiles, Nasser obtained military advantage while dooming the political option to failure. In Jerusalem it was argued, in the words of the director-general of the prime minister's office, "that there was no point in holding discussions with a country which did not honor its commitments." If Egypt could not be relied upon to adhere to the terms of a cease-fire, what possible value might there be in a peace agreement?[17]

Egypt: The Primacy of Honor

"Our dignity," Sadat proclaimed before the October War, "is absolutely priceless." He was expressing a general rule of Arab culture. Nothing is guarded more jealously than the Arab's reputation in the eyes of the group. No gain can compensate for a loss of face; no price is too heavy to regain it. Just as insecurity paralyzed Israeli diplomacy, the dictates of honor incapacitated Egypt. Indeed, for long the two imperatives appeared to be mutually exclusive, opposites that could never be attained in conjunction. Measures that Israel deemed vital for its safety perpetuated Egypt's humiliation; the satisfaction of Egyptian honor could be achieved only at the expense of Israel's security. Between the two poles negotiation remained suspended in lifeless immobility.

The outcome of the 1948 Arab-Israel War was a bitter pill for Egypt to swallow. On 15 May 1948 the Egyptian army, together with those of Syria, Iraq, Lebanon, and Transjordan, had invaded the newly declared state of Israel. By February 1949 the Egyptian forces had been soundly defeated and were on the verge of collapse in the Sinai when they were saved only by the diplomatic intervention of Britain and the United States. Years afterward (in August 1963), President Nasser could still urge his troops to prepare themselves "for the restoration of the rights of the Palestine people because the Palestine battle was a smear on the entire Arab nation. No one can forget the shame brought by the battle of 1948. . . ."[18]

Given the Arab ethos, the memory of the 1948 humiliation constituted a formidable psychological obstacle to entering formal peace negotiations with Israel. An armistice was one thing; a political settlement legitimizing the *status quo*—and therefore the bitter fruits of defeat—quite another. On the other hand, the Egyptians were quite capable of reading the political map. Israel, they realized, was here to stay, possessed a powerful army, and enjoyed the recognition of the great powers. Egypt had enough problems of its own without expending further blood and treasure on the question of Palestine. The problem of the Palestinian refugees displaced by the war was regarded as a serious question, but of a political rather than humanitarian nature—and therefore amenable to a political solution. (This was explained with brutal frankness in a secret talk between Egyptian and Israeli delegates at the Lausanne conference of the United Nations Palestine Conciliation Commission of April–May 1949. "Last year," the Egyptian pointed out, "thousands of people died of cholera in my country, and none of us cared. Why should we care about the refugees?")[19]

Torn between the contradictory impulses of pride and pragmatism, Egypt was prepared from the beginning to explore the possibility of an honorable accommodation with Israel. But there were three conditions that would have to be fulfilled if Egyptian face was to be saved. They remained basically valid and intact until 1977. First and foremost, Egypt could not, under any circumstances, appear to be the supplicant. In any context it would have to be treated as an equal partner. To be obliged to appear before the world as the defeated party, suing the victor for peace, would be utterly intolerable. Of course, within the context of an overall settlement, there might be trade-offs. Reciprocal concessions on points of detail—though not of principle—might be quietly made and presented in an acceptable form. But Egypt could never set its signature to a peace that had the slightest whiff of humiliation about it. Second, Egypt would need to have some kind of prior guarantee of satisfaction on certain irreducible points of principle. In the 1970s Sadat would define these as "honor, land, and sovereignty." In the earlier period Egypt also insisted on a solution *in principle* to the refugee problem. (As we shall see below, this was less than it sounded.) Finally, at least in the opening phase, direct talks would have to be kept secret. Until the Egyptians could be sure of an honorable outcome, face-to-face negotiations would be bound to carry the stigma of supplication. For the benefit of outside observers in general, and Arab brothers in particular, the only contacts would have to appear to be indirect, conducted through the good offices of a mediator, and therefore not implying formal recognition.

An idea of the essential elements of the Egyptian position at the beginning of the period can be obtained from the following conversation of May 1950 between an official of the American embassy in Cairo and Colonel Ismail Shirine, brother-in-law of King Farouk and principal Egyptian officer on the Mixed Armistice Commission. "Public sentiment in Egypt," he argued, "was still anti-Israel and . . . any government in Egypt which proposed peace would be in a delicate position." However, "something positive could be done if it were carefully handled with regard to the psychology of the people. He further believed that an Egyptian-Israeli peace would be followed almost immediately or simultaneously by negotiation of peace with Israel by other Arab countries."

There were three courses of action open to Egypt, Shirine continued: The first of these was war. In the circumstances, this was out of the question. The Egyptian army "had no equipment, no ammunition, and no transport." Israel was stronger than all the Arab states put together and "was in no danger of an attack from Egypt or any of the Arab powers." Later he added that "whatever genuine fear might exist in Israel concerning the Arabs, the fear of Israel by the Arabs was ten times greater." The second option was "to continue the present situation," but this was "potentially dangerous" and might work to Egypt's detriment. The final possibility was the establishment of peace. "Let's not kid ourselves," Shirine said. "Peace means recognition of Israel by Egypt and the other Arab countries. It means going back on our announced and sincerely meant principles but Egypt and the Near East must have peace." However, before there could be diplomatic and commercial relations, frontiers would have to be delimited; any gains made by Israel subsequent to the armistice agreement, especially on the Gulf of Aqaba, would have to be relinquished. As far as the refugees were concerned, he recognized that "there was no room for the refugees to return to in Israel."[20]

To overcome Egyptian inhibitions required great tact and sensitivity on the part of Israel. It was, after all, the victor. Now most Israelis were well aware of the humiliating effects of 1948, but only the school of thought associated with Moshe Sharett and a handful of other Arabists, foremost among whom was Eliahu Sasson, appreciated the need for painstakingly gaining the Arabs' confidence. Sharett's view was that the establishment of the State of Israel in the heart of the Arab world had been a powerful shock that it would take the Arabs time to adjust to. For its part Israel must patiently await the possibility of compromise and peace, while drawing the conclusion that "the less we demand peace, the more we expedite it."[21] But Sharett was virtually isolated, always on the defensive until his final defeat and dismissal in June 1956. The position of the majority led by Ben Gurion, strongly supported by the defense establishment and public opinion, was altogether different. Peace would come, in this view, only when the Arabs had been forcibly brought to the realization that Israel could not be destroyed. Yigael Yadin, chief of staff 1949–52, put it this way: The main obstacle between Israel and "the Arabs" was indeed emotional and not political, namely, "the insult of 1948." This alone rendered any compromise or concession futile. "Wounded pride and self-respect cannot be healed by concessions of secondary things on our part." Negotiation could never persuade the Arabs of Israel's right to exist. Only their conviction of Israeli strength could do that.[22]

This doctrine, which we can call that of "positions of strength," had certain obvious corollaries. One was the military strategy of massive reprisal, soon to dominate Israel's behavior toward its Arab neighbors. Another was the demand that negotiations be direct and be seen to be direct. Regardless of Egypt's susceptibilities, it had to be made to swallow the psychological reality of Israel—not as an act of philanthropy but as an acknowledgment of the inescapable necessities of power. Yet a third was a rejection of "prior conditions"; if the foundation of the State of Israel was in itself a humiliation, any sop to Egyptian pride would be necessarily pointless. On the contrary, it would be salutary for Egypt to abandon its illusions. Finally, since any outcome would simply reflect the immutable realities of the balance of power, there would be very little need to make concessions even at the negotiating table.

With each side insisting on its own principles, Egyptian-Israeli relations were effectively doomed to a generation of paralysis.

From the time of the Rhodes armistice negotiations of January–February 1949 onward, Egyptian and Israeli delegates met face to face. At first there had been reticence on the Egyptian part, but before long Ralph Bunche, the United Nations mediator, had both sides sitting alongside him in his hotel bedroom; and at the armistice signing, the heads of the two delegations were admiring family snapshots together.[23] The only precondition for such contacts was that they take place discreetly, out of the public eye. Eager to establish the principle of recognition, and also perhaps emphasize Egypt's anxiety for a settlement, Israeli sources were soon leaking news of these liaisons to the press. It was not long before this practice was gravely to interfere with the development of any genuine dialogue.

At the Lausanne talks which followed the success at Rhodes, Israelis and Egyptians met in secret on several occasions. Information on these encounters was subsequently leaked from both Israel's United Nations delegation (headed by Abba Eban) and the Lausanne delegation. The American State Department believed that these revelations had harmed the negotiations of the Palestine Conciliation Commission (PCC) and the possibility of separate informal talks between Israel and Arab delegations at Lausanne.[24] In January 1950 King Farouk authorized direct talks to take place in Ankara between Abdul Moneim Mustafa, the Egyptian representative to the PCC, and Eliahu Sasson, then Israel's envoy to Turkey (the two had talked for seven hours in a village near Lausanne the year before). The projected encounter was called off by the Egyptians with the appearance on 24 January of a detailed report in the Israeli newspaper *Hador*. "Datelined" Geneva—an obvious red herring—the story implied that the initiative for making contact came from the Egyptian side. It should be noted that *Hador* was a semi-official organ of the ruling Mapai Labor party, and it was inconceivable that such a report could have appeared without authorization from the highest level. As a result of the leak, the Egyptians were obliged, in the words of the American ambassador to Egypt, "to run for cover," denying any intention of direct negotiations with Israel. A new foreign minister in Cairo then opposed such contacts.[25]

In February and March 1952, a number of interesting signals of Egyptian interest in a settlement were picked up by the Israeli Foreign Ministry, from both its contacts and a study of the Egyptian press. On 20 March Ben Gurion decided to go public, telling a press conference that "internal dissension" in Egypt prevented peace with Israel but that he hoped that peace would soon come about. Strong denials that there was a possibility of peace were then published in the Egyptian press. Eliahu Sasson, whose advice on the Arabs had become more of an irritant than a stimulant to his superiors and who had accordingly been shunted off to Rome, was beside himself at his prime minister's unaccountable behavior. "Any declaration on our part," Sasson pointed out, "invites a negative and extreme response from the Arabs and postpones a renewal of contact for years." Israel was ensuring the failure of peace efforts with its own hands.[26]

Following the 23 July 1952 revolution in Egypt, there were in fact further contacts. Ben Gurion made a conciliatory speech on 17 August, and the Israeli chargé d'affaires in Paris, Shmuel Dibon, approached his Egyptian counterpart with the proposal of direct negotiations toward the establishment of peace. Informal discussions might precede these negotiations. When after ten days he had not yet received an answer, Dibon contacted the Egyptian diplomat and warned him that if no reply was forthcoming his government would be obliged to go public.[27] Not only did this clumsy threat indicate a quite inappropriate haste and lack of finesse in dealing with Egypt, it was hardly calculated to gain Egyptian confidence in Israeli discretion or awareness of Egypt's psychological necessities. Clearly, as far as Israel was concerned, negotiations and publicity were to be synonymous.

Again in February 1953, Egyptian Foreign Minister Fawzi used the opportunity of a visit to the Middle East by Ralph Bunche to indicate that he was interested in the possibility of talks with Israel. Bunche then flew to Israel, where he informed Sharett of Fawzi's statements. Sharett responded with an affirmation of willingness to meet with the Egyptians anywhere, anytime, assuring him that the talks would be kept absolutely secret. It did not take long, though, for the *New York Times* to get hold of the story, with the inevitable result that Egypt immediately denied that any such approach had been made.[28] This unfortunate habit of indiscretion has continued to the present day, dogging the "peace process" between Egypt and Israel.

The Struggle over Direct Negotiations

But it was in the coils of the issue of direct negotiations that Israeli and Egyptian sensibilities were to become most inextricably entangled, impeding all possibility of progress. For Israel the call for direct talks became a rallying cry of policy, encapsulating in a single slogan both apparent good sense and justice. For Egypt the taboo on sitting down with Israelis acquired almost theological dimensions. As the situation deteriorated along the Gaza Strip in the spring and summer of 1955, for example, procedural and substantive issues alike hindered the work of the Mixed Armistice Commission under the chairmanship of General Burns. At first Israel pressed, unsuccessfully, for a high level conference to discuss the improvement of security. But the harder it tried, the more fiercely the Egyptians resisted extending the scope or seniority of the discussions.

Various proposals were put forward in the commission to alleviate tension, although none came to anything. One potentially bright idea was the suggestion of a telephone link between the local commanders. Some, at least, of the incidents on the border were a product of misunderstanding between two jittery forces and might be prevented by such a "hot line." However, it was not long before metaphysics got in the way. At first Ben Gurion and Dayan insisted on a direct link, hoping to establish the greater principle of direct negotiations and *de facto* recognition. For the same reason the Egyptians opposed the idea. Under pressure from Burns they then agreed, on condition that the switchboard operator, the one who put through the calls, was a member of the United Nations observer force. When the rest of the Israeli government eventually accepted Sharett's argument that the Egyptians needed such a cover and that the main thing was that the two commanders talk directly to each other, the Egyptians took fright. They then objected to the prospect of a direct telephone conversation altogether, insisting that both sides would have to direct their remarks through the UN observer.[29]

Israeli insistence on direct negotiations was not, of course, simply a perverse caprice; nor was Egypt's refusal. The issues at stake emerged with great clarity during the course of the ill-fated Anderson mission of January –March 1956. Launched with high hopes by the United States in January 1956 in the aftermath of Nasser's ominous Czech arms deal, this was the last real chance for the settlement of Israeli-Egyptian differences before the Suez War. It had been planned in meticulous detail. Robert Anderson, a former assistant secretary of defense and secretary of the treasury, and personal envoy of President Eisenhower, would shuttle between Cairo and Jerusalem—in the manner of Henry Kissinger after the 1973 War—progressively narrowing the gap between the two sides. To the Americans it was obvious that this would satisfactorily meet the Egyptians' "psychological requirements" and held out the best chance of resolving the issues. Contingency plans were in hand for straightening the border by mutual adjustment, for resettling or compensating the refugees with financing by the international community, and for an Anglo-American guarantee against aggression.[30]

From all extant accounts of the mission, it is clear that the major stumbling block to progress was Ben Gurion's insistence on direct negotiations. Again and again during the course of the shuttle, he reiterated the point. At the very first session with Anderson—who had come from Cairo with tantalizing hints of possible concessions by Nasser—Ben Gurion left no doubt that, as he saw it, the Egyptian willingness to meet Israelis face to face was the acid test of Egyptian intentions: "The main question is whether there is a will to peace. I don't want to doubt it, but if there is any possibility of knowing, it will only be if the two sides meet together to discuss the issues that concern them. I see no other way." And later: "The meeting will be a decisive test of the seriousness of their goodwill. Without a meeting, we can only doubt Nasser's sincerity—whether he really aspires to peace."[31]

This argument, in essence, was the cornerstone of Israel's case over the years. Egypt's readiness to enter into direct negotiations and thereby acknowledge the legitimacy of the Jewish state was viewed as a condition of negotiations and not in itself negotiable. Nonrecognition was considered a symptom of an Arab inability to adjust to reality and even a synonym for a desire to "erase Israel from the map." As time went by, this issue loomed disproportionately large and became a matter of principle—the criterion for determining the Egyptian desire for peace. Congenitally suspicious at the best of times, the Israelis were only confirmed in their gloomy appraisal of Egyptian intentions by the latter's reluctance to negotiate face to face. The Egyptian response was to hang onto their refusal all the more tenaciously, seeing it as the last shred of a threadbare dignity, a bulwark against a dictated peace, a sole trump card in an otherwise meager hand.

Ben Gurion's second point in his talks with Anderson was that only Nasser's personal intervention could clear away the choking undergrowth of secondary detail. Anderson had argued for a step-by-step approach, but the Israeli prime minister wondered whether it might not be easier to tackle the big issues first. "If Nasser participates personally, and the entire scope of the problem is examined, it is possible that peace might be attained in ten days."[32]

Ben Gurion's perception that tough decisions in the Arab world could be made only at the highest level was borne out by his experience of dealing with King Abdullah after the 1948 War: the ruler of Transjordan had been able to cut through intractable problems at one stroke. If this was so, why waste time in aimless sparring with officials of a lower rank? The assumption was correct but the conclusion false. For the Egyptians, initial contacts were vital in order to sound out the Israeli position and insure against possible humiliation. In fact, the lesson that Egypt drew from Israeli negotiations with Abdullah was the opposite of Israel's. Face to face with Israeli negotiators, Abdullah had been forced to swallow a punitive and humiliating settlement, including the loss of territory. Israeli demands, Moshe Dayan later admitted, although just, were "by no means modest." When Abdullah asked for concessions in return, he was unceremoniously presented the facts as Israel saw them. "The time to have talked about concessions and compromise," Dayan told him, "was before the war, in order to prevent it. Now one had to bear the consequences and finish with it." News of the Israel-Jordan armistice agreement was received with shock by Abdullah's subjects, and the government was obliged to resign. On 20 July 1951 the king was assassinated on the steps of the El Aksa mosque in Jerusalem.[33] Hardly surprising, then, that the Egyptians were not falling over themselves with eagerness to mount the scaffold.

The third reason for Ben Gurion's insistence on face-to-face contact with Egypt derived from an unshakable faith, rooted in the Jewish intellectual tradition, in the power of reason. Untainted by the slightest trace of doubt in the absolute justice and essential *reasonableness* of the Zionist cause, he—and his successors—were supremely confident that they could bring the Arabs around to their point of view. General E. L. M. Burns, the Canadian commander of the United Nations observer force responsible for supervising the armistice agreements between Israel and its neighbors in the mid-1950s, was quick to grasp the depth of this conviction, so utterly incongruous in the passionate climate of Middle East politics. He rightly commented that the Israelis "had a fixed idea that if they could get the Egyptians, or any of the Arabs, to 'sit down with them,' they could win them to a complaisant—that is to say, peacemaking—attitude. I do not know what grounds the Israelis had for this confidence in their own charm and persuasiveness at the conference table."[34]

The Israelis' confidence—clearly incomprehensible to General Burns—derived from that age-old tradition of the Talmudic academy so formative in its effects on the development of Jewish culture. Grounded in the dialectical confrontation of keen legal minds arguing over abstruse points of law, the habit of reasoned exposition, a belief in the efficacy of forensic skills, carried over not only into the day-to-day conduct of politics but also into the Israeli approach to diplomacy. Though Ben Gurion, like other Zionists, had turned his back in contempt on the way of life of the "ghetto," he could not escape its implicit habits and assumptions. When Anderson moved from form to substance, bringing up the concrete problems of refugees and territory, he was crisply informed that these were only for discussion by the two sides. "They are so complex," Ben Gurion told him, "that I doubt whether any progress is possible without direct contact. . . . I believe I can see things as Nasser sees them, that I can convince him and he can convince me. . . . If we sit together we shall be able to understand one another."[35] The hands may have been the hands of the prime minister of the new Israel, but the voice was the traditional voice of Jewish reason.

No argument of Anderson's could shift Ben Gurion from his basic position. It was evident to the American envoy that in the face of this stand, even the most ingenious compromise proposals were so much wasted breath. After reporting back to President Eisenhower, he returned to Egypt for one last try at the beginning of March 1956. What was Nasser's reaction to the idea of an important Israeli nongovernmental personality, whose absence from his country would not be felt, coming to Cairo to negotiate? Nasser rejected the proposal. Abdullah's murder haunted the conversation like a specter. On four occasions Nasser returned to the subject: "I cannot stake myself and my Government on this game." Anderson had to understand "that in all the Arab countries there were people who would argue that this was against the good of the Arabs." Egypt could talk to the United States, and the United States might talk to Israel. But Nasser "could not take the risk of bringing an Israeli to Egypt."[36]

Israel's promises of secrecy were all very well, but Nasser could not conceal the loss of confidence in Israeli assurances that had resulted from the Gaza raid of the previous year. A "channel of communication" had existed, yet he had been "caught with his pants down." After that experience, he implied,

he could never be certain that Israel would not exploit direct contacts to destroy him. Anderson's fallback position—probably what he had envisaged all
along—was to suggest mediation through the good offices of the United
States. In the protocols of the mission, published by Ben Gurion before his
death, we have Anderson asking the Israeli prime minister what procedure
to adopt to put mediation into effect. Ben Gurion's answer is missing from
the published text.[37]

After the 1967 War, the demand for direct negotiations was one of the
three main planks of Israeli policy toward Egypt. The other two were territorial revision and the signing of a fully fledged peace treaty. "In Golda Meir's
eyes," one of the then prime minister's principal advisers has put it, "these
were not abstract principles but articles of faith that were absolute and unas-
sailable."[38] As in Ben Gurion's time, the seemingly peripheral procedural
point quickly developed into a central bone of contention. Since Israel would
put its cards on the table only in the physical presence of an Egyptian negotiator, and since no Egyptian negotiator would agree to meet face to face with
an Israeli, both parties were trapped in a Catch-22 situation.

United Nations mediator Gunnar Jarring, appointed to facilitate the implementation of Security Council Resolution 242 of 22 November 1967, was
faced with an insoluble dilemma. When shuttle diplomacy failed to get results, he invited the two governments to a peace conference on Cyprus. This
also fell through. In Egypt's state of demoralization and despair, the prospect
of direct negotiations was quite intolerable. With their territory under occupation, Egyptian leaders were convinced, they would be in the position of
an abject and helpless supplicant. "In any quarrel between two persons," Foreign Minister Mahmoud Riad told Ambassador Jarring, "any third party trying to separate them would naturally pull the weaker one away. In the dispute
with Israel, we were still the weaker party. Our problem was that if we took
one step backwards, we would fall into an abyss—therefore any attempt to
push us backwards would never achieve the desired peace."[39] The only innovation that would have satisfied Egypt was so-called proximity talks at
UN headquarters in New York. Instead of flying back and forth between
Cairo and Jerusalem, Jarring would install himself in Manhattan and move
between the Egyptian and Israeli permanent representatives. However, this
was unacceptable to Israel. The adoption of the idea by United States
Secretary of State William Rogers (in September 1969) lent it no extra
charm.[40]

The irony is that even when Sadat felt sufficiently secure and self-assured
to "break through the psychological barrier" and actually come to Jerusalem,
it rapidly transpired that open-ended, direct negotiations were still the last
thing on his mind. What he actually intended by the initiative was something
quite different: he was to hand down the Egyptian terms for a settlement en-
graved on tablets of stone—like Moses on Mount Sinai—and the Israelites

would have to decide whether to take them or leave them. No wonder the Israelis were confused. There was no precedent in the annals of international diplomacy for an undefeated party to be treated like a supplicant.

With hindsight we can see that the warning signs were present at the very first secret, exploratory meeting in Morocco between Dayan and Egyptian Deputy Prime Minister Tuhamy held on 16 September 1977. Reading from a written text, Tuhamy presented his country's overall conditions for a peace settlement. He ended, according to Dayan's account, with the following peremptory demand: "That's that. You can accept it or reject it, but there is no room for bargaining." On his return to Cairo, Tuhamy seems to have assumed that since Egypt's conditions were irreducible and axiomatic, they must be viewed as such by Israel. Certainly Sadat received this impression (and scholars have incorrectly repeated the "fact" of an Israeli "commitment" ever since). In Jerusalem itself on 19 November 1977, the first thing Sadat did was to make clear that he had nothing to add to his oft-declared public position, unchanged since 1971 and to be repeated from the podium of the Knesset: He was prepared to make peace in return for absolute Israeli withdrawal. Period. Mustafa Khalil clarified the point: Israel "had to understand that they did not wish the impression to be created that Egypt was conducting direct negotiations."[41]

Faced with this remarkable conception, Israel's leaders were at an utter loss. Here was what they had dreamed of for a generation—face-to-face meetings with their Egyptian counterparts. According to all their expectations, the two sides should now begin a dialogue, and the magic of "direct negotiations" would take over. This was how the game was played. When they discovered that they were simply supposed to sign on the dotted line, their reaction was one of amazement and disbelief. They most certainly did not share Tuhamy and Sadat's assumption that Israeli withdrawal from *all* of the Sinai was axiomatic. Dayan nowhere admits to making any such promise; Begin positively denies it, though he agrees that Sadat may have felt that it was implied. (It should be noted that Begin rejected a withdrawal to the so-called 4 June 1967 borders in his Knesset reply to Sadat.) Ezer Weizman, stating the general view, told Sadat to his face that his Knesset speech was an opening bid: "You started with the price high, with the aim of coming down later."[42] The Israeli government was convinced that in return for its withdrawal from most of the Sinai, it would be able to extract certain Egyptian concessions: the retention of civilian settlements in the Rafah salient including the new town of Yamit, and the Etam and Etzion airfields built after 1967.

Skepticism soon gave way to disillusionment and anger. Within weeks of Sadat's trip to Jerusalem, the old paralyzing mistrust reasserted itself. Dayan, missing the point, saw the Egyptians as issuing ultimatums rather than conducting negotiations. "Israel would not negotiate with a pistol at her temple."

Of the old confidence in the power of persuasion and the virtues of direct negotiations, only a shadow remained. Physical adjacency, without a meeting of minds, was not enough. At the Jerusalem convocation of the "political committee" in January 1978, the lack of communication between Israelis and Egyptians was so deplorable that an SOS was put out for American assistance. Secretary of State Cyrus Vance was drawn into the role of mediator. Just as Jarring and Rogers had proposed a decade before, Vance was obliged to shuttle between the rooms of the two sides in a search for common ground. Notwithstanding his efforts, the Egyptian delegation was withdrawn from Jerusalem. It would be another six months before the two sides met again. Sadat explained to his chief negotiator, Foreign Minister Kamel, on the latter's return from Jerusalem, that he had been afraid that Egypt would be maneuvered into making concessions.[43]

Israel never did work out what went wrong. Putting a brave face on it, Dayan claims in his memoirs that the source of the problem was to be found in the conservatism and rigidity of the Egyptian officials. Echoing Ben Gurion's old refrain, he writes: "The way to overcome obstacles was to move the discussions from the bottom to the top level, not the reverse"—in other words, the best way to restore momentum was to hold a summit conference.[44] But this was to ignore the failure of the previous three meetings with Sadat. As late as June 1978, Deputy Prime Minister Yigael Yadin reiterated the assumption that Sadat's speech was a "bargaining statement." If diplomacy was supposed to start with the ultimate demand, he plaintively wondered, "what are negotiations about?" He would be "depressed" if Sadat's attitude was take it or leave it. "I hope he doesn't mean this." If only he could talk to Sadat directly, "I am sure we would find a solution. One has to talk. I'm convinced that if direct negotiations are resumed, there is a chance for peace."[45]

On the other side of the fence, disillusionment also reigned. Although Sadat had met with the Israelis and broken through one "psychological barrier," the inhibitions in the way of the give-and-take of actual negotiation remained as powerful as ever. What Sadat really wanted was for the United States to save him from the intolerable prospect of direct negotiations. In February 1978, bitterly disappointed, he came to Washington. He was "dismayed," he told his hosts, by Israeli "haggling." Complaining about the Israeli preoccupation with "agendas and words," Sadat declared that he "would not negotiate directly with them until they were ready to meet his basic demands on withdrawal and a solution to the Palestinian question."[46] So much for Dayan and Yadin's faith in summit conferences. It was the end of the abortive, bilateral stage of the "peace process." From now on, at all subsequent meetings of Egyptian and Israeli delegations—at Leeds Castle in July, Camp David in September, and Blair House in October 1977—the procedure was to be triangular, namely, an American mediator moving between the two delegations. This was the approach that would bring peace.

With or without Preconditions?

Behind the profound Egyptian antipathy for direct negotiations with Israel was clearly the ever-present fear of humiliation, the intolerable prospect of playing the supplicant. There was also another, albeit related, factor, hinted at here by Sadat, which should be emphasized. Over the years Israel had always coupled an insistence on direct talks with the formula "without preconditions." There could be no entry price demanded by either party as a reward for entering discussions. Negotiations were to be open-ended, both sides putting forward their own proposals, with the assumption that they would arrive at a compromise "somewhere in the middle." This was the reason that Israeli governments, from the very first, always declined to draw maps or set out their demands in advance. (In the case of the Anderson mission cited above, we see Ben Gurion, in conformity with this long-standing principle, declining to be drawn out by the American intermediary.) From a pragmatic point of view, this made perfect negotiating sense; any definition by Israel of its minimal *desiderata* would have been taken by the other side as a maximal opening bid to be whittled down in subsequent bargaining. It was also associated with the Israeli belief, fostered by Arab hyperbole, that Arabs confused fantasy with reality. Any prior concession, Golda Meir argued as foreign minister, simply encouraged the Arabs "in their refusal to admit the realities of the situation."[47]

However, it was precisely the Israeli wish for unrestricted negotiations, in which either side would be perfectly free to raise any issue or demand it saw fit, that was most terrifying to the Egyptians. For there were some things that were not negotiable in Egyptian eyes, certain irreducible principles of justice and honor that were out of bounds to all discussion and could never be put up for auction. Rather than see these articles of faith sullied by profane debate, the Egyptians would prefer to forego negotiations altogether, no matter what the cost.

King Farouk's brother-in-law, Colonel Ismail Shirine, summed it all up as early as 1950; the following remarks could have been delivered at any time over the next twenty-eight years: "One hears, he said, that Israel wants peace and that she is ready to negotiate. When one asks the Israelis, however, what they have to propose as a basis for negotiation they merely say, 'Start negotiations with us and then you will see how benevolent we can be.' Egypt could not negotiate on this basis. Once negotiations were started they had to go on to completion. . . . Therefore, the items of negotiation must be agreed prior to their initiation."[48]

What, then, were the categorical imperatives of Egypt's foreign policy, the limits of its *non possumus*? First and foremost came the land; any concession of Egyptian soil was simply unthinkable. And at this point we return yet again to the womb of Egyptian culture: the immemorial life of the village. For the *fellah*, the land comes before everything. It is the source of his livelihood, the rock of his security, the well-spring of his prestige as a human being. The worst lot that can befall a peasant is to lose his land. In the village the most virulent, emotion-filled disputes are those over the ownership of land.[49] Anwar Sadat says it all in his autobiography. Writing of his childhood in the village, he movingly describes his sense of belonging to something beyond the family or even the village: the land. An adage of his grandmother's rang in his head: "Nothing is as significant as your being a child of this land. Land is immortal, for it harbours the mysteries of creation." His attachment to the land became the basis of his patriotism. By the time he left school he had acquired "a hatred for all aggressors, and a love and admiration for anyone trying to liberate his land."[50]

It is astonishing, given the Israeli willingness to suffer great hardship to re-claim, as they saw it, their own ancestral home, that they have been oblivious to this imperative on the Arab side. Yigael Yadin, ignoring any distinction between bedouin and peasant, argued that the nomadism of the "Arab" obvi-ated his attachment to any defined area. Modern borders, which were foreign creations, are unnatural and meaningless. Embracing Egyptian, Iraqi, and Palestinian in a remarkable generalization, Yadin believed that "the Arab people, in connection with their desire for unity, is more a people without a territory than it is a territory with a people." This view is representative—almost a cliché—of Israeli public opinion.[51] There is no question that since 1967 there has been utter incomprehension in Israel of the profound feelings aroused in Egyptians and others by the Israeli occupation of Arab lands.

The second treasured value of Egyptian foreign policy flows directly from the first: it is the principle of sovereignty. This implies the exclusive and indi-visible jurisdiction of the Egyptian government over its population, territory, and resources. Preoccupation with this factor is one of the key characteristics of Egyptian legal attitudes in the postcolonial era.[52] Any concept of power-sharing, limited sovereignty, extraterritorial rights, military occupation in any shape or form, is absolute anathema, an anachronistic relic of imperial-ism. Thus all Israeli (and, indeed, British, until 1954) ideas of "compromise" on these points were not only doomed to failure but also calculated to trigger the most deep-seated emotions. Joseph Sisco, the American diplomat, recalls that on the first occasion that he met Sadat in 1971, he made a plea for "com-promise" between Egypt and Israel (Sadat had just proposed a transitional agreement on the Suez Canal). At the mention of the word, the Egyptian president "hit the roof," associating it with the period of British colonialism.[53] Compromise: when an occupying power asks you to bargain over your own territory and rights.

The final imperative to take into account—and the most problematic—is the rights of the Palestinians. Although not a narrowly nationalistic value, the issue was very much a touchstone of Egypt's wider Arab affiliation. From the foundation of the Arab League in 1945, the question of Palestine was the main item on the agenda. Advocacy of justice for the Palestinians became synonymous with loyalty to the Arab cause. Any weakening of support, especially in the eyes of third parties, was seen as a dereliction of duty, a breaking of ranks. That said, it is clear that very often rhetoric and practice were two quite different things. Egypt had sufficient troubles of its own, and had paid a heavy enough price, to be free of guilt feelings where Palestine was concerned. From very early on, Nasser stated himself concerned mainly to secure a settlement that would leave his honor intact. In 1956, for instance, Nasser told Robert Anderson that Israel would have to agree "in principle" to accept those Palestinian refugees who wished to return to their homes. However, he would not object to administrative obstacles' being put in the way of their actual repatriation. Meanwhile, the United States could provide financial inducements or grants of land "to lure away those Palestinians made impatient by the delays."[54] The main thing, in other words, was to supply Egypt with a fig leaf behind which to conceal its modesty. What happened on the ground need bear no relation to the apparently impressive formal achievement which could be flourished before Egypt's fellow Arab states.

If there were to be any negotiations between the parties, therefore, Egypt would require guarantees in advance of indemnity on the issues of land and sovereignty—i.e., complete Israeli withdrawal—and at least the appearance of satisfaction in the matter of the Palestinians. It is interesting to note that the Egyptian concern to take out an insurance policy against possible disgrace is also an important feature of Japan's prenegotiating behavior. In a study of the Japanese style in international bargaining, Michael Blaker shows that Japan expends a tremendous effort in sounding out its opponent in a lengthy prelude to the opening of formal talks. Views are informally exchanged with the other side, information is gathered from third parties, and the chances of agreement are exhaustively assessed. Insofar as possible, the risk of an unexpected outcome is reduced by tying the hands of the adversary in advance. Devices used include narrowing the scope of subjects to be discussed, removing items inimical to Japanese interests from the agenda, and obtaining prior assurances that Japan's claims will be met.[55] The motive for this pattern of behavior is not hard to find. As an archetypal "high context," shame culture, in which the preservation of face is absolutely paramount, the Japanese possess an intense fear of submission, of the humiliation of failure. Thus both cultures, the Japanese and Egyptian, share a common wish to reduce the threat of an undesirable outcome and a consequent loss of face by laying down prior conditions for negotiation.

Over what is negotiable, Egyptians can bargain with the best of them; what Israel never grasped was that where their honor is perceived to be at stake, the prospect of bargaining is not only distasteful but profoundly distressing. In order to ensure that they would not be faced with this painful and quite unacceptable possibility, the Egyptians met the Israeli rejection of preconditions with an equal and opposite demand that Israel agree in advance to certain preliminary assurances. The form this insistence took is curiously reminiscent of the negotiating behavior of yet another high context culture—this time the Chinese.

The Chinese practice of negotiation is to begin by proposing agreement on generalities—the principles that are to govern the future course of talks—rather than on specifics. These principles are arrived at between the principals to the negotiation and may be very loosely formulated so as to leave the concrete details of the contract to subordinates. Lucian Pye, who makes this important observation, remarks that the Chinese approach is particularly hard for Americans to grasp since it flies in the face of their pragmatic assumption that progress is to be achieved by the incremental accumulation of agreement on points of detail. To get bogged down at the very start of talks in philosophical debate does not make sense as far as they are concerned. Should they, however, decide to humor their interlocutors by conceding what seem on the face of it to be vague platitudes, they may be unpleasantly surprised later on when they discover the Chinese referring back to the agreement in principle in order to extract substantive concessions.[56]

Although Professor Pye based his conclusions on the study of commercial negotiations, they are fully corroborated by Henry Kissinger in his account of the talks with Chou En-lai that preceded the epoch-making Shanghai communiqué of February 1972 (and which was in itself a declaration of principles and not an exhaustive treaty). "Confidence had to emerge," Kissinger writes, "from conceptual discussions." More like two professors of philosophy than international statesmen, the men spent many hours "giving shape to intangibles of mutual understanding." Petty bargining was altogether out of place at this level. Indeed, "sharp trading," as Kissinger quickly realized, would be suicidal. The two sides could hope to establish a sound and fruitful relationship only by achieving overall compatibility of purpose. The details could be filled in at a later stage.[57]

As Kissinger himself realized, the Chinese style was precisely that favored by the Egyptians. Both Sadat and Chou En-lai, he observes, were more interested in "philosophical understanding" than in agreement on details.[58] This stress was no mere personal foible of President Sadat's. In February 1966, at a low point in Egyptian-American relations, Nasser had sent a message to President Johnson asking for "one thing" only. It was not wheat or aid. "What we want, and we think it is the key to everything, is understanding. We don't want anything more than understanding." This was quite incomprehensible at the time to the Americans.[59] Kissinger's genius was to appreciate the importance of adopting an approach consonant with Egyptian needs. In fact, he admits that the first time he heard the Egyptian plea for "open hearts"—in September 1972, before the Yom Kippur War—he understood "too little about Egyptian psychology . . . to respond with comparable humanity." The next occasion on which he was to hear the refrain was in January 1974, after the war had taken place. Only then, as he was invited into Sadat's study, did Kissinger realize that the Egyptian leader was absolutely sincere when he told him that they must first reach agreement on principles.[60]

For all its outward drama and exhilaration, the Sadat visit to Jerusalem was a profoundly disturbing experience for the Israeli government. When they attempted to get down to the "nitty-gritty," substantive discussion of the issues and procedures, they found Sadat evasive and uncomfortable. He was not, as we have seen, ready for negotiations in the sense understood by Israel. "The important thing," he told them, was to arrive at "an agreed programme." This was what the Knesset speech was all about. It was never intended as a blueprint, but as a philosophical declaration of first principles. With lofty disregard for detail, the *Rais* defined the concepts that must underpin a settlement: an end to the occupation of Arab lands; the rights of the Palestinians; the right of countries to live in peace; the resolution of conflict through peaceful means.[61] All else would be mere commentary.

In further contacts over the next few weeks, the Egyptians used every opportunity to get their message across: Sadat was ready for full peace with all the trimmings. Yet first there had to be a declaration of principles to serve as a basis for negotiations. It did not have to be very detailed, but it must contain two fundamental features: "agreement in principle to withdrawal from all the occupied territories and a solution of the Palestinian problem."[62] This mystified the Israelis. Why waste time on generalities? Was not the main thing to get on with the specifics? "Every side wants to deal with details," Begin pronounced, "not only general declarations." Dayan suggested, with sturdy commonsense, that discussions concentrate "on practical proposals rather than on new formulae and paper declarations."[63] Where Sadat was prepared to bypass the excruciatingly difficult and contentious Palestinian issue with a sweeping proclamation, Begin was determined to tie Egypt down with preclusive detail. It was, as Kissinger had anticipated with Chou En-lai, a suicidal way of doing things. At Ismailia in December, to which Begin had come armed with elaborate proposals for the future of the West Bank (the autonomy plan), Sadat did his best to steer discussion away from detail and back to "big business." He appealed again for a declaration of principles. It was to no avail. Here was a classic cross-cultural conundrum: what one side took for granted, did not even think about, was incomprehensible to the other.

Not until the closing stages of the Camp David conference in September 1978 did it dawn on the Israeli government that the Egyptians meant exactly what they said and were not seeking a pretext to evade real talks or obtain bargaining advantage. Over the entire period, the two sides were stuck in a rut of utter incomprehension. In the end the Camp David accords gave Egypt what it had called for all along: a preliminary declaration of principles. And at the heart of the document lay Israeli agreement to complete withdrawal from the Sinai and recognition of the legitimate rights of the Palestinian people. The final peace treaty of March 1979 was to be an extrapolation of these first principles.

VII

DEADLOCK
ISRAEL AND EGYPT NEGOTIATE

Bargaining, the act of bidding for the purpose of exchange, is one of those pursuits seemingly common to all mankind. Like most other social institutions it is marked by considerable cross-cultural diversity. From one society to another, the shared label can be seen to conceal a wide range of variations in style, tempo, and etiquette. Nor does bargaining necessarily perform the same social function for different cultures. Throughout the Middle East, bargaining is far more than just a cold mechanism of the market. It is a pastime enjoyed and valued in its own right, a forum for human relationships, a mechanism of social integration. Bargaining, as one bazaar merchant put it, "is not a matter of saving a few piastres, but a custom, a traditional way of life. If you don't haggle it shows that you don't value the goods or the seller. Get into a taxi; it has a meter—but you still have to bargain with the driver over the price. It's in the blood; do you understand?"

There is nothing offensive about haggling, as many Western visitors to the Middle East seem to think. On the contrary, it is expected, and its absence causes disappointment. As the bazaar merchant suggested, it may actually be seen as a sign of good faith. It is certainly an opportunity for pleasurable conversation and hospitality. Only notables do not bargain, as a sign of their superior status.[1]

According to William Quandt, Egypt's negotiating style exemplifies two Middle Eastern traditions. One is indeed that of the bazaar or *suk*. But there is another parallel model that is very different, the "tribal or bedouin approach." Egyptians, as we have argued, are acutely sensitive to matters of honor or "face," the reputation of the individual in the eyes of his group. Imputations to one's honor are intolerable; face-saving is all-important. And where one's standing and self-respect are at stake, according to Quandt, the *suk* model of bargaining is quite inappropriate. Rigid insistence on principle replaces haggling; instead of face-to-face negotiation involving the risk of loss of face, mediation through the good offices of a prestigious and trusted intermediary is the accepted mode of conflict resolution.[2]

Both approaches have been equally confusing for Israelis. When the Jews

134

arrived in Palestine, they were certainly no strangers to commerce. For generations, trading of one kind or another had been their major occupation, whether in Eastern Europe or the Middle East. It was precisely against this aspect of diaspora life that the Zionist movement set its face. The mercantile talents of the Jew were far from a source of pride. On the contrary, they were viewed, in a bitterly negative light, as an aberration, the unfortunate consequence of economic discrimination by the majority. Barred from land ownership or the professions, the Jew had been forced into the role of middleman. As such his relationship with the Gentile was that not of an equal but of a buffer, a shock absorber between the peasant and squire. It was not a comfortable posture, nor did it acquire the Jew social status. Zionism accepted the tendentious designation of this role as nonproductive and parasitical, a legitimate object of contempt. In their own land, it was argued, the Jews, free at last, would turn their backs on the market place. In the economy of a Jewish state every man could do that for which he was best fitted.

It is against this background that one must appreciate the meaning of international negotiation for Israel's political elite. Negotiation in the international arena, when Israelis find themselves faced by representatives of "the nations," is essentially a stressful experience. At one level, especially if the issues at stake touch upon national defense, it evokes all the familiar fears and insecurities. But it is also strongly associated with the market place of the *shtetl*, the East European township. Here the Jews found the source of their livelihood at the expense of their wider integration in society. If anything, the market was a symbol of the Jew's marginality. It was a place where the Jew and the Gentile were locked, not in companionship but in antagonism. The peasant customer of today might be the assailant of tomorrow. Bargaining, moreover, was all too often equivalent to sharp practice: not a pleasurable pastime, but part of a struggle for survival in a hostile environment. To summarize, where bargaining has positive connotations for the Arab, for the Israeli it is reminiscent of a rejected and despised way of life.

Zionism was a deliberate and concerted effort to dispose of the habits of the diaspora. Haggling with the Gentile represented all that was felt to be most discreditable in the minority status of the Jew. Moral rehabilitation was to be sought in the soil, factory, or profession of arms, not in commerce. There is no question that the State of Israel has changed the range of occupational possibilities available to the Jew. Cultural traits, though, are less easily disposed of. In the domestic political system, the bargaining tradition retains its hold. Shlomo Aronson rightly points to the predominance of "habits of compromise, give and take, and common gains."[3] The 1984 and 1988 electoral agreements between Likud and Labor, setting up governments of national unity notwithstanding the ideological chasm dividing the two sides, remarkably exemplify this truth.

When it comes to negotiation with the Arabs, with their formidable reputation for haggling, Israelis rediscover their distaste for bargaining. Deprecating

Sadat's important peace proposal of 4 February 1971, General Haim Herzog, former chief of military intelligence (and from 1983 president of Israel), professed himself offended by some of its terms. "This atmosphere of Middle East market bargaining is rather typical and emphasizes one of the problems which face Israel—or indeed anybody else—in negotiations with the Arab world."[4] Shlomo Gazit, another intelligence chief, patronized the Egyptians to their faces: "I'm a man who doesn't know how to negotiate," he told the members of a military delegation in January 1978. "I understand that our negotiations are being conducted the way things go at the market of Khan-al-Khalil—starting high in order to come down later."[5] If this mixture of superciliousness and cultural myopia was to mark Israel's attitude in negotiating with Egypt, trouble was clearly in store.

Opening Moves

Contrasting Israeli and Egyptian approaches to the inaugural phase of negotiations were to provide an initial source of confusion. A classic dilemma was involved: the connection between one's opponent's opening bid and the minimal outcome he would settle for. Put another way, what element of his offer was truly negotiable?

When Egyptian negotiators conform to the *suk* model, it has been natural for them, in Quandt's words, "to start with opening positions that are quite far from the positions that they expect to accept when the negotiations have reached an end." Israeli practice, relative to that of Egypt, has invariably been to avoid making a grossly inflated opening offer. A posture would be adopted which, while leaving some limited room for maneuver, was not all that far from the final, fallback position—the minimal acceptable line of retreat. Should circumstances permit, Israel's preferred strategy was deliberately to eschew the philosophy of the petty dealer—asking a high price to give the customer a fictitious discount. This approach is well exemplified by the 1949 armistice negotiations with Abdullah. It was decided in advance not to "ask for a mountain in order to settle for a mouse," or to "indulge in Oriental haggling," but to put forward a proposal and stand by it.[6]

Were this optimal strategy ruled out, Israel was prepared to allow itself some scope for concession, but it did this with a great show of reluctance and to a limited extent only. Israeli instincts are exemplified by the following high-level exchange of opinions between the director-general of the foreign ministry, Walter Eytan, and Foreign Minister Sharett from December 1952. At this time thought was being given to the possibility of negotiations with Egypt in which Egyptian demands for a territorial link with Jordan through the Negev desert would loom large. In Eytan's view, Israel should oppose the corridor idea "through fire and water" (the Hebrew term carries the connotation of self-sacrificial resolution). He then surprisingly went on to argue that in this way any eventual agreement to free passage would seem like a great concession. Sharett agreed. Were Israel to be confronted with the choice of either peace with Egypt or the inviolability of the Eilat wedge, it would be difficult to maintain an absolutely negative position. They would then have to seek a compromise outcome. While Israel's strategy was never put to the test at the time in actual negotiations, there were numerous exploratory contacts. As their opening offer, Sharett and his colleagues always presented their opposition to any surrender of territory in the Negev in the intransigent tone suggested by Walter Eytan.[7]

How this approach worked out in practice can be seen from the various negotiations of the 1970s. Describing the government's consultations in advance of the 1974 disengagement talks with Syria, Dayan (then minister of defense) professed regret that not only content but also tactics had to be considered. This was necessary, first because the Syrians were notoriously unyielding bargainers, and second because the American mediator had to be given something in reward for his pains. Dayan's further remarks are most revealing: "For us," he wrote, "the difficulty with this kind of bargaining was not simply that we viewed it as undignified, but that it put us in an invidious position vis-à-vis the Israeli public. There are no secrets in Israel. Thus if we took a particular negotiating stand, it would be widely known. Later, if we dropped our sights, we would be accused of political surrender." Accordingly, the first line presented by the Israeli negotiators was scarcely a few hundred meters west of the "absolute minimum line" beyond which Israel would not withdraw under any circumstances. (This should be contrasted with Syria's opening demand for the return of half of the Golan Heights—an area of hundreds of square kilometers.)[8]

The reasons that Israel views the strategy of the inflated opening bid with distaste are, therefore, a mixture of principle and domestic political necessity. On the one hand, it is seen to be below Israel's dignity—all right for Orientals but not for a people that has left the market place behind it. On the other hand, it is understood—in the light of bitter experience—that in the heightened atmosphere of fear and suspicion that characterizes Israeli public opinion on defense matters, substantial concession would be equated with endangering the security of the state.

A third point should be added. Any initial suggestion of flexibility would imply a margin of safety Israel, whether government or man in the street, simply does not feel it has. Better to propose a plan fairly close to the limit of the acceptable and then fight a tenacious rearguard action, eking out any concessions in very small amounts. In this way one might retain one's credibility and self-respect, while stressing the limited room for maneuver at one's disposal. Thus the obduracy which, as we shall see, is such a striking feature of Israel's negotiating behavior is inherent in its starting position.

Israel's first acquaintance with Egyptian practice was made at Rhodes in 1949 during the armistice negotiations. In this particular case, cross-cultural

incompatibility made little difference to the final outcome of negotiations because the dimensions of the Egyptian defeat and especially the overwhelming
need to extract the beleaguered Faluja garrison left Egypt with little real
room for maneuver. Egypt's opening gambit still came as something of a
shock to the Israeli negotiators: it was to demand Israeli agreement to the
appointment of an Egyptian military governor at Beersheba, which was fairly
and squarely within Israeli territory. When this proposal was laughed out of
court, the Egyptians put in the claim for a governor at Bir Asluj, a collection
of mud huts to the south of the town. In the end UN mediator Ralph Bunche
prevailed upon Israel to agree to a demilitarized zone at the site, as a face-
saving concession to Egypt. Walter Eytan, leader of the Israeli delegation,
drew the rueful lesson from the episode that in future Israel would also have
to start out with "far reaching and even fanciful demands," otherwise it would
"not get very much in the end. This whole business," he added, "consists of
oriental bargaining. When the Egyptians finally agreed to drop their demand
for a Civil Administrator in Bir Asluj, Bunche at once chalked it up as a concession to their credit and demanded an equivalent concession from us."[9]

Despite the "lesson" of Rhodes, the imperatives described by Dayan invariably proved more compelling. Of course, Israelis were theoretically aware
of the virtues of tactical bidding, but found it difficult to overcome deep-
seated cultural constraints. In January 1974, a little more than two months
after the Yom Kippur War, Israel put forward a plan of "disengagement" in
the Sinai. It did contain a certain margin of concession but was presented
to Dr. Kissinger, mediating between Egypt and Israel, as "without flexibility." This was, he notes, "characteristic Israeli negotiating style." In response
to Kissinger's argument that he could not deal with Sadat on a take-it-or-
leave-it basis, the Israeli cabinet simply turned the original scheme into a
fallback position and proposed an even more rigid opening stand.[10]

At the Camp David talks of September 1978, which everybody knew were
a make-or-break opportunity for the success of the "peace process," and were
the culmination of all Israel's experience of negotiating with Egypt, Sadat's
stiff opening price—which included a demand for reparations—still caught
Israeli negotiators unawares. By then, one supposes, they surely should have
known better. Moshe Sharon, a government adviser on Arab affairs, recalls
that on the eve of the conference "Begin told his associates that Sadat was
a modern man and that one should not bargain with him as though one were
in a market. Right at the beginning of the talks one should make clear the
maximum extent of one's concessions."[11] Begin was to be sorely disappointed.
At the opening session, Sadat presented the detailed draft of an overall agreement which went back on all the concessions made or hinted at in prior contacts and reiterated the most inflexible of Arab positions. Extraordinarily
enough, Egyptian Foreign Minister Kamel actually considered his president's
strategy to be excessively moderate. He advised him to adopt an even
"tougher" opening stand than envisaged in order to obtain greater "elbow-

room" in the face of "pressure designed to secure concessions from the outset." Sadat disagreed, clearly more aware than Kamel of what the market would bear.[12]

Still, the Israeli team was left at an utter loss as to Sadat's intentions. Begin saw the Egyptian draft as a ploy to "force Israel to break up the conference and incur international condemnation." Ezer Weizman and the others were equally shocked. Dayan, who had been dealing with Arabs at both the private and official levels for most of his life, was no less puzzled about the Egyptian intention. Was it indeed an opening gambit, or was it to be made public as a demonstration of Egypt's unflinching defense of the Arab cause?[13]

The Israeli approach was no less deceptive for Egypt. Saadia Touval observes that Egypt was seriously misled about the limits of Israeli concessions in Kissinger's ill-fated attempt to achieve a second disengagement agreement in March 1975.[14] We learn from the memoirs of Israel's then prime minister, Yitzhak Rabin, that in return for a peace treaty he was prepared to withdraw from most of the Sinai. His second preference was for a solemn Egyptian declaration of nonbelligerency, for which Israel would withdraw to a line bisecting the desert. Failing either of those two alternatives, of which he doubted the feasibility, he was prepared to settle for a "mini-accord"—a limited withdrawal in return for a consolidation of the cease-fire. Either way, it was clear that Egypt would not settle for much less than the Abu Rodeis oil fields on the Gulf of Suez and the strategic Mitla and Giddi passes, which control the approaches to the Suez Canal.

In two ill-advised interviews in the run-up to the shuttle, Rabin candidly sketched out a position which actually reflected his true views but would inevitably be perceived by Egypt as an opening offer to be whittled down. To *Ha'aretz* on 3 December 1974, Rabin admitted that the demand for a nonbelligerency agreement was unrealistic. In a second interview with ABC television in February, Rabin gave notice that "in exchange for an Egyptian commitment not to go to war . . . the Egyptians could get even the passes and the oil fields." If this was Rabin's opening position, it could mean in Egyptian eyes only that (a) he would settle for less than a declaration of nonbelligerency, and (b) Egypt could expect to receive at least the passes and the oil fields. Rabin had stripped himself naked even before negotiations had got underway. Since this was actually his fallback position, he had left himself with no cards to bargain with.

As Touval correctly argues, "the rules of the game" required that both sides make concessions during the course of the shuttle, above and beyond anything "given away" beforehand. Adopting precisely these tactics, Egypt opened the bidding with an extravagant opening proposal. Israel would withdraw hundreds of kilometers to within twenty kilometers of the international boundary; Egypt would advance to a line east of the strategic passes; while a demilitarized zone would separate the two sides. Having left himself the whole of the Sinai peninsula to maneuver in, Sadat, from then on, could afford to be generous. Rabin, in contrast, had provided himself with little to give away apart from a handful of transparently artificial demands for a cessation of the propaganda war and the passage of Israeli cargoes through the Suez Canal. Worst of all, and to the utter confusion of the Egyptians, Israel—in the absence of a full-blown nonbelligerency agreement—refused point-blank to concede the Mitla and Giddi passes to Egypt. With the world accusing Israel of intransigence, the shuttle ended in abject failure.[15] To demonstrate that the breakdown was a result of miscalculation and not the clash of irreconcilable interests, Kissinger returned to the Middle East six months later, in August 1975, and this time succeeded in mediating an accord satisfactory to both sides, including an Israeli descent from the passes.

Middle Game

The intermediate stage of Egyptian-Israeli negotiations has been marked by dogged and drawn-out rearguard actions on the part of Israel. Compared with their Egyptian counterparts, Israeli negotiators tend to a slow rate of progress, acute sensitivity to the security implications of any moves, hesitant and piecemeal concessions resisted until the last possible moment, and a propensity to legalism. The Egyptian style is uncompromising on issues of high principle—the land and sovereignty—and, while tactically tenacious, ready for the unexpected and advantageous concession.

Some of the differences between the two sides can be immediately accounted for in terms of their respective political cultures, especially as reflected in the structure and practice of government. For their part Israeli cabinets rest on finely balanced coalitions in which the prime minister is no more than a first among equals. Cabinet ministers can rarely be dismissed, because they owe their position, not to prime-ministerial preference, which can be subsequently withdrawn, but to the autonomous support of their own parties or party factions, which cannot—without a government crisis. Political necessities apart, democratic habits of consultation run deep, and leaders are highly accessible and responsive to subordinates. Major decisions can be reached only by consensus and, if they outrun the public mood, run the real risk of being repudiated in parliament. On issues touching on national security, any Israeli negotiator has, moreover, to prove to skeptical colleagues and a highly strung public opinion that he has gone to the very limit in resisting unnecessary concessions on his own part while wringing the very last ounce from his opponent.

In contrast, the Egyptian president stands at the head of a relatively compliant and authoritarian regime. With due regard to the formidable practical constraints to which he is subject, the *Rais* enjoys, within the system, undoubtedly wide prerogatives. He can appoint or dismiss ministers at will, is not vulnerable to a vote of no confidence in parliament, and has a formidable security and propaganda apparatus at his disposal. Public opinion has shown itself pliable to government directives on matters of foreign policy. Consent rather than consensus is the pattern. All this implies that while it would be a mistake to overrate the president's willingness to intervene in routine negotiations conducted by the bureaucracy, let alone to overrule his officials, he has greater freedom to make timely and crucial negotiating decisions than his Israeli counterparts. Thus he is in a far better position to bargain tactically and to regulate the pace of negotiations without reference to domestic political imperatives.

The practical effect of these differences is readily apparent. President Carter observed it at first hand: "While at Camp David," he wrote, "Sadat wanted to make Egypt's decisions himself, did not like to have aides present when he was with me, and seemed uncomfortable when they were around him. His closest advisers, the Vice President and Prime Minister, were in Cairo managing the affairs of Egypt. Throughout our stay at Camp David, Sadat spent little time with his staff. In contrast, Begin relied heavily on his aides and advisers." Not only that, but as the talks approached their climax, a threefold division emerged within the Israeli delegation between Dayan, Weizman, and Begin on the key issue of withdrawal.[16]

Within the Israeli system, this kind of principled disagreement would have to be resolved by argument—albeit of the most intense kind—rather than the exercise of prime-ministerial authority. As it happens, Begin's opposition to withdrawal was not the dominant voice; nor was the Dayan view that withdrawal should take place only after an extended period. The ultimately decisive argument was that of Defense Minister Weizman, the politically weakest member of the triumvirate, who believed that Israeli settlers should leave the Sinai if parliament voted in favor. United States National Security Adviser Zbigniew Brzezinski's perception that the Israeli "team" lacked negotiating cohesion, or that there was a "political contest" between Dayan and Weizman, involved a series of culture-bound judgments:[17] First, Israelis are not "team players" in the American sense. Second, fierce disagreement within Israeli governments is the rule rather than the exception and no evidence, one way or the other, of power play; neither Dayan nor Weizman disputed Begin's leadership in a formal sense—they did not need to in order to make their voices heard. Third, Israel is able to make tough decisions only by thrashing them out in open debate; no Israeli prime minister is able to impose the kind of hierarchical discipline on his subordinates that an American or Egyptian president can. And if he did, it would ensure the failure, not success, of his policy. Even Ben Gurion, with all his immense prestige and authority, was shackled by political constraints. His view did carry particular weight, but he could never dictate policy. On many occasions he was overruled in cabinet.

American and Egyptian impatience with Israel's convoluted and contentious method of decision-making, therefore, though natural, was misguided and unhelpful. Sadat's assessment during the long gap in substantive negotiations that lasted through the spring and summer of 1978, that he could somehow undermine Begin's leadership—by cultivating leader of the opposition Shimon Peres, by attacking the Israeli prime minister in the media, and by parading his friendship with Ezer Weizman—was equally mistaken. Former Foreign Minister Kamel's report that Sadat actually approached the Americans with the idea of "toppling" Begin, suggests a complete misreading by Sadat of the Israeli political map. Vigorous debate, criticism, and even crisis are the stuff of Israeli democracy, not proof of its degeneracy. Alfred Atherton's refutation of Sadat, namely, that Begin enjoyed majority support in the Knesset and that personal attacks would have only an adverse effect, was much nearer the mark.[18] To the extent that Sadat's faulty grasp of Israeli domestic debate misled him into believing that he could somehow reach agreement with Israel while bypassing the Begin government, it clearly contributed to the delay in the peace process. For all Israel's own misjudgments of Egyptian necessities, a settlement was going to be achieved only by the resumption of dialogue and not by the imposition by one side of its views on the other.

In addition to a political system which leaves the leadership limited powers of discretion, Israel brings to negotiations an obsession with security that makes sense only in the light of the historical vulnerability of the Jewish people. This emerges in the form of very deep suspicion of the opponent (and even the mediator), reluctance to move too fast before every possible implication has been weighed, and a degree of emotional involvement which is not always well concealed. The man who best understood Israeli complexes was, not surprisingly, Henry Kissinger, himself a Jewish refugee from Nazi Germany. He rightly perceived the "premonition of catastrophe burnt deep into the soul of a people that has lived with disaster through the millennia of its history, and the worry that if it once yielded to pressure it would invite an unending process of exactions."[19] Less sympathetic outsiders have found Israel's sense of insecurity frankly hard to credit in the light of its evident military supremacy and the general assumption that it has possessed nuclear weapons since the early 1960s. Thus, while Israel might be objectively stronger, militarily, than Egypt, subjectively it felt itself weaker. Egypt, the product of thousands of years of uninterrupted settlement, has seen countless conquerors come and go, outlasting them all. Not surprising that Israel's security concerns should long have been viewed as a mere pretext for expansionism.

Hence the paradox of the post-1973 series of negotiations. Although convinced that it had defeated Egypt on the battlefield, Israel conducted itself at the negotiating table with a shrill defensive-mindedness verging on the paranoid. The pattern was established as early as the cease-fire negotiations of October 1973 which terminated hostilities in the Yom Kippur War. It entailed haggling over the slightest concession; avoiding any compromise that was not absolutely essential; and settling only when other parties had reached the very limits of exhaustion. Over the crucial issue of the encircled Egyptian Third Army, effectively trapped on the east bank of the Suez Canal by Israel's invasion of the west bank, Israel consented to allow essential supplies through only in the face of an American ultimatum. It was easier for Israel to be coerced into agreement, to be able to claim before parliament and public opinion that there was no other alternative, than to concede of its own free will.[20]

In the 1975 negotiations for a second disengagement agreement, Israel fought a stubborn and protracted campaign in an effort to extract the best possible deal and to demonstrate for everybody's benefit that it was no pushover. As we have already seen, the first stage of the talks ended in deadlock. Kissinger was right in his judgment, conveyed to the Egyptians, that the Rabin government's domestic base was too insecure to be able to take serious decisions without prolonged deliberation.[21] As anticipated, the long interval before the resumption of negotiations in August did help Israel to digest the implications of failure in terms of relations with both Egypt and the United States.

It is no coincidence that Israel also needed "time out" for reflection and internal debate during the abortive 1971 contacts over an interim agreement and the 1978 negotiations. Frustrating as this may be for other participants, Israel simply cannot be rushed into what it perceives to be fateful decisions. Quandt, at the time a staff member of the American delegation at Camp David, was right when he complained to Weizman: "You Israelis! You always accept our proposals—but it's always six months too late, and you pay dearly for it!" But petulance or impatience on the part of Egypt or the United States was not going to help. Presidents and officials might come and go; the Nile and the Mississippi would serenely roll on. Israelis, however, never take for granted that "there'll always be an Israel." A single miscalculation, they feel, and the precarious experiment that is the third Jewish commonwealth might come to an abrupt and tragic end. "A peace settlement will shape the character of the State of Israel for many years," was how one Israeli general put it in 1978. "What's called for is to draw it out as long as possible—there's no sense in being overhasty. That could provoke crisis and dissension."[22]

When the disengagement talks resumed in August 1975, the Israeli government, though more aware of the limits of the possible, was certainly no less painstaking in its approach. "During those ten days [21–31 August]," Rabin recalled, "we held daylong—and occasionally nightlong—discussions, and there were times when we felt we were flogging a dead horse. Five hours might be spent discussing a stretch of sand one hundred meters long. It was a supreme test of our patience, persistence, and even our physical endurance. Wisely, skillfully, patiently, Kissinger inched his way forward between Sadat's difficulties and mine, between proclamations from each side that 'this is our final concession.'"[23]

Careful comparison of the Hebrew and English versions of the above extract reveals a curious omission in the English edition. The following sentences have been deleted: "Myriads of words were aired. We split hairs for hours on end over every trifling clause."[24] The Hebrew term for hair-splitting is the same word used for that meticulous process of textual analysis, casuistry, and dialectics—*pilpul*—traditionally used in Talmudic study. There is no point in speculating why Rabin should have preferred to avoid this reference in the English edition. What is clear, though, is that of all the features of Israeli negotiating style, this is the most characteristic.

Stress on Israeli legalism should not give the impression that Egypt (or, still less, the United States) has been negligent of legal niceties. Egyptian negotiators have shown a high degree of professional competence and the ability to wage a skilful and determined campaign over the phraseology of agreements. They are certainly not in the business of making juridical gifts to the Israelis or anyone else. No, what is referred to by Israeli legalism is something over and above mere textual precision and the adroit negotiation of a favorable document. There is no virtue in technical sloppiness. Legalism, rather, implies two unusual patterns of behavior: the reliance on legal expedients— formulas and instruments—to achieve objectives which go beyond the realistic scope and function of international law; and an obsession with words for their own sake—an excessive and unjustified preoccupation with semantics.

To anyone familiar with the Jewish tradition of Talmudic scholarship, the Israeli approach to international law comes as no surprise. Every Talmudic text has a virtually word-by-word commentary, and every commentary itself gives rise to a host of primary, secondary, tertiary, and so on commentaries in a theoretically infinite regression. Study entails the loving interpretation of text, painstaking cross-referencing and comparison of alternative explanations, analysis of every conceivable aspect of a problem—including the consideration of deliberately remote contingencies—culminating in a solution in which apparently contradictory views are demonstrated to be reconcilable within an overall synthesis. Among secular Jews, especially the Zionists, Talmudic study fell into disrepute for its otherworldliness, its tendency to sterile scholasticism and verbal quibbling. However, it still flourishes in hundreds of academies in Israel and the diaspora, has undoubtedly contributed to the extreme litigiousness of Israelis, and is their deeply ingrained method of textual analysis.

Henry Kissinger has called negotiating with Israel, not entirely tongue-in-cheek, "ordeal by exegesis." In the first place Israeli negotiators much prefer to have a written draft to work with. They are not happy with grand conceptual speculations and generalizations. "I am not interested in theoretical formulas," was how Yitzhak Shamir put it. Negotiation then consists in debate over, and painstaking examination of, each term and alternative term in the draft until a final, satisfactory version is arrived at. The Talmudic heritage makes itself felt in the search for meanings behind meanings, an extreme preoccupation with remote contingencies, and what Gideon Rafael has called "overnegotiation"—continuing to quibble beyond the point at which diminishing returns set in.

Meir Rosenne, the legal adviser to the foreign ministry at the time of Camp David, notes that the aim of a treaty is to prevent future misunderstanding and to leave no doubt as to whether or not an infringement has taken place. Every moment dedicated to legal precision is time well spent.[25] This is true so far as it goes. What he and his fellows tend to overlook is that in the real world a treaty is the starting point and not the culmination of a relationship, and can neither legislate against uncertainty nor act as a substitute for good will. If one does not trust one's partner to honor his word, why reach an agreement with him in the first place?

In the final analysis one is forced to conclude that Israel's overreliance on legal instruments and formulas is in effect a mechanism for overcoming a deep-seated mistrust and fulfilling a subjective need for reassurance. Aharon Barak, Israel's attorney-general and a key participant in the Camp David talks, admitted as much when he remarked that many of the Israeli positions had no intrinsic merit but were "essentially psychological in origin."[26]

Had they been left alone with the Israelis at Camp David, it is doubtful whether the Egyptians would have had the forbearance to keep going. American solicitude and tolerance were sorely needed. Always ready with a new draft, alternative formulations, a slightly different turn of phrase, the United States could also provide the sort of authoritative and comforting interpretation of a text (in the form of a side letter or memorandum of understanding) without which Israel would not commit itself. (This technique had proved itself indispensable during negotiation of the 1974 and 1975 disengagement agreements.)

Anticipating Israeli legalism and Egyptian posturing, the United States delegation wisely decided to discard its clients' own, improbable, texts and work with an American draft agreement on the table. Each side would react, separately, to points in the document, and the Americans would then generate a fresh formulation. Carter would take this proposal to Sadat for quick approval or slight modification and then present it for Israeli appraisal. This method fitted in very well with Israel's favored approach. According to President Carter, he would spend "hours or days working on the same point."

> Sometimes, in the end, the change of word or phrase would satisfy Begin, and I would merely inform Sadat. I was never far from a good dictionary and thesaurus, and on occasion the American and Israeli delegations would all be clustered around one of these books, eagerly searching for acceptable synonyms. Would the Israelis withdraw "out of" certain areas or "into" military encampments? What was meant by "autonomy," "self rule," "devolution," "Palestinian people," "authority," "minor modifications," "refugees," "insure, ensure or guarantee," and so forth? The Egyptians were never involved in these kinds of discussions with me.[27]

Begin and the Israeli delegation were in their element, absorbed, as Brzezinski saw it, in "esoteric legal argumentation," conducting a tenacious debate over every tittle and jot. The security of the State of Israel was always uppermost in their minds.[28] This was no legal seminar but a struggle for survival, a battle to be waged from street to street, like the Warsaw ghetto uprising.

Faced with what he regarded as Israeli haggling over minutiae, Sadat became increasingly restive. As a dignitary and a man of honor struggling for the restoration of his land, this was exactly, as Quandt correctly perceives, the kind of negotiation most uncongenial to him and from which he had withdrawn the previous January in disgust. In his view the leaders should agree on the principles of a just peace and leave the drafting to the experts. By the eleventh day of the conference he was at the breaking point and prepared to go home. Only a heartfelt appeal from the president of the United States persuaded him to stay on.[29] Was this a gambit, like Disraeli's waiting train at the Congress of Berlin? Hardly, since Sadat received no concession for staying. Israel had strayed very close to the edge. Lucky indeed is the state that can look out into the void, knowing that it has a superpower friend waiting at the bottom of the cliff to catch it.

End Game

The closing stages of an Israeli-Egyptian negotiation can be characterized as a last-ditch Israeli effort to dot the *i*'s and cross the *t*'s—in short, to obtain maximum specificity. Ambiguity is shunned, and written commitments are insisted upon. Egypt displays a greater tolerance for ambiguity *where called for* and may seek to avoid public embarrassment by informal understanding. What is not made as translucent and explicit as possible, Israelis argue, but is left to the mercy of future Egyptian benevolence, is unlikely to be honored. Wrong, argue the Egyptians: the more formal you want it, the less likely you are to get it. Trust us.

Neither side, of course, has a monopoly of virtue in the matter. Every negotiation has to be taken on its own merits in the light of circumstances; and the success or failure of an agreement will anyway be contingent on subsequent political realities. Whereas in one case a lack of detail may dilute or obviate an obligation, simply inviting future confusion and bitterness, in another case ambiguity may serve a larger purpose by saving face or permitting an intractable obstacle to be bypassed. There are no hard and fast rules; whether one prefers preclusive detail to constructive ambiguity is, in the final analysis, a question of judgment—and instinct.

It is at this point that cultural conditioning enters the picture. On the whole, Israelis attach a high value to semantic accuracy as an end in itself. This is both the thrust of their legal tradition and, rational or not, their means to tie down an opponent in whose reliability they have gnawing doubts. And, as we emphasized in our discussion of modern Hebrew, Israelis are more comfortable with a directness that leaves little to the imagination than with allusiveness. Specificity has also reflected the need to have as tangible and watertight an agreement as possible to reassure a skeptical public that all those concessions were worthwhile.

For their part the Egyptians have less faith in the irrevocably binding powers of contract. In the words of the Arabic proverb: "Peace comes from understanding, not agreement." If there is trust, a contract is superfluous; if trust is absent, an agreement cannot help. At the same time Egypt, as a high context culture, is in its element with indirectness, the pregnant silence tacitly implying an otherwise embarrassing consent, the subtle hint that may be acceptable where the explicit statement would offend. Ambiguity has thus appealed to Egypt as a way of reconciling the conflicting pulls of national expediency and loyalty to the wider Arab cause. It can conceal, or at least minimize, the shame which Arab purists will see as inherent in any deal made with the Jewish state.

All Israeli-Egyptian agreements since 1973 have had to find the middle way between obscure versus precise or implicit versus explicit formulations. The pattern was set as early as November 1973 in the negotiations for a binding cease-fire agreement after the Yom Kippur War. In essence the accommodation rested on a careful balance of advantage initially agreed upon between Henry Kissinger and President Sadat: A corridor would be opened up along the Cairo-Suez road to permit the resupply of the encircled Egyptian Third Army; although the route passed through Israeli-controlled territory, this fact would be disguised by placing the checkpoints under UN control; the Egyptian blockade of the Straits of Bab el-Mandeb at the entrance to the Red Sea would be lifted, provided Israel made only "moderate" use of them; there would be an exchange of all prisoners of war.

In order to save Egyptian face, it was necessary to maintain a certain fuzziness about the exact details of these arrangements. What Sadat could accept in practice, he could not agree to formally. As Kissinger understood, "too many public concessions would hurt his position with his Arab brethren." The lifting of the blockade would be unpopular; Sadat would find it highly embarrassing to acknowledge the fact of Israeli control over the Cairo-Suez road; and a detailed schedule of the resupply of the Third Army "would have brought home its plight to every Arab." If the cease-fire were to be a humiliation for Egypt, what possible chance would there be of progressing toward a political settlement which, after all, was the ultimate prize to aim for?

All Israeli instincts militated against this imprecision. There should be a firm timetable for the exchange of prisoners. What was meant by "moderate" use of the straits? By how much and how often was the Third Army to be resupplied? Who controlled the road, Israel or the UN? Pleas to avoid humiliating the Egyptians fell on deaf ears. On the contrary, a badly shaken Israel had its own psychological requirements: let Egyptian dependence on Israeli grace be emphasized. Finally, public opinion had to be considered, and Israel, amidst all its sorrows, was in the run-up to an election. Private assurances would cut little ice with an electorate vigilant to any hint of a "sell-out."

In this kind of "dialogue of the deaf," all hinges on the presence and ingenuity of a "cultural interpreter," able to explain each side to the other and tender assurances the rivals themselves cannot provide. Left to their own devices, the former combatants might, willy-nilly, have resumed hostilities. Hence, to mitigate Israeli suspicions, the United States agreed to an Israeli-American memorandum of understanding spelling out in detail the exact terms of the cease-fire. It was this authorized interpretation which gave Israel the confidence to withdraw its objections to the original accord. In the event, the memorandum of understanding was never invoked, proving, as Kissinger wryly observed, "that the parties had understood each other much better" than their "raucous posturing" had suggested.[30]

As long as Kissinger's "step-by-step" diplomacy was underway, it was possible to resolve Israeli-Egyptian discord on the relative merits of specificity and explicitness with American reassurances. And should a problem later arise in the implementation of one of the interim accords, the United States was always there to lend a helping hand. For instance, Israeli experts were less than happy with the 1975 military annex specifying the dispositions of the Egyptian and Israeli armies in the Sinai under the terms of the second disengagement agreement. For three days they fought unsuccessfully for an exact definition of the size and structure of the units permitted in the limited force zones. (The relevant clause simply referred to "Eight [8] standard infantry battalions.") When Israeli surveillance flights subsequently detected some technical infringements of this provision—arising from a rather flexible Egyptian interpretation of what constituted a "standard infantry battalion"—all hell broke loose in Israel, with the news soon leaking to the media. While the experts could say "we told you so," general perceptions of Egyptian unreliability were reinforced. What was an essentially trivial episode could have had unfortunate consequences for the "peace process" had the United States not intervened to resolve the dispute.[31]

Once interim arrangements gave way to negotiations for a full-blown peace, it became harder to bridge the cultural gap between Egyptian and Israeli sensibilities. Without exaggeration it can be said that subjective, rather than substantive, factors were the major obstacle in the path of progress in the long months between Sadat's Jerusalem visit and the Camp David summit. Two issues were the focus of dispute: the future of the Palestinians and the question of withdrawal. True, both sides profoundly differed on the solution to these problems. But Egypt was prepared to obfuscate any disagreement in the short term in order to clear the way for bilateral negotiations on a treaty of peace; Israel was not. Thus, while President Sadat strongly pressed for a rapid declaration of principles, including a general expression of readiness to solve the Palestinian problem, Prime Minister Begin preferred to meet the issue head on. Far from postponing confrontation, he insisted on premature preclusion. Where the former sought a vague, face-saving formula for the benefit of the Arab world, the latter, intolerant of the unsatisfactory ambiguity of this device, wished to preclude all future uncertainty.

It was at Ismailia in December 1977 that the breadth of the gap between the two sides became apparent. Eschewing all preliminary discussion on general principles, Begin had arrived in Egypt with a comprehensive blueprint on the future of the West Bank: the autonomy plan. At the first meeting of the Egyptian and Israeli delegations, he plunged straight into detailed exposition. In vain Sadat tried to steer him round to a discussion of "big business." All that was required at this point, the *Rais* indicated, was a brief communiqué of two or three lines. There was no need "to go into details" on behalf of the Palestinians. As Sadat had informed Israel before the conference, via the United States, he could go ahead with a bilateral peace, but only within a wider framework—a declaration of principles, "formulated in general terms . . . which could give him the necessary defense against domestic and external criticism, and enable him to conduct practical negotiations . . . for a peace treaty."[32] But this was precisely what Israel was not prepared to concede.

On two occasions, attempts were made to produce a satisfactory formula. On 4 January 1978 a worried President Carter flew to Aswan for lengthy talks with his Egyptian counterpart. The resultant statement contained nothing Israel had not already or would not in the future agree to: peace based on normal relations; "withdrawal by Israel from territories occupied in 1967"; a resolution of the Palestinian problem which would "recognize the legitimate rights of the Palestinian people and enable the Palestinians to participate in the determination of their own future." To meet Israeli objections, no reference was made to *the*—implying *all the*—territories occupied by Israel, or to a Palestinian state. The statement, to be known as the Aswan formula, could have been the basis for an Israeli-Egyptian declaration of principles.[33]

Again in July 1978, the so-called Kreisky-Brandt statement, known to have Sadat's approval, reiterated exactly the same points. As in January, Israel's reaction was dismissive. Dayan believed that the "worthlessness" of the formula was demonstrated by Austrian Chancellor Kreisky's admission that "it had been made deliberately vague so that both sides could read into it whatever they wished."[34] Surely this was the whole point of the exercise!

Until the very last days of the Camp David conference, the Israeli delegation continued to see the autonomy plan as the necessary condition for an agreement with Egypt. Only when failure stared it in the face did it realize, with American prompting, that fudging was the only way to bridge the gap between the two sides on the Palestinian question. (The other great issue, the principle of full withdrawal from the Sinai, was conceded.) Were an agreement to be reached at all, Dayan now recognized, major differences of opinion would have to be either left unmentioned or covered up with "vague formulae which each side could interpret in its own way." All hope of ensnaring the Egyptians in entangling detail evaporated. Ditching all his preconceptions, Dayan accepted that the problem was "more one of words and formulae than of substance."[35]

The resultant accord—intended to provide the "framework" within which an Egyptian-Israeli peace treaty would be negotiated—was basically an elaboration of the Aswan and Kreisky-Brandt formulas and included every one of the principles rejected by Israel in January and July. On the West Bank Israel made substantial concessions and obtained few of the binding elements of the original autonomy plan. It agreed that "representatives of the Palestinian people should participate in negotiations on the resolution of the Palestinian problem in all its aspects"; and that the subsequent solution would "recognize the legitimate rights of the Palestinian people and their just requirements."

As for the other substantive issues—Jerusalem, the settlements, the future prerogatives of the Israeli army, the very nature of authority in the area—all were shrouded in a decent veil of obscurity. Sometimes the positions of both sides were included simultaneously, further adding to the ambiguity. The whole effort, in fact, had been an extraordinary waste of time. No substantive agreement had been achieved; all the principal differences remained; even the mechanism for progress that was determined on proved to be a broken reed. If anything, Israel had conceded more than it needed to; the idea of a five-year transitional regime for the West Bank, though constructive in itself, did not square with the Likud government's real intention—which was to consolidate Israel's hold over the area. The Aswan formula would have served the needs of the Likud at lower cost, and without the complicating and embarrassing effect of American involvement.

When it was all over—and Sadat had basically achieved what he had wanted all along, only far, far too late to draw other Arab states into the "peace process"—there were still those on the Israeli side who remained convinced of the ingenuity of their formulations. A more realistic assessment was provided by Begin's *chef de cabinet* and the chairman of the committee that had prepared the position papers for Camp David, Eliahu Ben-Elissar. Looking back, he acknowledged that the very "genius" of the accord lay in its lack of clarity, since in this way Israel and Egypt were able to negotiate a bilateral peace within a relatively short time.[36] It had taken a long time, but light had finally dawned.

Mediation

Camp David was not a summit conference in the usual sense of the term. Up to the end, as Dayan recognizes, the two leaders found no common language; they could hardly bear to be in the same room together. Such meetings as there were between them were fraught with tension. Solutions did not emerge from direct negotiations, but as a result of the resourceful and untiring efforts of the American delegation and particularly President Carter, shuttling back and forth between Israelis and Egyptians.[37] Camp David, and the outstanding contribution of the United States to the success of the "peace process"—from the time of the 1973 cease-fire to the February 1989 agreement on Taba—confirm the indispensable role of a mediator in the Egyptian-Israeli relationship. It is a remarkable fact that *every single negotiation* ever conducted between the two parties has made use of a mediator. And in most cases that mediator has been a representative of the United States. (In 1949, at Rhodes, there was a United Nations mediator, American Ralph Bunche; and the United Nations and the Red Cross have also been helpful on other occasions, for instance, with prisoner exchanges.) The presence of a mediator did not always ensure success, but his absence surely guaranteed failure.

How is one to explain this noteworthy phenomenon? Out of the gloom of dissonance that otherwise envelops Israeli-Egyptian relations shines a single ray of light, the two parties' common tradition of mediation. In both Arab and Jewish cultures, the intermediary plays a central role in delicate negotiations in general and the resolution of conflict in particular.

Throughout the Arab world, resort to the mediator—in Arabic *wasta* or *wasit*—is the culturally sanctioned mechanism for solving disputes between individuals or groups. Chosen from among neutral and prestigious dignitaries, the mediator (or mediators) performs a complex set of tasks, from intervention to terminate violence, via arbitration of grievances, to final reconciliation—*sulh*. In traditional communities, resort to mediation is much more important than resort to law. In fact, and this is an essential point, mediation is not intended to serve some abstract concept of justice; its purpose is to find a formula that will save the face of both parties so that communal life can continue. Where the feud threatens social cohesion, mediation preserves it. What would be humiliating and unacceptable if offered by one's opponent can be swallowed if proposed by a respected third party.[38] In inter-Arab state relations, mediation, rather than resort to international law or arbitration, has proved to be the foremost procedure for conflict resolution. The secretary-general of the Arab League has come to assume a particularly important role in this respect. But at various times Saudi Arabia, Egypt, and other Arab states have been called upon to perform this duty.[39]

Traditional Jewish culture also fostered a whole range of roles and institutions which, though not identical to the *wasta*, overlap with it. The *borer*, or arbitrator, existed throughout the history of the Jewish diaspora. In the absence of autonomous Jewish courts, civil disputes would be referred to this institution for adjudication or compromise, rather than to the local courts. The *shtadlan*, literally "one who exerts himself" or intercedes on another's behalf, was another typical diaspora figure who, by virtue of wealth or standing, had access to the ruling power. Acting as a representative of the Jewish community, he would use his skills as advocate or diplomat to defend its interests.[40]

Among many Israelis the *shtadlan* is looked down upon as another reminder of ghetto life. Nevertheless, as with so many other traditional institutions, he often turns out to be indispensable in practice. Certainly the mediator or broker, whether in business or social life, is still a familiar figure to Jews in Israel and elsewhere. He sometimes makes an appearance in Israeli politics in the mediation of interparty disputes. Israeli governments, in the absence of diplomatic relations with the USSR, frequently resorted to the good offices of friendly statesmen or businessmen, such as Harold Wilson, François Mitterrand, or Armand Hammer, to intercede on behalf of Soviet Jewry. Even in the United States it has been quite common for the Israeli government to make use of the services of well-connected American Jews known to have the ear of the president. (Leon Charney, a wealthy New York lawyer, acted as a go-between, for example, between Ezer Weizman and Jimmy Carter during 1978 and 1979; this, notwithstanding Weizman's denigration of the *shtadlan* "as a vestige of the mentality that characterized the Jews of the pale of settlement in Russia, where they lived under the protection and authority of their local overlords. I find it an alien attitude, reflecting a ghetto mentality.")[41]

Where direct negotiations were invariably calculated to arouse all those cross-cultural disharmonies enumerated in this book, mediation provided a striking basis of cultural compatibility upon which to build. Whether he was called Ralph Bunche, Henry Kissinger, or Jimmy Carter, the *shtadlan/wasta* was the only feasible way out of the Egyptian-Israeli impasse. Only a statesman of international stature, acceptable to both sides, held the key to unlocking the dungeon of mistrust, miscommunication, and misunderstanding to which Egypt and Israel seemed eternally doomed.

The functions of the mediator were as indispensable as they were numerous. First and foremost he could bring to the attention of the prospective suitors the very possibility of a match. When states lack an established channel of communication, they necessarily acquire a distorted impression of each other's views; they may not even be aware of each other's willingness to settle. President Carter saw Arabs and Israelis trapped into immobility by their lack of a common language: "they can't make enough positive statements publicly to convince their adversaries that the talks will be successful because, if they do, in the process, they are giving away their playing cards in advance." This is where a mediator such as the United States could help—listening for any indication from either side of an interest in a settlement.

Once negotiations got underway the mediator had to display a rare collection of talents: He had to play the part of interpreter, faithfully translating the needs, psychological as well as substantive, of both sides to each other so that they might obtain a realistic assessment of what the market could bear. He had to serve as a conduit, passing on constructive proposals that the rivals would be unable to put forward themselves for fear of a humiliating slap in the face. As Carter emphasizes, no Arab leader wants to "put forward a proposal to the other adversary and be rebuffed. It's a deep embarrassment and loss of face if you make a proposal and you have it rejected publicly."[42] The mediator also had to act as a filter or censor, straining out proposals that were obviously unacceptable, and which would retard rather than advance the prospect of a settlement, presenting others in the best possible light; all the while, as Henry Kissinger explains, helping to "soften the edges of controversy and provide a mechanism for adjustment on issues of prestige."[43]

As the talks approached their climax, the mediator had to be ready to come forward with compromise proposals of his own to bridge the gap—or, to present a suggestion which, hard to swallow from an opponent, might be acceptable coming from the mediator. Time and again, negotiations that seemed doomed to fail at the last moment, because pride stood in the way of some minor but crucial concession, were saved by talks late into the night at which the saving formula would be pulled from the hat by the trusted mediator. Face was always a crucial factor with the Egyptians.

With the Israelis, the final obstacle, which only the United States could overcome, was also psychological: the agony of decision itself—the unpalatable need to choose between the known and the unknown. To exchange concrete assets for a promissory note, to have to trust a historical adversary, was excruciatingly painful for Israel. At this point the United States could nudge Israel in the right direction, not because the latter could be forced to accept an agreement that it genuinely feared would threaten its survival—states cannot be coerced into suicide—but because, as Henry Kissinger perceptively observed, "Israel sometimes finds it easier to shift the responsibility for difficult choices to its great ally than to make the decision itself."[44]

The final service of the mediator was to underwrite the agreement—and this, in the final analysis, is why only the United States, and not the European Community or the United Nations, was suited for the part. Obligations that Egypt could not formally undertake toward Israel could be informally made to the United States. Assurances, in the form of American guarantees, could be given of the signatories' compliance. Agreed interpretations, always needed with Israel, could be supplied. Military equipment and financial inducements could be thrown in to sweeten the pill. Only a superpower, with the absolute trust of both sides and the resources to boot, could possibly assume these onerous commitments.

Excursus: The Sadat Initiative of 4 February 1971

Exemplifying many of the incompatibilities described here, Sadat's proposal of 4 February 1971 for an interim agreement on the Suez Canal was the great missed opportunity of the period between the 1967 and 1973 wars.

It also demonstrated the consequences of the absence of an active and authoritative mediator. The original concept of a partial settlement was first floated by Israeli Defense Minister Moshe Dayan in the autumn of 1970. On the face of it the situation held more promise than at any time since June 1967. Nasser, whom Israel considered an obstacle to peace, had just died (on 28 September) and, thanks to the albeit abortive Rogers initiative, a cease-fire was in effect along the Suez front. A thinning out of military forces on both sides of the canal, in Dayan's view, coupled with the clearing of the waterway and the resumption of maritime traffic, could defuse tension and provide an added element of stability. Kissinger suggests that Dayan saw the idea as a way of forestalling further Israeli withdrawals, but the defense minister was too shrewd not to understand that any withdrawal would constititute a precedent and that the reopening of the canal would create a new reality in which possibilities for progress that had not existed before would suddenly appear more feasible. There would have to be, though, a formal Egyptian commitment ending the state of belligerency; after Egyptian infringements the previous August of the standstill provisions of the cease-fire, only a written agreement would be acceptable.[45]

Sadat, not long in the presidential palace, was seriously interested. Obviously his ultimate aim was to bring about Israeli withdrawal from the Sinai and not simply to recreate a new *status quo* from which only Israel could benefit. Nevertheless, successful negotiations had started out from less promising points of departure. The main thing at this stage was to release Egyptian-Israeli relations from the deadlock which, like the ships trapped in the Suez Canal, they had been consigned since the Six Day War. As I shall argue, his tactics for achieving this initial objective were to concede implicitly what he could never accept explicitly and to bypass immediately insoluble problems by cloaking them in constructive ambiguity.

On 15 January 1971, Israel was informed by the United States of an approach made by a close friend of Sadat to Donald Bergus, head of the U.S. Interest Section in Cairo (the American embassy had been closed since 1967). The unofficial feeler—clearly intended to prepare the ground for a later official initiative—went as follows: Israel would withdraw about forty kilometers to the Mitla Pass; Egypt would thin out its forces west of the canal, leaving its air defenses intact; there would be an exchange of prisoners of war; the cease-fire would be extended; most important, the Suez Canal would be opened to "free passage to all ships"—this latter tantalizingly hinting at possible Israeli inclusion.[46]

Sadat unveiled his formal, public offer on 4 February. Looking back, he always dated his peace strategy to this speech, delivered before the National Assembly. Egypt, he said, agreed to extend the existing cease-fire by a period of no more than thirty days, ending on 7 March 1971. During this period Israeli troops were to be "partly withdrawn from the east shore of the Suez Canal, as the first step towards the submission [by Israel] of a time-table for the implementation of the entire Security Council Resolution [242]. If this should happen, we shall be ready to begin work on clearing the Canal for the benefit of international navigation and the world economy."[47]

Israel's immediate reaction was a mixed one. On the positive side, it was undeniable that Sadat's move was a negotiating offer. This was underlined in an Egyptian message to the State Department which was passed on to Israel. Sadat's principal motive was "to defuse the prevailing danger." "He wanted a serious discussion with Israel conducted through the good offices of the United States and not through Jarring."[48] However, when Israel examined the proposal in detail, there seemed to be too many discouraging elements. Prime Minister Golda Meir's reaction was critical and suspicious. In an NBC television interview recorded on 5 February, she poured scorn on its basic premise—the reopening of the canal. Israel had long ago agreed to this. She did not know why Sadat thought that this was something he was giving to Israel. He had not even mentioned peace. All he wanted was for Israel to begin to pull back. The crucial question, which Meir addressed to the Egyptian president, was this: "Are you prepared, if we come to an agreement on all outstanding problems, to sign a peace agreement with us and to put an end to belligerency?" Her more considered reaction, delivered in a speech to the Knesset on 9 February, was less abrasive but substantively the same. Though she wondered how one could clear the canal while the threat to renew the war was still in force, she was ready to discuss the opening of the waterway with Egypt, even as a separate issue. Nevertheless, withdrawal in isolation from the other provisions of UN Resolution 242 seemed a strange conception. There should be a peace agreement and the fixing of secure and recognized boundaries.[49]

What Meir and her government missed entirely was the tacit dimension of the Egyptian proposal. With Israel in occupation of his land, Sadat could never commit himself in writing to an unlimited armistice. Actually he was offering something much better—if not the form, then the substance of an end to belligerency. After all, a mere piece of paper could always be torn up. Reopening the canal, Sadat explained in a later interview, would create "a whole new atmosphere"; the canal cities "would come to life again"; "a real momentum for peace would be underway."[50] He did not refer, though he might have, to Egypt's need for the canal revenues and the important stake the international community had in any arrangement.

The second and more serious point overlooked by Israel was that progress could be made only by obscuring the shape of any final agreement. As Sadat makes clear above, the main thing was to break the deadlock; before one could even begin thinking about an overall settlement, confidence had to be established. The premature definition by both states of their ultimate objectives would simply nip the initiative in the bud. Egypt would be bound to demand Israel's full withdrawal to the pre-1967 war borders, while Israel would reiterate its old insistence on "secure and recognized boundaries" (a

euphemism for territorial revision). With both sides entrenched in their established positions, the deadlock would simply be reinforced.

It was precisely in order to prevent this eventuality that Sadat deliberately
refrained in his speech of 4 February—unlike Meir in her reply—from char-
acterizing the final borders. All he referred to was the implementation of Security Council Resolution 242, knowing full well that Israel and Egypt differed on its interpretation. Sadat's eloquent omission was not lost on his own
foreign minister, Mahmoud Riad, who warned him before the address that
"many countries would assume we had retracted from our insistence on a
total withdrawal."

While Israel was still struggling with this first revelation, Egypt then came
out, at the foreign-ministerial level, with a second, no less revolutionary departure from past policy. In an *aide-mémoire*—an official government
document—presented to UN mediator Gunnar Jarring on 15 February for
transmission to Israel, Egypt effectively answered Meir's objections of 5 and
9 February: were she to commit herself to full withdrawal and a just settlement of the refugee problem, Egypt would be "ready to enter into a peace
agreement with Israel." Here it was in black and white.

By this time Israel was becoming thoroughly confused with the contrasting
facets of the Egyptian initiative—which, from Sadat's point of view, were essential to its success. Sadat was in fact playing the game at two levels. At
one level, bypassing the foreign ministry (remember Riad's objection to the
4 February speech), he was offering an interim agreement based upon constructive ambiguity. It would be separate from an overall settlement and
would not, therefore, need to enter into knotty questions of an ultimate nature. It would have to be negotiated by the political echelon and would be
intended to establish confidence. At a second level, conducted through established channels, Egyptian thinking on the detailed juridical nature of any final
settlement could be laid out. Inevitably, this would remain faithful to Egypt's
historical official positions. But it was not, as Sadat had informed Israel via
the Americans, on the immediate agenda. (See above: "He wanted a serious
discussion with Israel conducted through the good offices of the United States
and not through Jarring.") What could be communicated in this formal way
was a solemn and binding reply to Israel's insistence on a contractual peace
as the conclusion of the overall process.

Israeli ears were simply not attuned to this contrapuntal subtlety.
Mordechai Gazit, Meir's *chef de cabinet* at the time, complains in his own
memoir of the episode that Egypt made no attempt to "direct attention" to
its readiness to reach a peace agreement while Israel was deliberating its own
answer. He also suggests that by not preparing Jarring or the Americans for
their change of course, they made it look as if it was "not considered of great
importance to them."[51] Clearly, Israel had overlooked the importance of the
Egyptian *aide-mémoire* of 15 February.

To make matters even more complicated for Israel, President Sadat then gave an interview to *Newsweek* which had the effect of compounding bewilderment with suspicion. In the original version, published on 22 February, Sadat agreed with his interviewer, Arnaud de Borchgrave, that Egypt would conclude a *peace treaty* with Israel provided various conditions were met (thereby answering Meir's skepticism and neatly linking his 4 February speech and the 15 February *aide-mémoire*). He also set out his opening bid for an interim agreement: Israeli forces should withdraw to a line stretching from Ras Muhammad on the Red Sea to El Arish on the Mediterranean coast. However, in the Arabic version of this interview, distributed by Egypt's official Middle East News Agency on 16 February, there were various emendations. Instead of "peace treaty," it merely spoke of "conditions of peace" (*salaam* rather than *sulh*). An affirmation by Sadat of Israel's inviolability and political independence, and right of navigation through the Suez Canal, was omitted. The restoration of Palestinian rights was added to Egyptian conditions for an overall settlement.[52]

Quite unwittingly, and with the best will in the world, Sadat had mixed together all the ingredients of a first-class dialogue of the deaf between a high context and a low context culture: ambiguity and allusiveness (the reference on 4 February to UN Resolution 242 rather than the international boundary); an important nonverbal element (opening the canal rather than a declaration of nonbelligerence, the loaded use of different communicatory mediums—the presidential speech, the bureaucratic document, the magazine interview); oversubtlety (use of diverse channels, broadcasting different versions of the same message for different audiences); a high opening price (offer of a 30-day ceasefire, call for a deep withdrawal). Israel's response was sadly predictable. First, instead of perceiving the revolutionary substance of the Egyptian messages, Israel concentrated on nitpicking, semantic detail—thereby missing the forest for the trees. Second, it confused what was negotiable—the length of the cease-fire, the depth of the interim withdrawal—with what was nonnegotiable—the principle of full withdrawal. Third, its whole approach was suffused with mistrust; in the end the initiative came to be viewed as a trap and not an opportunity. Paralyzed by uncertainty, suspicion, and fear, the Israeli government was unable in the time available to summon up either the will or the unity to return a decisive reply. By the time it got around to doing so, events had moved on.

Pundits and ministers alike made hay with the *sulh-salaam* distinction, quite ignoring the main point, which was that Sadat was offering Israel a contractual peace. In *Davar*, the semi-official organ of the ruling Labor party, the disparity between the English and Arabic versions of the *Newsweek* interview was seen as "considerably modifying" the importance of the original text. *Salaam* ("condition of peace," rather than *sulh*, "reconciliation") was "an expression without clear or binding significance." One Israeli commentator went so far as to claim that by peace Sadat meant a "peace based on the non-existence of the State of Israel." Israel Galili, a key minister in the Meir cabinet, exemplified the cross-cultural dissonance at the heart of the matter. Launching into an exhaustive textual analysis of all the documents involved, and even bringing in United Nations resolutions dating back to 1948, he accused the Egyptians of cleverly using "cloudy formulations that leave them with the option of denying entirely their readiness to enter into a peace agreement." Yitzhak Rabin, Israel's ambassador to Washington, and another influential player, damned the initiative as bearing Sadat's "evasive imprint." Finally, Golda Meir cast it into outer darkness. Yes, she affirmed, President Sadat was the first Egyptian leader to say that he was "prepared to make peace." "At least, he said it. But does he mean it?"[53]

Over the next few months, Israel and Egypt set out their terms for an interim agreement in greater detail. Each side, of course, had its own requirements, but these were by no means unbridgeable (and by December 1971 Israel had conceded some of the Egyptian conditions). The one fundamental gap that could not be spanned was Israel's reluctance to leave the boundary issue shrouded in that fog of obscurity in which Sadat wished to cloak it for the time being. Foreign Minister Eban was prepared for a noncommittal formulation on borders, only to be defeated in cabinet. "It is best that things be clear, without doubts," explained Minister Galili. He was supported by Dayan and Rabin. Meir remained skeptical altogether. In a memorandum of 19 April, Israel submitted its initial thoughts on an interim agreement to the United States. It contained the crucial and invariant proviso that any first-stage withdrawal should in no case be construed as "a commitment of withdrawal to the international boundary." It also included the demand for an end to the state of belligerence and a cease-fire of unlimited duration.[54]

By then Sadat was becoming restive. His proposal of 4 February, which had been intended to bypass the as yet intractable question of final borders, had bogged down in a sterile debate on this very issue. Speaking to the National Assembly on 20 May, he protested at "philosophical arguments," "word games" and "[empty] talk." He was "no longer disposed to exchange messages to and fro."[55] Israel—through no fault of its own—knew no other way to negotiate.

The way out of this impasse should come as no surprise in the light of this chapter: there would have to be mediation at the very highest level. Direct talks were out. Sadat did not conceal the humiliation of a situation in which "the starting point for every Israeli attitude is that we were defeated and they can, therefore, dictate whatever they want." But neither did he fail to make clear his wish for active American involvement in the negotiation. He complained on 16 September that the United States had so far been a mere "mailman": "they come to us, sit with us, listen to us, and then go to Israel and listen to them, and then return to us with their replies. . . ." The "mailman" was Assistant Secretary of State Joseph Sisco. A talented diplomat, he was simply not senior enough to play the sort of role envisaged by Sadat (and also, incidentally, such Israelis as Ambassador Rabin). Unfortunately, a solution was never found to this problem. With hindsight Gazit regretted that the United States failed to "appoint a personal representative authorized to handle the mission personally and continuously." The ideal candidate would have been President Nixon's national security adviser, Henry Kissinger. But neither he nor anyone else in the adminstration saw much urgency in the Middle East situation. Vietnam, the USSR, and the People's Republic of China all had a higher priority. As a result the initiative dragged on inconclusively, eventually to succumb from sheer neglect. It was a sad end to the best—and last—chance of a settlement before the 1973 War.[56]

VIII

CONCLUSION

At the root of the Arab-Israeli conflict, there is unquestionably a substantive clash between hitherto incompatible claims to the same land. As King Solomon judged in the case of the infant, compromise—in this case division of the land—was for long unacceptable to the indigenous inhabitants. But onto this unpromising stock the first Arab-Israeli war grafted an additional element of international contention. The local confrontation of Palestinians and Jews expanded into a regional dispute between the Jewish state and the neighboring Arab states. At first the prospects for the resolution of this international conflict seemed promising. Indeed, the 1949 armistice agreements concluding the 1948 War were expressly seen as a first step to the "restoration of peace." For some years afterward both sides assumed that sooner or later—there might be disagreement over the timing—a settlement would be arrived at.

In the event, the conflict dragged on, through four more wars and countless border clashes, for over a generation until, in a breathtaking initiative, Israel's principal antagonist, Egypt, resolved to break out of the deadlock. On the face of things it was difficult to account for the delay. What had Egypt or Israel to gain from such a protracted and debilitating contest? Above all else, both sides needed quiet development and the consolidation of their independence. Instead of peaceful construction they had squandered their blood and treasure merely to arrive back at their original point of departure. Nothing achieved in 1979 could not have been realized thirty years before.

It has long been an axiom of certain observers of the Arab-Israeli dispute that conflict between Israel and its neighbors is inevitable and that therefore nothing Israel does can make much difference. "There was no misunderstanding between Jew and Arab, but a natural conflict," wrote Vladimir Jabotinsky as early as 1923. This book begs to differ. What was true for the local relationship of Jewish settlers and Arab villagers did not necessarily hold at the state level. On the contrary, it should have been clear from the 1930s on that however much Arab states might sympathize with the plight of their Palestinian brethren, there was certainly no automatic identity of interests between them. In certain conditions *raison d'état* might even militate in favor of accommodation with the Jews. Thus King Abdullah of Transjordan could arrive at an informal understanding with the Jews over the West Bank of the Jordan in 1947–48; Israel might make itself ready to defend Jordan's independence (in the face of a Syrian invasion) in 1970; and more recently and unlikely still, Syria and Israel might even find themselves on the same side in the Lebanese imbroglio—in opposition to Yassir Arafat's Palestine Liberation Organization. The study of international relations teaches that the convoluted logic of statecraft may be a better guide to state behavior than common sense.

A second erroneous belief, following from the first, is that "psychological" factors have played only a negligible role in the outcome of the diplomatic process. If two states do share certain common interests, it is assumed, these will inevitably emerge regardless of the skill, or lack of it, of attendant diplomats. In fact, this version continues, excessive enthusiasm or exaggerated empathy with one's opponent's point of view might be positively harmful. Were this curious claim to be true, it is hard to understand what diplomats have occupied themselves with for centuries. It utterly ignores the crucial point that for shared purposes—if only to avoid war, let alone cooperate in peaceful endeavor—to emerge, they must first be perceived, communicated, and agreed upon. The history of Egyptian-Israeli relations amply demonstrates that the success of diplomacy cannot be taken for granted. Between the cup of common interest and the lip of actual accommodation there has been an unending series of mishaps and impediments—a succession of miscalculations, misperceptions, and misunderstandings. Unfortunately, the seemingly congenital repulsion between Israelis and Egyptians continues despite a decade of formal peace.

What, then, is the explanation for this phenomenon? The argument of this book is that Israel and Egypt suffer from a very high degree of cultural incompatibility. Each culture is virtually a closed book for the other. Imprisoned in mutually exclusive conceptual worlds, complex ecologies of assumption and habit, neither society is able to bridge the gap dividing it from the way of life of its neighbor. Why, oh why, Mohamed Ibrahim Kamel wondered at Camp David, could not Israel "live like any other country of the Middle East"?[1] But surely the beginning of diplomatic wisdom is precisely a recognition that others are different and have a right to be so? Failure to do this condemns the contending parties to a "dialogue of the deaf," a state of affairs when even the best-intentioned attempts at communication shatter against a barrier of incomprehension.

Egyptian and Israeli cultures are the opposing products of millennia of utterly different social circumstances, historical experiences, and religious conditioning. But for the Zionist revolution, which sought to transfer the Jewish people from the waters of Babylon and the Pale of Settlement to the shores of the Sea of Galilee and the Mediterranean, Egyptians and Jews would have had very little to do with each other. That they should have become neighbors and opponents is an unkind trick of fate. Rarely can two such incongruous partners have been thrust into unwilling embrace.

Where Egyptian culture is a product of the village community, wresting its livelihood, over a long history of uninterrupted settlement, from the land, Jewish culture evolved in the small township known in Eastern Europe as the *shtetl*. Egyptian culture takes the collective imperative as its guiding motif. Within this framework, the extended family provides the paradigm for most of life's activities, defining one's values and expectations. Individual autonomy is subordinated to the needs of the group. Conformity is the predominant ethic. Jewish culture departs from a different premise. The Jewish family is nuclear; the concept of the clan as a focus of loyalty is unfamiliar. Thus the Jew's allegiance is owed to the wider Jewish community, a community of fate and faith rather than work—of survival in hostile human surroundings, rather than sustenance in an inimical natural setting. Fierce Jewish communal consciousness is balanced by the assiduous cultivation of personal autonomy.

From this underlying bifurcation, much else follows. Egypt is a shame culture, in which one's standing and reputation in the eyes of one's fellows count for everything. There is no greater offense than to strike at a man's honor. Saving face is a categorical imperative. Revenge, whether to restore personal or family honor, is a common cause of violence. Great pains are therefore taken in speech and behavior to avoid possible injury. Good manners have evolved into a fine art. Elaborate codes of decorum govern the various areas of human contact—including visiting, bargaining, meeting, and parting—in order better to maintain social harmony. In contrast, Israel is a guilt culture. Self-esteem is a product less of outward appearances and social approval than of the internalized dictates of one's own conscience. Since shaming is far less of a sanction, there is correspondingly less resort to violence to restore face. Nor is there the Egyptian emphasis on decorum. On the contrary, Zionism's egalitarian ideology and the effect of mass immigration have strongly downgraded the role of the social graces. Courtesy tends to be marked by its absence.

When it comes to communication, whether verbal or nonverbal, the two cultures also part company. Edward T. Hall's well-known distinction comes in useful here. Egypt exemplifies many of the features of the so-called *high context* culture, in which the cues and circumstances surrounding an articulation may be as significant as its overt message. Since abrasive confrontation or the embarrassment of a refusal is to be shunned as disruptive of a brittle social harmony, circumlocution and indirect allusion loom large. Acute sensitivity to the nuance and nonverbal gesture is acquired. Israel, for its part, fits rather into the category of the reciprocal *low context* culture. Sharp disagreement and ungilded bluntness are preferred to emollient evasiveness. There is little need for tacit clues and nonverbal hints. Indeed, indirectness is more likely to annoy and confuse than to be appreciated for its subtlety.

The Koran and Talmud have fostered equally divergent literary and intellectual traditions. As the unmediated word of God, the Koran has acquired unrivaled sanctity and authority. Learning by rote, not discussion, has been the custom in Koranic schools. This hardly encourages innovative thinking, since revealed truth is both unalterable and definitive. Declamation of the holy verses has a central role in religious worship, reinforcing the power of the spoken word. Embellished and often exaggerated hyperbole has long been a prominent feature of Arab discourse. Subservience to authority is another heritage of Islam reflected in the Koran. For its part, Judaism has inherited quite different habits from its sacred texts. The functional equivalent of the Koran is not the Bible but the Talmud. In the Jewish tradition, Talmudic study is seen as the epitome of divine worship. Literacy and the exercise of the intellect are thus elevated to a ritual level. On the other hand, the Talmud is not so much a heavenly last word, more a compilation of rabbinical debates, rulings, and commentaries. It is not to be learned by heart or declaimed but critically analyzed, argued over, endlessly interpreted. The fine point of logic is more appreciated than the rhetorical flourish. Textual analysis becomes second nature. Since there is no final and definitive exegesis of a passage of Talmud, scope is left for personal innovation. Authority is approached with a critical and far from deferential eye.

The gulf between Egypt and Israel is at its widest on the issue of attitudes to the stranger. Throughout history Egypt has been subject to frequent invasion and foreign rule. But in the end the Egyptian way of life has demonstrated an extraordinary ability to emerge unscathed from the experience. Between the desert and the Nile, village life is regulated by an unvarying calendar. True, modern Egyptians have acquired a natural resentment of foreign interference in Egyptian affairs or of incursions on their land and sovereignty. However, this is combined with the charm, pliability, and self-confidence that derive from a comforting sense of their country's massive resilience. The lot of Israelis is diametrically opposed. No tribal memory of continuous settlement for them, but of exiles and expulsions. No historical guarantee of survival but an oppressive consciousness, after the Holocaust, that the worst—national extinction—can indeed happen. No easy confidence with the stranger—the *goy*—but the abrasive and defensive manner of the world's victim. Zionist hopes that a state of their own would cure the Jews of their persecution complex—and the Gentiles of their anti-Semitism—have not been sustained. More than forty years after Ben Gurion's declaration of independence, Israelis remain as tortured and insecure as ever.

The chemistry that has resulted from contact between the Egyptian and Israeli ethoses has proved highly volatile. Conflicting approaches to the very role of language have provided an initial and recurrent source of confusion. An Egyptian tendency to see language as a social lubricant, as important for dispensing good will and preventing friction as for transmitting dry facts, has proved misleading for Israelis conditioned to view language in a mainly informational, instrumental light. *Plus ça change, plus c'est la même chose.* During the 1954 Cairo trial of Egyptian Jews accused of working for Israel, the Egyptian consul in Milan "spontaneously"—and deceptively—comforted his Israeli counterpart with the assurance that not only would blood not be spilled, but no one would be sentenced to life imprisonment. It was and they were. Years later, the Egyptian consul in Eilat, overwhelmed by the horror of the October 1985 Ras Burka massacre of Israeli tourists by an Egyptian soldier, concocted a fantastic account of the episode featuring an Egyptian officer who, at risk to his own life, saved the lives of two Israeli children.[2] In both cases an Egyptian official preferred to please his audience rather than present an unpalatable truth. Such well-meaning inaccuracy has extended to the highest echelons of the Egyptian government, with obvious repercussions for Egyptian credibility.

Even graver consequences have resulted from the emphasis of Arabic-speakers on the expressive, declamatory aspect of language. Egyptian leaders have often striven for rhetorical effect and public enthusiasm at the expense of international tranquillity. More at home with a low-key presentation, Hebrew-speakers may well take verbal immoderation at its face value. Gratuitous abuse of Israel has never failed to poison the atmosphere, exacerbating crisis and hindering détente. Again the invariance of the phenomenon is noteworthy. How could he cooperate in any peace initiative, Nasser protested to the British ambassador in May 1955, when he had not long ago told his troops in Sinai that they should "hate the Israelis"? And this was nothing compared to what was being broadcast, day in and day out, over Cairo Radio. A generation later, in January 1987, Egyptian Defense Minister Abdel-Halim Abu Ghazala was reported to have told the Defense and National Security Committee of the Egyptian parliament that despite the 1979 peace, Israel was still his country's "principal and sole enemy," adding that Egypt and Syria, acting in unison, could "crush" Israel and regain Arab rights. Did he really mean this literally? Was this practical politics? In 1987—as in 1955, or 1967, for that matter—this kind of ringing declaration could only complicate matters unnecessarily. It weakened the hand of Israeli moderates and prompted Israeli Prime Minister Shamir's fatalistic reflection that "no peace lasts forever."[3]

Yet another subjective source of friction has been the typical Israeli preference for plainspokenness as opposed to the Egyptian instinct for indirectness. Time and again, particularly during the peace negotiations of 1978–79, Egyptian diplomats were distressed by maladroit Israeli moves. Not all Israelis are tactless, but it takes only one unfortunate remark to spoil a meeting, whether of officials or private citizens. Whatever the provocation, it was neither constructive nor very realistic, following the Ras Burka killings, for Israeli minister Arens to call for an immediate apology and a full report within a few days—or else. With an Arab leader, the ultimative demand that he swallow his pride is more likely to be counterproductive. Nor did the abbreviated timetable insisted upon by Arens make much sense in a Middle Eastern context. Of course, self-righteous Egyptian attempts to minimize the tragedy did not help much either. Within an alarmingly short time, years of painstaking diplomatic efforts to improve the atmosphere of relations were disrupted. Israeli ambassador in Cairo Sasson complained of the impossibility, in the circumstances, of maintaining a public, high-level dialogue through which the sides could try to understand each other's problems.[4]

The contrast between Egypt's high context and Israel's low context cultures has had other implications for the conduct of diplomacy. Crowded along the banks of the Nile, Egyptians have acquired, of necessity, acute sensitivity to the nonverbal nuances of human contact and a strong sense of social propriety. Israeli society, in the tradition of Zionist (and also, some would argue, Hasidic) egalitarianism, has acquired neither of these attributes. One might say that if Egyptians are people-oriented, then Israelis are word- or thing-oriented. This disparity has made itself particularly felt in the area of tacit and symbolic communication.

To get anywhere in Egypt requires cultivating personal contacts and ties of friendship. Anonymity is anathema. The wheels of business and diplomacy alike are oiled by the impulse to accommodation that comes only from personal acquaintance and obligation. All too often, Israelis have neglected this factor. If diplomacy is about objective interests, the drawn-out social preliminaries required by Arab diplomacy have seemed like so much wasted time, or even an excess of zeal. Warning against giving a prematurely official character to social contacts established with the Egyptian ambassador in Brussels in 1956, Eliahu Sasson argued that negotiations could take place only when the time was ripe, otherwise one would simply frighten off one's partner. The Syrian-born envoy's advice was ignored. Typically, Eliahu Elath (at the time ambassador in London, and the senior diplomat involved) saw "no point in continuing unless the ambassador proposes something substantial that will appear to us serious and practical."[5] Since 1977 Israeli leaders such as Ezer Weizman and Shimon Peres have, encouragingly, grasped the importance of "the personal touch." Others have not.

As befits a culture in which courtesy and decorum figure so prominently, protocol and the nuances of political hospitality have often been manipulated by Egyptian diplomacy to make political points. It was not by chance that Egypt's ambassador to Belgium, Ahmed Ramzi, drank a toast with the Israeli consul at a reception in May 1956 in the presence of other members of the diplomatic corps. "*Qu'est-ce que cela signifie?*" wondered a Belgian minister.[6] One of the ways that Sadat communicated his step-by-step process of accommodation with Israel after the 1973 War was via the use of protocol. What started at kilometer 101 on the Cairo-Suez road, when Generals Gamasy and Yariv met to discuss a cease-fire, was completed four years later on the day Sadat landed on Israeli soil.

Unfortunately, since the exchange of ambassadors in February 1980, Egypt has been unable to resist the temptation to make nonverbal points by regulating the pace and scope of the normalization of relations. "Cold peace"—an isolated ambassador with no access to the Egyptian media, and minimal

people-to-people contacts—was not quite what the Israeli ethos, weaned on
the messianic prophecies of Micah and Isaiah, had in mind. Mubarak's withdrawal of his ambassador to Israel in 1982 (after the Sabra and Shatilla massacre of Palestinians by Christian militiamen) may have been the least he could
do in an invidious situation. To Israeli public opinion hungry for "true
peace," it seemed like bad faith, reinforcing prejudice and dampening any
willingness to extend the peace process. The signing of the Taba *compromis*
(agreement on the terms of arbitration) in September 1986 restored an Egyptian ambassador to Tel Aviv and greatly improved the standing in Cairo of
Israeli ambassador Moshe Sasson. It would be have been yet more helpful
if Egypt could have resolved to detach the substance of normal ties with
Israel—trade, tourism, routine diplomatic work—from the inevitable ups and
downs of high-level politics.

If Egypt has misused the symbolism of peace, Israel has too often disregarded the symbolic dimension of war. For Israel to bomb the Iraqi nuclear
plant "Osirak" (on 7 June 1981) a couple of days after a meeting between
President Sadat and Prime Minister Begin was bound to be embarrassing,
suggesting prior Egyptian knowledge of the raid and even complicity. Israel
then repeated the performance in October 1985, flying along more than one
thousand kilometers of the Egyptian coast to bomb the PLO headquarters
in Tunis—Tunisia, incidentally, being one of Egypt's only friends in the region. "They—the Arabs, both enemies and friends—say that either we
helped you or else we have lousy radar capabilities, probably the former,"
complained a former senior officer in the Egyptian air force to an Israeli jour-
nalist after the raid. "Whatever, you place us in an impossible position. How
can we, after you bomb Tunisia, which was just as bad as Begin bombing the
Iraqi reactor two days after meeting with President Sadat, be expected to be
warm to you? We have to show you a cold shoulder."[7] Not surprising, then,
that Egypt should require explicit assurances that Israel would stay its hand
after the Istanbul synagogue massacre of September 1986, before agreeing
to go ahead with a Peres-Mubarak summit.[8]

Opposing attitudes to the meaning of violence have dogged Israeli-
Egyptian relations from the outset. On the whole Israel, in the classical Western tradition of *Realpolitik*, has viewed military force as a legitimate instrument of state policy to be wielded to achieve political gain. Military strikes
are supposed to "signal" warnings to an enemy and create expectations on
the basis of which he can make choices about his future course of action. He
is seen as a "rational actor"; that is, one capable of comparing the value of
his conduct to the pain of the anticipated punishment. If the latter outweighs
the former, he will modify his behavior.

However, in a high context, shame society, such as Egypt, violence frequently performs a *socially expressive* as well as an *instrumental* role. Incentives and disincentives do, of course, influence one's decisions. But neither
can the intangible, psychic significance of violence be ignored. The victim of

violence has been not only materially damaged, but also dishonored and therefore diminished in his own eyes and those of society. To this he can never reconcile himself, whatever the schedule of material gains and losses. So he, in his turn, will take revenge as a means to wipe out shame "though the heavens fall." To live shamefully may be worse than not to live at all—an incomprehensible point of view to the low context individual.

Given their difference in perspective, it is hardly surprising that Egypt and Israel should have been puzzled by each other's use of force. As far as the Egyptians were concerned, Israel's policy of retaliation was disproportionate and humiliating, conforming to none of the traditional conventions of revenge. From the early 1950s onward Israeli military action was supposed to provide Egypt with incentives to conform to Israeli wishes—whether to block off Palestinian infiltration, surrender in the War of Attrition, or sit down at the conference table. Israeli leaders believed, following Ben Gurion, that there was no logical contradiction between the use of force and overtures for peace. Not only did this strategy fail, it was also counterproductive. The definitive answer to it was given by Nasser to Richard Crossman: "Tell [Ben Gurion] he cannot force me to make peace. He cannot force peace."[9]

What Israel in fact did was to ensure the exacerbation of the conflict: The reprisal raids on the Gaza Strip aborted successive mediation attempts and drew the Czech arms deal and the 1956 Sinai campaign in their wake; the "lessons" of 1966–67 inflicted on Jordan and Syria precipitated the Six Day War; the deep penetration bombing of Egyptian cities in 1970 sent Nasser off to Moscow for Soviet pilots and SAM missiles. But the most serious miscalculation came before the 1973 War. Israeli rationality could not accommodate the possibility of a seemingly suicidal attack launched to restore Arab self-respect. Despite warnings of the most explicit kind from President Sadat that war would follow if "Arab psychology" was ignored, Israel's foremost Arabists in the defense and foreign ministries and academia ruled that "no Arab leader has an interest to make war, in order to lose it." For the foreseeable future, Israel's deterrent power would thwart the danger of a fresh outbreak of fighting.[10]

For its part, Egypt has been consistently mistaken about the limits of Israeli tolerance. First, it ignored the maddening effect of random violence against civilians on Israeli opinion. Ras Burka was the latest example of a cultural myopia which first made itself felt in the fedayeen raids of the 1950s. A common Egyptian reaction to expressions of Israeli anguish was that they were a malicious fabrication of the news media. Second, Egyptian leaders tended to misjudge the threshold of Israeli threat perception and therefore the possibility of successful deterrence, for instance in 1955–56 and 1966–67. Israel's chronic sense of insecurity invariably had the effect of magnifying even minimal shifts in the strategic balance, whether real or imagined, into anticipations of imminent annihilation. Thus a destabilizing asymmetry was inserted into the core of the Egyptian-Israeli relationship. Nasser's hope after the September 1955 Czech arms deal that fruitful negotiation was now more likely proved the reverse of the truth.

Israel's obsession with security is deeply rooted in Jewish experience, a product of historical vulnerability and persecution culminating in the Nazi Holocaust and Arab invasion of 1948. All this is quite remote from the Egyptian experience. Nasser thought that the scale of the Holocaust had been exaggerated by Israel for propaganda purposes. Sadat's foreign minister Mohamed Kamel wondered why the Jews had not stayed where they were— in post-Holocaust Europe—altogether. The latter's account of the March 1978 Israeli invasion of Southern Lebanon in reply to a PLO assault in which thirty-five civilians died, reflects at one and the same time outrage at a typically disproportionate Israeli response, and indifference to the original provocation, described as a "daring operation."[11]

In the diplomatic sphere, Israeli insecurity translates itself into a pervasive mistrust. "All the world's against us" is a national assumption that quickly acquires the nature of a self-fulfilling prophecy. It creates a formidable psychological resistance to even entering negotiations, let alone bringing them to a successful conclusion. In the 1953–54 period, Egyptian feelers, including two notes from Colonel Nasser, were dismissed as maneuvers designed to protect Egypt's flank while it was engaged in crucial negotiations with Britain. In 1955, after Egypt had shown itself interested in various American and British offers of mediation, Israel argued that it was all a ruse to gain time to digest newly supplied Soviet weapons while preparing for war. In 1971 Sadat's initiative for an interim agreement on the Suez Canal was squandered on the grounds that his motive was simply to regain the Sinai in order to attack Israel in more favorable circumstances. In the 1980s Mubarak has been portrayed as grudgingly maintaining the 1979 peace treaty to ensure American aid, while awaiting his moment to abrogate it. More than a decade after Sadat's Knesset speech, an expectation of Egyptian bad faith still pervades broad sectors of Israeli opinion.

Another long-standing obstacle to a settlement was the conflicting dictates of Egyptian pride and Israeli preconceptions. Convinced at an early stage of Egyptian unreliability and defective grasp of reality, Israel insisted that negotiations would have to be direct and without prior conditions. Only in this manner could Egypt be brought to face up to the fact of Israel's existence. This became the acid test of Egyptian good will. (It still is the official Israeli position vis-à-vis both Jordan and Syria.) Backing it was the concern that any great power mediator would be biased in favor of the Arabs. One suspects that it also reflected underlying Jewish assumptions about the power of reason: that rational men could always arrive at a mutually acceptable compromise.

What Israel overlooked was that Egypt, as a shame culture, could never enter negotiations with an unfamiliar and militarily superior opponent without a high degree of confidence in its ultimate success. Kamel's 1978 comment that "one should know where a road leads before starting out on a journey," is apropos.[12] Either out-and-out failure or an agreement excessively favorable to Israel would result in a loss of face before the Arab world. To avoid these distressing possibilities, the Egyptian instinct was to seek the psychological shelter of a powerful protector-cum-intermediary and prior assurances that their minimum terms would be satisfied. A face-to-face confrontation with Israel in the conference chamber was anticipated with profound apprehension. The forthright style of Israeli negotiators did nothing to quiet this fear. Sadat did not come to Jerusalem, as he endlessly reiterated, to "haggle" but to present his irreducible terms for a settlement. After the breakdown of brief, direct talks in January 1978, all subsequent negotiations leading up to the March 1979 peace treaty were conducted through the good offices of the United States. Moreover, Egyptian insistence on a preliminary declaration of principles, at first rejected by Israel out of hand, was ultimately conceded in the shape of the Camp David "framework for peace."

One obvious way out of the deadlock to which Egypt and Israel's contradictory "psychological" requirements consigned them was to work to establish greater mutual confidence over an extended period of time. But this flew in the face of Israel's low context dislike of inconclusive and ambiguous situations. Better to bring the matter to a head by clear-cut demands for proof of Egyptian good will. "We are not prepared," it was decided in 1953, "for a drawn-out game of empty promises for the future and insist on testing [Egypt's] intentions in a practical manner." Free passage through the Suez Canal and a high level meeting were among the proposed tests.[13] Similar tests have been required ever since. In 1986 these consisted of a Peres-Mubarak summit, the return of an Egyptian ambassador to Tel Aviv, and progress on "normalizing" relations.

The Egyptian approach, in contrast to that of Israel, has always been to opt for a more relaxed process of confidence-building. It is from the intimate and exclusive personal relationships of the traditional community—and their equally jealous rivalries—rather than the brisk, anonymous transactions of Western business practice, that Egyptian diplomacy takes its cue. Confidence is not bestowed lightly. It is a delicate plant to be watered and nurtured before bearing fruit. "Ripeness is all." Faced by the request of his Israeli colleague in May 1956 for direct negotiations, Egyptian ambassador Ahmed Ramzi counseled patience. "The day will come when that will happen, but now is still too early, for the psychological ground has not been prepared."[14] Sadat's step-by-step strategy after the 1973 War was based on precisely this approach. Israel's preference was to jump straight to nonbelligerency. "What's the hurry?" Egyptians still answer when asked why they do not speed up normalization. To the impatient Israeli mind, the call for protracted confidence-building reeks of an evasive unreliability.

Negotiation is one area of international intercourse in which the effect of cultural dissonances has been appreciated for some time. Particular attention has been paid to the glaring difficulties faced by Western negotiators in their dealings with collectivist cultures such as those of China or Japan. In the Egyptian-Israeli case, the high context–low context dichotomy has been compounded by Israel's hypersensitivity on security matters. A premonition that one false move might spell catastrophe permeates Israeli behavior at every stage of a negotiation.

Egypt's opening gambits, from the armistice talks of 1949 onward, have usually left considerable leeway for maneuver. Proposals for interim agreements in 1974 and 1975 called for much deeper Israeli withdrawals than were subsequently agreed to. Egypt's opening proposal at Camp David, including a claim for war damages, was also demonstrably far from a last word. One may speculate that claims to the Negev, which were a feature of Egyptian discourse in the 1950s, fell into the same category. Israel's reaction has invariably been one of discomfort. Experience has not blunted the surprise of being faced with what seem like exorbitant demands, or helped Israel to distinguish the negotiable from the irreducible elements of the Egyptian position. Meanwhile, Israel, preoccupied with the narrowness of its margin of survival and also constrained by a vigilant public opinion, has staked out an opening position leaving relatively little room for subsequent withdrawal.

In the middle and end games of a negotiation, the logic of these rival strategies works itself out. For Israel, the dogged rearguard action and the belated and grudging concession eked out to extract the maximum advantage have nicely corresponded to its sense of vulnerability. Particular emphasis is placed, in the scholastic tradition of Jewish learning, on contractual precision and fine shades of meaning. Enormous effort is invested in shutting off possible loopholes, as though legal expedients could in themselves preclude infringement of an agreement. In 1979, for instance, Israel at first insisted that the security provisions of the peace treaty specify the position of every Egyptian guard post in the Sinai.[15] Egypt, for its part, having left itself greater freedom of action, can afford more self-confident and expansive maneuvering. The utility of ambiguous formulations to fudge over disagreement and save face is fully appreciated. The different foreign policy decision-making processes, that of Israel diffuse and argumentative, that of Egypt centralized and deferential, reinforce these respective tendencies. At this stage, faced by Israeli tenacity and delaying tactics, Egyptian negotiators begin to indicate signs of discomfiture. Requests for face-saving gestures are put forward with increasing insistence.

In the final analysis, though, ultimate agreement has always depended upon the intervention of a third party. Where mistrust, misunderstanding, and pride have precluded direct contact and then hindered negotiation, the good offices of a mediator have proved indispensable as a channel of communication. Luckily, both cultures assign a decisive role to the mediator—in Arabic *wasta*, in Hebrew *shtadlan*—in the task of conflict resolution. It is one of their few points of convergence. At no time are his services more essential than in the last act of a negotiation. He can suggest the saving formula to bridge the last few inches separating the parties, underwrite the final accord, and provide compensation for possible loss. The 1979 negotiations could not have been concluded without President Carter's shuttle; the multinational force, a crucial element of the Sinai security arrangements, required Secretary of State Alexander Haig's intervention; Israel's final withdrawal from the Sinai in 1982 called for Deputy Secretary Walter Stoessel.

After more than ten years of direct diplomatic contact, the Israeli-Egyptian relationship continues to depend on the good offices of the United States. Formal relations and greater mutual contact have only partly mitigated the effects of cross-cultural dissonance. The recently resolved Taba dispute well exemplifies the continuing failure of the parties to transcend their differences without outside assistance. Under the terms of the final settlement, signed on 26 February 1989, this small resort enclave on the Gulf of Aqaba was returned to Egypt, and a hotel on the site was purchased by the Egyptian government. Various arrangements were agreed upon facilitating the access of Israeli tourists. However, had the Israeli government appreciated Egypt's profound sensitivity over the issues of land and sovereignty, and had it conducted negotiations in a more flexible manner, very much better terms might have been achieved. Moreover, years of unnecessary and unproductive bitterness and friction might have been avoided.

At an early stage it was clear that Israel had a tenuous claim in law to Taba, from which it had withdrawn, significantly enough, in both 1949 and 1957. Begin had unwisely granted the concession to build a hotel on the site before the final withdrawal from the Sinai. But in 1982 President Sadat, precisely in order to prevent what was essentially a secondary problem in itself from becoming a major bone of contention, suggested a reasonable compromise. In return for acknowledgment of Egyptian sovereignty, Israel would be allowed to lease the area for ninety-nine years. "And what will happen afterward?" was Begin's response. On the eve of international arbitration, another compromise—again posited on an Israeli concession of sovereignty, a *sine qua non* as far as Egypt was concerned—was suggested: joint ownership of the hotel. This was also turned down by an Israel locked into intransigence.[16] Throughout the protracted talks, American mediation was, as usual, indispensable. Assistant Secretary Richard Murphy was the hero of the hour in the negotiation of the 1986 *compromis*; the final Taba agreement depended on the untiring efforts of Abraham Sofaer, legal adviser to the State Department.

Taking Egyptian-Israeli relations in their entirety over the whole period, a compelling picture emerges of mutual bewilderment and missed opportunity. While different observers would doubtless disagree about the precise weight to assign to the role of cross-cultural dissonance as opposed to personality factors, surrounding circumstances, or objective conditions in any particular instance, its overall salience cannot be doubted. There have been leaders in both camps who appreciated the need to communicate to the other side in a language that side could understand: Sadat made a genuine attempt to penetrate Israel's security concerns; Sharett and Weizman were equally sensitive to Egyptian "psychological" requirements. But foreign relations between nations are not conducted on a one-time basis by lone individuals. Culture is of the essence because in the long term policies are evolved and sustained by governments—communities of officials—rooted in the assumptions and attitudes of the societies from which they spring and to which they are ultimately answerable.

An Egyptian-Israeli *modus vivendi*—a minimal relationship of "live and let live"—was always feasible. After 1948, all the wars were the result of decisions taken only after diplomacy had failed to disentangle subjective fears, suspicions, and frustrated aspirations. Neither the success nor the failure of diplomacy was preordained. Without the involvement of the United States at the very highest level after 1973, it is inconceivable that a peace treaty would have been arrived at. Similar engagement in 1971, by the admission of the participants themselves (including Sadat, Kissinger, and Mordechai Gazit), might have been equally efficacious. In the future it will doubtless also be indispensable.

Whether or not Egypt and Israel can ever hope to achieve a peace "like that between Belgium and Holland" is a moot point. The two countries are heir to utterly disparate traditions and have different orientations and dreams. Even the concept of "peace" means something different to the two of them. However, as many examples of accommodation between ideological opponents over the centuries demonstrate, this is not essential. Neither has the right or the means to convert the other to its way of life—to become "more Western" or "more integrated into the Middle East." It is sufficient for them to live alongside each other on mutual sufferance at a minimum, toleration and a degree of functional cooperation at a maximum. A stable international order does not have to rest on love, only on recognized "rules of the game," stable deterrence, and, most important, unencumbered communication.

Since 1979 these conditions have been fulfilled in part. The peace treaty and subsequent agreements and understandings have established a normative framework of relations. Diplomatic mechanisms and procedures are in place to resolve disagreements before they degenerate into full-scale conflict. For all the confusion and anger surrounding the Ras Burka massacre and the Taba dispute, they were defused through diplomatic means. This is not to say that, at the time of writing, serious objective difficulties do not remain. There are elements in both Egypt and Israel who consider the 1979 settlement a mere provisional cease-fire: Egyptians who cherish a final settling of accounts with the usurper, Israelis who value the West Bank over Israel's commitment under the Camp David accords to solve the Palestinian problem. The

Egyptian government does not conceal its rejection of the thesis that it has signed a "separate peace" with Israel. It is doubtful whether the present state of affairs can continue indefinitely unless the settlement is expanded to take in Syria, Jordan, and the Palestinians. For this to occur requires painful decisions on the part of Israel.

Nevertheless, having said all that, we must finally return to the question of communication. It is not a sufficient condition for reaching or maintaining a settlement. But it is a necessary condition. In its absence there is no chance of accommodation. This book has described the dialogue of the deaf that results from cross-cultural incomprehension. If its argument is even partly correct, it follows that intelligible dialogue depends upon a mutual effort, at a societal, not just individual, level, to surmount the cultural barrier. And the first step in this process is a raising of consciousness: without the awareness that there is a problem, there can be no attempt to find a solution.

Some have achieved greater insight as a result of the peace treaty. Shmuel Meltzer was deputy mayor of Eliat on behalf of the Likud party. As a result of his many visits to Egypt and dealing with Egyptians, he succeeded in grasping the essential point that the biggest obstacle to peace and development is "the mentality barrier." In Meltzer's words, "Neither understands the other, and everyone talks like a deaf man. Each side thinks it knows what the other is thinking, and they're both wrong." In order to break down the barrier, he suggests extensive use of television. An Israeli TV relay station, for instance, could be established on the border with Egypt so that Egyptians could see more of the Israeli way of life. He would also like Jerusalem to broadcast more programs on the Arab world to domestic audiences.[17]

People do not need to be taught to hate and mistrust each other in the Middle East. They do need to be encouraged to acquire a better understanding of their neighbors' hopes and concerns. This will not occur spontaneously. It will require educational programs in schools and universities, language-learning, and extensive contact at all ages and in as many areas as possible. Intercultural communication should be taught as a subject in its own right. Among others, businessmen on both sides of the border would benefit from courses in the professional customs and practices of the other side. Government officials and diplomats should certainly be trained in intercultural skills.

Samuel Lewis, U.S. ambassador to Israel 1977–1985, believes that even the U.S. Department of State has been amiss in preparing foreign service officers in the art of negotiating with other cultures. He is convinced that American cultural unmindfulness contributed to the failure of the U.S.-mediated talks between Egypt and Israel for a five-year period of autonomy for the West Bank and Gaza Strip, mandated by Camp David, which began in August 1979. The United States, in the view of Ambassador Lewis, should not have insisted on Western-style, face-to-face talks between Israeli and Egyptian negotiators. Rug merchants might haggle face to face, but when it came to matters of honor in the Middle East, individual parties in a dispute did not make concessions in each other's presence. "We really didn't understand this." This error of American diplomacy should come as no surprise, Lewis adds. The Foreign Service Institute, the teaching arm of the State Department, has only a one-week course in negotiations, offered twice a year to twenty-six students, and two three-day workshops a year.[18] Culture is mainly an incidental adjunct to language studies.

At this point the reader may object that if the mighty United States is placing insufficient emphasis on intercultural negotiating skills, Egypt and Israel can hardly be expected to do better! But this is an excuse, not a justification. In the final analysis, it is first and foremost up to the immediate disputants to understand and overcome their diplomatic shortcomings. After all, the ultimate price for the failure of the autonomy talks—and all the other failures referred to in this book—was paid by Israel and Egypt, not by the United States.

The final word should be given to an Israeli diplomat, Eliahu Sasson, who early on appreciated the need for unencumbered communication between Jews and Arabs on the basis of mutual respect and heightened cross-cultural awareness:

> The people of Israel did not rent an apartment in Israel but built themselves a house in this part of the world and must develop and live in it for ever. The prerequisite for a tranquil, constructive, and happy life is to find a common language with our neighbors in all senses and fields, whether those neighbors are good or evil, advanced or retarded, friends or foes. We have no choice. . . . for we cannot live by the sword alone. . . .[19]

NOTES

I. Cairo and Jerusalem

1. *The Jerusalem Post*, 12 Sept. 1986. Professor Ann M. Lesch of Villanova University points out that of those visiting Israel, there were very few tourists as such. Most were officials, journalists, and especially Palestinians with Egyptian laissez-passers.

2. David Ben Gurion, *Yihud Veyiud* (Hebrew. Tel Aviv: Ma'arakhot, 1971), p. 174.

3. United States National Archives, Department of State Documents (hereafter *SD*) 674.84A/5–650, 6 May 1950; Israel State Archives, Foreign Ministry Papers (hereafter *IFM*) 2410/2/a, 19 Oct. 1951, 17 Mar. 1952.

4. Walter Eytan, *The First Ten Years* (New York: Simon and Schuster, 1958), p. 58; *IFM* 2410/2/a, 17 Mar. 1952; British Public Records Office, Foreign Office Papers (hereafter *FO*) 371/115867, 1 Apr. 1955 and 371/115885, 28 Nov. 1955; Miles Copeland in *The Times* (London), 24 June 1971; see also *Al Hamishmar* magazine supplement (Hebrew), 12 June 1986, p. 7.

5. *IFM* 2451/1/b, 8 Dec. 1952.

6. *FO* 371/115882, 17 Nov. 1955.

7. Hermann F. Eilts interview, 19 Aug. 1985; Ismail Fahmy, *Negotiating for Peace in the Middle East* (Baltimore: Johns Hopkins University Press, 1983), p. 254; *IFM* 2453/12, 14 Aug. 1951.

8. Henry Kissinger, *Years of Upheaval* (London: Weidenfeld and Nicolson and Michael Joseph, 1981), p. 842; *The Jerusalem Post*, 22 Feb. 1985.

9. Ezer Weizman, *The Battle for Peace* (New York: Bantam, 1981), p. 132; Moshe Dayan, *Breakthrough* (London: Weidenfeld and Nicolson, 1981), p. 100; Ezer Weizman interview, *The Jerusalem Post* Magazine, 16 Nov. 1984, p. 3; Samuel Lewis at United States Institute of Peace seminar, 10 Nov. 1988; Hermann Eilts interview.

10. Edward T. Hall, *The Silent Language* (New York: Doubleday, 1959); idem, *The Hidden Dimension* (New York: Doubleday, 1966); Glen Fisher, *Mindsets* (Yarmouth: Intercultural Press, 1988).

11. Quoted in Michael D. Olien, *The Human Myth* (New York: Harper and Row, 1978), p. 293.

12. Ruth Benedict, *Patterns of Culture* (Boston: Houghton Mifflin, 1934), p. 46.

13. Clyde Kluckhohn, "The Study of Culture," in D. Lerner and H. D. Lasswell (eds.), *The Policy Sciences* (Stanford, Calif.: Stanford University Press, 1951), p. 86; idem, *Mirror for Man* (New York: Fawcett, 1957).

14. For instance, John C. Condon and Fathi S. Yousef, *An Introduction to Intercultural Communication* (New York: Bobbs-Merrill, 1975); Richard W. Brislin, *Cross-Cultural Encounters* (New York: Pergamon, 1981); Stephen Bochner (ed.), *Cultures in Contact* (Oxford: Pergamon, 1982); William B. Gudykunst and Young Yun Kim, *Communicating with Strangers* (Reading, Mass.: Addison-Wesley, 1984).

15. Rosita D. Albert and Harry C. Triandis, "Intercultural Education for Multicultural Societies," *International Journal of Intercultural Relations*, vol. 9 (1985), pp. 319–337; Margaret L. Cormack, "American Students in India: Ambassadors or Cultural Polluters?" *International Studies Quarterly*, vol. 17 (Sept. 1973), pp. 337–358; Geert Hofstede, "Lessons for Europeans in Asia" (2 parts), *Euro-Asia Business Review*, vol. 1 (Dec. 1982), pp. 37–41; vol. 2 (Jan. 1983), pp. 38–47; Howard F. Van Zandt, "How to Negotiate in Japan," *Harvard Business Review*, vol. 48 (Nov.-Dec.

1970), pp. 45–56; Byron J. Good, "The Heart of What's the Matter: The Semantics of Illness in Iran," *Culture, Medicine, and Psychiatry*, vol. 1 (1977), pp. 25–58.

16. For instance, Adda B. Bozeman, *Politics and Culture in International History* (Princeton: Princeton University Press, 1960); idem, *The Future of Law in a Multicultural World* (Princeton: Princeton University Press, 1971); idem, "Law, Culture, and Foreign Policy: East versus West," *Asian Affairs*, no. 2 (Nov.-Dec. 1973), p. 109; idem, "Iran: Foreign Policy and the Tradition of Persian Statecraft," *Orbis*, vol. 23 (Summer 1979), pp. 387–402; idem, "Statecraft and Intelligence in the Non-Western World," *Conflict*, vol. 6 (Mar. 1985); R. P. Anand (ed.), *Cultural Factors in International Relations* (New Delhi: Abhinav, 1981), pp. 100–101; Lucian Pye, *Chinese Commercial Negotiating Style* (Cambridge, Mass.: Oelgeschlager, Gunn and Hain, 1982), pp. 5–8, 21–23, 78; Akira Iriye, "Culture and Power: International Relations as Intercultural Relations," *Diplomatic History*, vol. 3 (Spring 1979), pp. 115–128; Anthony Marc Lewis, "The Blind Spot of U.S. Foreign Intelligence," *Journal of Communication*, vol. 26 (Winter 1976), pp. 44–55; Hiroshi Kimura, "Soviet and Japanese Negotiating Behavior: The Spring 1977 Fisheries Talks," *Orbis*, vol. 24 (Spring 1980), pp. 43–67; Michael K. Blaker, "Probe, Push, and Panic: The Japanese Tactical Style in International Negotiations," in Robert A. Scalapino (ed.), *The Foreign Policy of Modern Japan* (Berkeley: University of California Press, 1977), pp. 55–101; Masao Kunihiro, "U.S.-Japan Communications," in Henry Rosovsky (ed.), *Discord in the Pacific* (Washington, D.C.: Columbia Books, 1972), pp. 164–167; Ogura Kazuo, "How the 'Inscrutables' Negotiate with the 'Inscrutables': Chinese Negotiating Tactics vis-à-vis the Japanese," *The China Quarterly*, no. 79 (Sept. 1979), pp. 544–545; Glen Fisher, *International Negotiation: A Cross-Cultural Perspective* (Yarmouth: Intercultural Press, 1980).

17. Fisher, *Mindsets*, pp. 68–69.

18. Raymond Cohen, *International Politics: The Rules of the Game* (London: Longman, 1981), p. 61.

19. K. J. Holsti, "Along the Road to International Theory," *International Journal*, vol. 29 (Spring 1984), p. 360.

II. Egypt and Israel

1. Shimon Shamir, "Egypt: Political Characteristics," lecture delivered at a conference on Egypt, Jaffee Center of Tel Aviv University, 3 June 1986. I am also grateful to Professor Robert F. Hunter of Tulane University for his comments on this paragraph.

2. Jacques Berque, *Egypt: Imperialism and Revolution* (London: Faber and Faber, 1972), pp. 66–67.

3. P. J. Vatikiotis, *The History of Egypt*, 3rd ed. (London: Weidenfeld and Nicolson, 1985), p. 4; Berque, p. 54.

4. Anwar el-Sadat, *In Search of Identity* (London: Collins, 1978), p. 3.

5. Hamed Ammar, *Growing Up in an Egyptian Village* (London: Routledge and Kegan Paul, 1954), p. 48; S. D. Goitein, "Individualism and Conformity in Classical Islam," in Amin Banani and Speros Vryonis (eds.), *Individualism and Conformity in Classical Islam* (Wiesbaden: Otto Harrassowitz, 1977), pp. 3–17.

6. Sania Hamady, *Temperament and Character of the Arabs* (New York: Twayne Publishers, 1960), pp. 70, 92; Hisham Sharabi, "Impact of Class and Culture on Social Behavior: The Feudal-Bourgeois Family in Arab Society," in L. Carl Brown and Norman Itzkowitz (eds.), *Psychological Dimensions of Near Eastern Studies* (Princeton: The Darwin Press, 1977), p. 246; Yassin El-Sayed, "The Egyptian Character and the

Civilizational Significances of the October War," paper given to an International Symposium on the October War, Cairo, 27–31 Oct. 1975, pp. 10–11.

7. Hamady, pp. 28–32.

8. Raphael Israeli, *The Public Diary of President Sadat*, part 1 (Leiden: E. J. Brill, 1978), p. 64.

9. Sharabi, pp. 247–250.

10. Raphael Patai, *The Arab Mind*, revised ed. (New York: Charles Scribner's Sons, 1983), pp. 90–96, 101–106.

11. Ammar, p. 35.

12. Henry H. Ayrout, *The Egyptian Peasant* (Boston: Beacon Press, 1963), pp. 112, 143–144.

13. Ibid., p. 145; Hani Fakhouri, *An Egyptian Village in Transition* (New York: Holt, Rinehart and Winston, 1972), pp. 109, 111.

14. E. T. Hall, *Beyond Culture* (New York: Anchor Press, 1976).

15. Sharabi, pp. 252–255; Hamady, pp. 75–77; Nadia Abu-Zahra, "Material Power, Honour, Friendship, and the Etiquette of Visiting," *Anthropological Quarterly*, vol. 47 (1974), p. 126.

16. John Boman Adams, "Culture and Conflict in an Egyptian Village," *American Anthropologist*, vol. 59 (1957), pp. 226–227.

17. Ammar, pp. 52–53.

18. Israeli, p. 64.

19. Mohamed Ibrahim Kamel, *The Camp David Accords* (London: KPI, 1986), pp. 286, 315–316.

20. Vatikiotis, p. 24; Ammar, p. 34.

21. G. E. Von Grunebaum, *Islam*, 2nd ed. (London: Routledge and Kegan Paul, 1961), pp. 7, 25.

22. Ahmed M. Gomaa, "The Egyptian Personality—Between the Nile, the West, Islam, and the Arabs," in Shimon Shamir (ed.), *Self-Views in Historical Perspective in Egypt and Israel* (Tel Aviv: Tel Aviv University, 1981), pp. 33–34.

23. L. Melikian, "Authoritarianism and Its Correlates in the Egyptian Culture and in the United States," *Journal of Social Issues*, vol. 15 (1959), pp. 58–69.

24. Walter Laqueur, *A History of Zionism* (London: Weidenfeld and Nicolson, 1972), pp. 308–314.

25. Moshe Lissak, "Israeli Political Culture," *Skira Hodshit* (Hebrew), vol. 31, no. 8/9 (1984), p. 74.

26. See Charles S. Liebman and Eliezer Don-Yehiya, *Civil Religion in Israel: Traditional Religion and Political Culture in the Jewish State* (Berkeley: University of California Press, 1983).

27. Shlomit Levi and Elihu L. Guttman, *Values and Attitudes of Students in Israel* (Hebrew. Jerusalem: The Institute of Applied Social Research, 1976), pp. S4, 38; Ofira Seliktar, "Continuity and Change in the Attitudes towards the Middle East Conflict: The Case of Young Israelis," *International Journal of Political Education*, vol. 3 (1980), p. 148.

28. Mark Zborowski and Elizabeth Herzog, *Life Is with People: The Jewish Little-Town of Eastern Europe* (New York: International Universities Press, Inc., 1952), p. 227; Shlomo Swirski, "Community and Meaning of the Modern State: The Case of Israel," *Jewish Journal of Sociology*, vol. 18 (1976), p. 129; Gad Ya'acobi, *The Jerusalem Post*, 23 Jan. 1987, p. 7.

29. See Ruth Landes and Mark Zborowski, "Hypotheses concerning the Eastern European Jewish Family," *Psychiatry*, vol. 13 (1950), pp. 447–464.

30. Ron Shouval et al., "Anomalous Reactions to Social Pressure of Israeli and So-

viet Children Raised in Family and Collective Settings," *Journal of Personality and Social Psychology*, vol. 32 (1975), pp. 477–489.

31. Itai Zak, "Modal Personality of Young Jews and Arabs in Israel," *The Journal of Social Psychology*, vol. 109 (1979), pp. 3–10.

32. Quoted in Shlomo Avineri, *The Making of Modern Zionism* (New York: Basic Books, 1981), p. 154.

33. Quoted in ibid., p. 200.

34. Yael Dayan, *My Father, His Daughter* (Tel Aviv: Steimatzky, 1985), pp. 90–91.

35. "Are We Israelis Polite?" symposium in *Ma'ariv* (Hebrew), 6 Mar. 1970.

36. Quoted in Avineri, p. 214.

37. See Yehoshafat Harkabi, *The Bar Kochba Syndrome* (Chappaqua, N. Y.: Rossel Books, 1983).

38. Avineri, p. 277.

39. David Vital, "Continuity and Change in the Jewish People after the Establishment of the State of Israel," in Shamir, pp. 87–88.

40. Numbers 33:53.

41. See Itzhak Galnoor, "Israel's Polity: The Common Language," *The Jerusalem Quarterly*, no. 20 (Summer 1981), pp. 65–82.

42. Charles S. Liebman, "Attitudes toward Jewish-Gentile Relations in the Jewish Tradition and Contemporary Israel," *Kivunim* (Hebrew), vol. 25 (1984), p. 8.

43. *Nazi Conspiracy and Aggression* (Washington: United States Government Printing Office, 1946–48), vol. 5, document 2738-PS.

44. Rita Rogers, "The Emotional Climate in Israeli Society," *American Journal of Psychiatry*, vol. 128 (1972), pp. 988–992. See also G. H. Grosser et al. (eds.), *The Threat of Impending Disaster* (Cambridge, Mass.: MIT Press, 1964).

45. Chaim Schatzker, "The Holocaust in Israeli Education," *International Journal of Political Education*, vol. 5 (1982), pp. 75–82; Charles S. Liebman and Eliezer Don-Yehiya, "The Dilemma of Reconciling Traditional Culture and Political Needs: Civil Religion in Israel," *Comparative Politics*, vol. 16 (1983), pp. 63–65.

46. Charles S. Liebman, "Myth, Tradition, and Values in Israeli Society," *Midstream* (Jan. 1978), pp. 44–53.

47. James W. Gillespie and Gordon W. Allport, *Youth's Outlook on the Future: A Cross-National Study* (New York: Doubleday, 1955), p. 31; Seliktar, pp. 148–149.

48. Schatzker, p. 78.

49. *FO* 371/115887, 9 and 19 Dec. 1955.

50. *Ha'aretz* (Hebrew), 8 Feb. 1985.

51. *The Jerusalem Post* Magazine, 27 June 1986, p. 17.

III. Arabic versus Hebrew

1. Harry Hoijer, "The Sapir-Whorf Hypothesis," in idem (ed.), *Language in Culture*, American Anthropological Association Memoir Series, no. 79 (Dec. 1954), p. 93.

2. David H. Laitin, *Politics, Language, and Thought* (Chicago: University of Chicago Press, 1977), pp. 162, 210–213.

3. E. T. Hall, *Beyond Culture* (New York: Anchor Press, 1976); Stella Ting-Toomey, "Toward a Theory of Conflict and Culture," *International and Intercultural Communication Annual*, vol. 9 (1985), pp. 76–77.

4. Hamady, *Temperament and Character of the Arabs*, p. 36.

5. Michael Gilsenan, "Lying, Honor, and Contradiction," in Bruce Kampferer (ed.), *Transaction and Meaning* (Philadelphia: Institute for the Study of Human Issues, 1976), pp. 191–219.

6. Shaul C. Sohlberg, "Social Desirability Responses in Jewish and Arab Children in Israel," *Journal of Cross-Cultural Psychology*, vol. 7 (1976), pp. 301–314.

7. El-Demerdash Abdel-Meguid Sarhan, *Interests and Culture* (New York: Bureau of Publication, Teachers College, Columbia University, 1950).

8. Bernard Geis, *Uneasy Lies the Head: The Autobiography of King Hussein of Jordan* (n. p., 1962), p. 93.

9. John Bagot Glubb, *A Soldier with the Arabs* (London: Hodder and Stoughton, 1957), pp. 377, 385, 335. Also see Humphrey Trevelyan, *The Middle East in Revolution* (London: Macmillan, 1970), pp. 31, 33.

10. Ismail Fahmy, *Negotiating for Peace in the Middle East* (Baltimore: Johns Hopkins University Press, 1983), pp. 3, 264; Mohamed Ibrahim Kamel, *The Camp David Accords* (London: KPI, 1986), pp. 313–314.

11. Moshe Dayan, *Avnei Derekh* (Hebrew. Tel Aviv: Yediot Akhronot, 1976), p. 199. See also C. L. Sulzberger, *Seven Continents and Forty Years* (New York: Quadrangle, 1977), p. 208.

12. Y. Harkabi, "Basic Factors in the Arab Collapse during the Six-Day War," *Orbis*, vol. 11 (1967), pp. 688–689. On the Nasser-Hussein conversation see Patai, *The Arab Mind*, pp. 102–104.

13. Moshe Dayan, *Mapa Khadasha* (Hebrew. Tel Aviv: Ma'ariv, 1969), pp. 48–49.

14. Foreign Broadcasting Information Service, *Daily Report*, 21 Sept. 1962, no. 185.

15. Y. Harkabi, "Arab Ideology of the Conflict," in G. C. Alroy (ed.), *Attitudes toward Jewish Statehood in the Arab World* (New York: American Academic Association for Peace in the Middle East, 1971), p. 92.

16. T. G. Fraser (ed.), *The Middle East, 1914–1979* (London: Edward Arnold, 1980), p. 117; Daniel Dishon (ed.), *Middle East Record III, 1967* (Jerusalem: Israel Universities Press, 1971), pp. 271–272; Daniel Dishon (ed.), *Middle East Record IV, 1968* (Jerusalem: Israel Universities Press, 1973), pp. 211, 214; Mahmoud Riad, *The Struggle for Peace in the Middle East* (London: Quartet, 1981), pp. 66–73.

17. Mohamed Heikal, *The Road to Ramadan* (London: Fontana, 1976), p. 52.

18. E. Shouby, "The Influence of the Arabic Language on the Psychology of the Arabs," in Abdulla M. Lutfiyya and Charles W. Churchill (eds.), *Readings in Arab Middle Eastern Societies and Cultures* (The Hague: Mouton, 1970), p. 700.

19. Sharabi, p. 69; Hamady, p. 44.

20. Barbara J. Koch, "Presentation as Proof: The Language of Arab Rhetoric," *Anthropological Linguistics*, vol. 25 (1983), pp. 47–60.

21. Clifford Geertz, *Local Knowledge* (New York: Basic Books, 1983), pp. 109–114.

22. Koch, pp. 55–56.

23. See Dale F. Eickelman, *The Middle East* (Englewood Cliffs: Prentice-Hall, 1981), pp. 235–241.

24. I am indebted for this idea to Dr. Tova Cohen of Bar-Ilan University. Tova Cohen, "The Activation of 'Simultaneous Reading' in Hebrew Poetry as an Example of the Use of 'Interpretive Strategies.'"

25. E. T. Prothro, "Anglo-American Differences in the Judgement of Written Messages," in Lutfiyya and Churchill, pp. 704–712.

26. United States National Archives, Department of State, Document 674.84A/5–450, 4 May 1950.

27. Raphael Israeli, "'I, Egypt': Aspects of President Anwar Al-Sadat's Political Thought," *Jerusalem Papers on Peace Problems*, no. 34 (1981), pp. 117–143.

28. Anthony Nutting, *Nasser* (London: Constable, 1972), p. 37.

29. Kamel, p. 365.

30. Fahmy, p. 266; Riad, p. 306; Sadat, p. 308.

31. David Ben Gurion, *My Talks with Arab Leaders* (Jerusalem: Keter, 1972), p. 281.

32. Yehoshafat Harkabi, *Arab Attitudes to Israel* (London: Valentine and Mitchell, 1972), p. 129.

33. Ezer Weizman, *The Battle for Peace* (New York: Bantam Books, 1981), pp. 146, 201.

34. Israeli State Archives, Foreign Ministry Papers 2453/20, 21 Dec. 1954; Raphael, p. 38; Maurice Orbach, "The Orbach File: First Visit to Cairo," *New Outlook*, October 1974, p. 23.

35. Ben Gurion, pp. 297, 301.

36. Henry A. Kissinger, *Years of Upheaval* (London: Weidenfeld and Nicolson and Michael Joseph, 1982), p. 212.

37. Carl von Horn, *Soldiering for Peace* (London: Cassell, 1966), p. 82; Alec Seath Kirkbride, *A Crackle of Thorns* (London: John Murray, 1956), p. 102.

38. Baruch A. Margalit and Paul A. Mauger, "Aggressiveness and Assertiveness: A Cross-Cultural Study of Israel and the United States," *Journal of Cross-Cultural Psychology*, vol. 16 (1985), pp. 497–511.

39. Mark B. Adelman and Myron W. Lustig, "Intercultural Communication Problems As Perceived by Saudi Arabian and American Managers," *International Journal of Intercultural Relations*, vol. 5 (1981), pp. 349–363.

40. E. A. Levenston, *English for Israelis* (Jerusalem: Israel Universities Press, 1970), pp. 11–13.

41. Gideon Rafael, *Destination Peace* (London: Weidenfeld and Nicolson, 1981), p. 216.

42. Aharon Cohen, "How to Talk to the Arabs," *New Outlook*, no. 7 (1964), p. 13.

43. Moshe Sharett, *Yoman Ishi* (Hebrew. Tel Aviv: Ma'ariv, 1978), vol. 3, pp. 633, 640.

44. Ibid., p. 837.

45. Moshe Dayan, *Breakthrough* (London: Weidenfeld and Nicolson, 1981), p. 78.

46. Interview with Hermann F. Eilts, U.S. Ambassador to Egypt 1973–79, 19 Aug. 1985; Boutros-Ghali interview in *Yediot Ahronot Weekend Supplement*, 6 Nov. 1987.

47. Dayan, p. 143; Kamel, p. 216. See also Eitan Haber et al., *The Year of the Dove* (New York: Bantam, 1979), pp. 211–212.

48. Kamel, pp. 350–353, 360. There is no mention of this episode in Dayan's own account.

49. Haber et al., pp. 134–135.

50. E. L. M. Burns, *Between Arab and Israeli* (London: George C. Harrap, 1962), p. 132.

51. "How to Speak to the Arabs," *Middle East Journal*, vol. 18 (1964), p. 146.

52. Kamel, pp. 63–64; Cyrus Vance, *Hard Choices* (New York: Simon and Schuster, 1983), p. 201. See also Riad, p. 310.

53. Weizman, pp. 182, 186. Also see p. 329.

54. Lord Gore-Booth (ed.), *Satow's Guide to Diplomatic Practice*, 5th ed. (London: Longman, 1979), p. 1.

IV. Israelis and Egyptians Face to Face

1. Rivka Yadlin, *Dyukan Mitsri* (Hebrew. Jerusalem: Magnes, 1986), p. 7.

2. James A. Bill and Carl Leiden, *Politics in the Middle East* (Boston: Little, Brown, 1979), pp. 151–163; Mohammad Talaat Al Ghunaimi, *The Muslim Conception*

of International Law and the Western Approach (The Hague: Martinus Nijhoff, 1968), pp. 65–66.

3. Interview with Lucius D. Battle, 13 Aug. 1985; John S. Badeau, *The Middle East Remembered* (Washington, D.C.: The Middle East Institute, 1983), pp. 236–237.

4. Ismail Fahmy, *Negotiating for Peace in the Middle East* (Baltimore: Johns Hopkins University Press, 1983), pp. 275, 299–300; Mohamed Ibrahim Kamel, *The Camp David Accords* (London: KPI, 1986), pp. 315–316; Jimmy Carter, *Keeping Faith* (New York: Bantam, 1982), p. 342.

5. Fahmy, pp. 135–136; Anwar Sadat, *In Search of Identity* (London: Collins, 1978), p. 242; Kamel, p. 37.

6. *Newsweek*, 25 Mar. 1974, p. 16. Also see ibid., 13 Dec. 1976, p. 25.

7. Fahmy, p. 46. Also see William R. Brown, *The Last Crusade* (Chicago: Nelson-Hall, 1980), pp. 300–301.

8. "How to Speak to the Arabs," *Middle East Journal* (1964), p. 146. On Sasson's background and pre-1948 dealings with Arab leaders, see Eliahu Sasson, *Baderekh El Hashalom* (Hebrew. Tel Aviv: Am Oved, 1978).

9. *The Jerusalem Post*, 14 Sept. 1986, p. 8; Weizman interview, *The Jerusalem Post Magazine*, 16 Nov. 1984, p. 4; Kamel, pp. 142–143, 322.

10. Eilts interview.

11. El-Demerdash Abdel-Meguid Sarhan, *Interests and Culture* (New York: Columbia University, College of Education, Bureau of Publications, 1950), p. 91.

12. Mara B. Adelman and Myron W. Lustig, "Intercultural Communication Problems As Perceived by Saudi Arabian and American Managers," *International Journal of Intercultural Relations*, vol. 5 (1981), p. 357.

13. Alec Seath Kirkbride, *A Crackle of Thorns* (London: John Murray, 1956), p. 32.

14. Fahmy, p. 136.

15. Joe Haines, *The Politics of Power* (London: Jonathan Cape, 1977), p. 11.

16. Fahmy, p. 87; Henry Kissinger, *Years of Upheaval* (London: Weidenfeld and Nicolson and Michael Joseph, 1982), pp. 949–950.

17. Abba Eban, *An Autobiography* (London: Futura, 1979), p. 144.

18. Ibid., p. 547; Rafael, p. 320.

19. Fahmy, pp. 164–165.

20. Quoted in T. G. Fraser (ed.), *The Middle East, 1914–1979* (London: Edward Arnold, 1980), p. 156.

21. Dayan, p. 102; Weizman, pp. 122–124.

22. Nitza Ben-Elissar, *Kriat Yam Suf* (Hebrew. Jerusalem: Edanim, 1982), pp. 76, 87, and chapter 7 in general.

23. E.g., in *Yediot Ahronot* (Hebrew), 26 Mar., 6 Apr. 1980.

24. *The Times* (London), 4 Nov. 1981.

25. Golda Meir, *My Life* (London: Futura, 1976), p. 330.

26. Majid Khadduri, "International Law," in Majid Khadduri and Herbert J. Liebesny (eds.), *Law in the Middle East* (Washington: The Middle East Institute, 1955), esp. pp. 359–360.

27. Israeli, *The Public Diary of President Sadat*, p. 33.

28. Iliya Harik, *The Political Mobilization of Peasants* (Bloomington: Indiana University Press, 1974), pp. 140–141, 158.

29. David Ben Gurion, *Yihud Veyiud* (Hebrew. Tel Aviv: Ma'arakhot, 1971), pp. 173–174.

30. United States National Archives, Department of State, Document 674.84A/9–852, 8 Sept. 1952; Israel State Archives, Foreign Ministry Papers (hereafter *IFM*) 2453/20. See entire file.

31. Ibid., 674.84A/1–1453, 14 Jan. 1953; 674.84A/2–1753, 18 Feb. 1953; *Davar* (Hebrew), 4 July 1986, p. 18.

32. *Al Hamishmar* magazine supplement (Hebrew), 12 June 1986, p. 18.

33. *IFM* 2453/20, 25 May 1953.

34. British Public Records Office, *FO* 371/102733, 18 May 1953.

35. Ibid., 1 Aug. 1953.

36. Dan Hofstadter (ed.), *Egypt & Nasser*, vol. 3, 1967–72 (New York: Facts on File, 1973), pp. 164–171.

37. *Le Monde*, 8 Apr. 1970, p. 1.

38. Ibid., 19 Feb. 1970, p. 2.

39. Ibid., 8 Apr. 1970, p. 1.

40. Yeshayahu Ben-Porat, *Sihot* (Jerusalem: Edanim, 1981), p. 36; *The Jerusalem Post*, 7, 9 Apr. 1970.

41. *Divrei Haknesset*, vol. 57, 1970 (Hebrew. Jerusalem: State Printer, 1970), pp. 1572–1574.

42. Ibid., pp. 1576–1577.

43. Harold Saunders, *The Other Walls* (Washington: American Enterprise Institute, 1985), p. xvi.

44. Sadat, p. 274.

45. Eitan Haber et al., *Shnat Hayonah* (Hebrew. Tel Aviv: Zemora, Beitan, Modan, 1981), p. 131.

46. Kamel, p. 22.

47. Weizman, p. 125.

48. Ibid., pp. 316–318.

49. Ibid., p. 330; Haber et al., p. 207.

50. Kamel, pp. 223–225.

V. When Deterrence Fails

1. *Yediot Ahronot* (Hebrew), 9 Oct. 1985; *The Jerusalem Post*, 11 Oct. 1985.

2. *Yediot Ahronot* (Hebrew), 24 Jan. 1986.

3. *The Jerusalem Post*, 13, 14 Mar. 1986.

4. Bernard Geis, *Uneasy Lies the Head: The Autobiography of King Hussein of Jordan* (n. p., 1962), p. 24.

5. Dane Archer and Rosemary Gartner, *Violence and Crime in Cross-National Perspective* (New Haven: Yale University Press, 1984), appendix, "Comparative Crime Data File: Nations"; Simha F. Landau and Israel Drapkin, *Ethnic Patterns of Criminal Homicide in Israel: Final Report* (The Hebrew University of Jerusalem, Institute of Criminology, 1968), pp. 9, 10.

6. Harold W. Glidden, "The Arab World," *American Journal of Psychiatry*, vol. 128, Feb. 1972, p. 985.

7. Mark Zborowski and Elizabeth Herzog, *Life Is with People* (New York: International Universities Press, 1952), p. 152.

8. Charles R. Snyder et al., "Alcoholism among the Jews in Israel: A Pilot Study," *Journal of Studies on Alcohol*, vol. 43, 1982, p. 626.

9. See Nahum Goldmann, *Memories* (London: Weidenfeld and Nicolson, 1969), p. 289; Menachem Begin, *The Revolt* (New York: Dell, 1977), pp. 25–26, 60, 85.

10. J. Goldberg, Y. Yinon, and A. Cohen, "A Cross-Cultural Comparison between the Israeli and American Fear Survey Inventory," *Journal of Social Psychology*, vol. 97 (1975), pp. 131–132.

11. *Yediot Ahronot* (Hebrew), 18 June 1982.

12. Ehud Ya'ari, *Egypt and the Fedayeen, 1953–1956* (Hebrew. Givat Haviva: Center for Arab and Afro-Asian Studies, 1975), pp. 9–14.

13. Ibid., p. 15; interview with General Y. Harkabi, chief of Israeli Military Intelligence 1955–59.

14. Ya'ari, pp. 11–12.

15. *ISA* 2456/3, 6 Jan. 1956.

16. Ibid., 2453/20, 9 Mar. 1954.

17. Moshe Sharett, *Yoman Ishi* (Hebrew. Tel Aviv: Ma'ariv, 1978), vol. 2, p. 591; Moshe Dayan, *Story of My Life* (London: Sphere, 1976), p. 308.

18. Elmore Jackson, *Middle East Mission* (New York: W. W. Norton, 1983), p. 114.

19. Sharett, p. 591.

20. Dayan, *Story of My Life*, p. 183; Moshe Dayan, *Avnei Derekh* (Hebrew. Tel Aviv: Yediot Ahronot, 1976), pp. 114, 147. The latter is the very much expanded original version of *Story of My Life*.

21. Sharett, vol. 4, p. 1001.

22. Shlomo Aronson and Dan Horowitz, "The Strategy of Controlled Retaliation—The Israeli Example," *State and Government* (Hebrew), vol. 1 (1971), p. 81.

23. *The Jerusalem Post*, 4 Sept. 1955.

24. Dayan, *Avnei Derekh*, pp. 115, 187; Sharett, vol. 2, pp. 591, 1001; Gideon Rafael, *Destination Peace* (London: Weidenfeld and Nicolson, 1981), p. 43.

25. *The Jerusalem Post*, 4 Sept. 1955.

26. *ISA* 2456/3, 6 Jan. 1956.

27. Rafael, pp. 38–45; Maurice Orbach, "The Orbach File," parts 1 and 2, *New Outlook*, Oct. 1974 & Nov.-Dec. 1974; Elmore Jackson, *Middle East Mission* (New York: W. W. Norton, 1983). Material on the Orbach mission is in *ISA* 2453/20 and 2453/21.

28. Humphrey Trevelyan, *The Middle East in Revolution* (London: Macmillan, 1970), p. 11.

29. Alec S. Kirkbride, *A Crackle of Thorns* (London: John Murray, 1956), pp. 71–72; Ahmed Abou-Zeid, "Honour and Shame among the Bedouins of Egypt," in J. G. Peristiany (ed.), *Honour and Shame: The Values of Mediterranean Society* (London: Weidenfeld and Nicolson, 1965), pp. 245–259; Pierre Bourdieu, "The Sentiment of Honour in Kabyle Society," in ibid., pp. 190–241; Nicholas G. Onuf, "Reprisals: Rituals, Rules, Rationales," Princeton University, Center of International Studies, Research Monograph no. 42, July 1974, pp. 22–28.

30. Sharett, vol. 3, p. 799.

31. Jackson, p. 41.

32. *ISA* 2410/2/b, 25 Jan. 1956.

33. E. L. M. Burns, *Between Arab and Israeli* (London: George C. Harrap, 1962), p. 76.

34. *The Jerusalem Post*, 12, 14 May 1967; *New York Times*, 13 May 1967.

35. Shlomo Aronson, *Conflict and Bargaining in the Middle East: An Israeli Perspective* (Baltimore: Johns Hopkins University Press, 1978), pp. 58–59.

36. Hanoch Bartov, *Dado: Forty-eight Years and Twenty Days* (Tel Aviv: Ma'ariv, 1981), p. 91.

37. *Ma'ariv* (Hebrew), 2 June 1972.

38. Moshe Dayan, *Avnei Derekh*, p. 399. There is no mention of this in the English-language version of the book: *Story of My Life* (London: Weidenfeld and Nicolson, 1976).

39. Dan Schueftan, "Nasser's 1967 Policy Reconsidered," *The Jerusalem Quarterly*, 3 (1977), p. 132.

40. Zuhair Diab (ed.), *International Documents on Palestine, 1968* (Beirut: Institute for Palestine Studies, 1971), p. 319; Yitzhak Rabin, *Pinkas Sherut* (Hebrew. Tel Aviv: Ma'ariv, 1979), p. 133. There is no mention of this in the English-language version of the book: *The Rabin Memoirs* (Boston: Little, Brown, 1979), p. 67.

41. See Schueftan, pp. 132–134.

42. Indar Jit Rikhye, *The Sinai Blunder* (London: Frank Cass, 1980), p. 71.

43. U Thant, *View from the UN* (London: David and Charles, 1978), p. 480. Also see Nasser interview in *Look*, 19 Mar. 1968.

44. Yitzhak Rabin, *Pinkas Sherut*, p. 136.

45. Benjamin Geist, "The Six Day War" (Ph.D. thesis submitted to the Hebrew University of Jerusalem, 1974), p. 124; Thant, *View from the UN*, pp. 481–482, 485.

46. Rabin, *Pinkas Sherut*, pp. 139, 146.

47. Walter Laqueur and Barry Rubin (eds.), *The Israel-Arab Reader*, 4th ed. (London: Penguin, 1984), p. 202.

48. Ibid., pp. 173–174.

49. Diab, *International Documents on Palestine, 1968*, p. 320.

50. Abba Eban, *An Autobiography* (London: Futura, 1979), p. 331.

51. Laqueur and Rubin, p. 176.

52. Mohamed Heikal, *The Cairo Documents* (London: Mentor, 1973), pp. 215–216.

53. Geist, p. 247. See also Eban, p. 321, and Rabin, *Pinkas Sherut*, p. 138.

54. Eban, pp. 332–334; Amit quoted in Geist, p. 113; Allon quoted in *The Jerusalem Post*, 15 June 1972; Golda Meir, *My Life* (London: Futura, 1976), p. 302. See Benjamin Geist, "A Question of Survival: The Holocaust Syndrome in 1967," *International Journal*, vol. 28 (1973), pp. 630–647.

55. Rabin, *Pinkas Sherut*, p. 161; Eban, p. 349.

56. Eban, pp. 319–320.

57. Ibid., p. 321; Rabin, *Pinkas Sherut*, pp. 133, 138; Laqueur and Rubin, p. 176.

58. Eban, pp. 326, 327; Rabin, *Pinkas Sherut*, p. 144.

59. Eban, p. 329; Fuad Jabber (ed.), *International Documents on Palestine, 1967* (Beirut: Institute of Palestine Studies, 1970), pp. 9–10.

60. Laqueur and Rubin, p. 202.

61. Anthony Nutting, *Nasser* (New York: E. P. Dutton, 1972), p. 398.

62. Diab, p. 320.

63. Geist, pp. 163–164; Mahmoud Riad, *The Struggle for Peace in the Middle East* (London: Quartet, 1981), pp. 19, 22.

64. *The Sunday Telegraph*, 21 Oct. 1973.

65. Harold Nicolson, *Diplomacy*, 3rd ed. (London: Oxford University Press, 1969), p. 123.

VI. Obstacles to Negotiation

1. *The Jerusalem Post* Magazine, 16 Nov. 1984, p. 3; *Yediot Ahronot* (Hebrew), 2 Nov. 1984, p. 4.

2. Dayan, *Breakthrough*, p. 68.

3. Ben-Porat, *Sihot*, p. 235.

4. Boutros Boutros-Ghali, *The Arab League, 1945–1955* (New York: International Conciliation, 1955), pp. 85–86.

5. See Ehud Ya'ari, *Mitsraim Vehafedayin*, Arab and Afro-Asian Monograph Series no. 13 (Hebrew. Givat Haviva: Centre for Arabic and Afro-Asian Studies, 1975).

6. Maurice Orbach, "The Orbach File (part two): Second Visit to Cairo," *New Outlook*, Nov.-Dec. 1974, p. 11.

7. Moshe Sharett, *Yoman Ishi*, vol. 3 (Hebrew. Tel Aviv: Ma'ariv, 1978), p. 689.

8. Ibid., p. 690.

9. Ibid., p. 633.

10. Ibid., p. 716.

11. Ibid., p. 1056.

12. Eban, p. 252; Mordechai Gazit, "The Peace Process, 1969–1973: Efforts and Contacts," *Jerusalem Papers on Peace Problems*, no. 35 (1983), pp. 17–18.

13. Yigal Allon, *Masakh Shel Hol*, 2nd ed. (Hebrew. Tel Aviv: Hakibbutz Hameuhad, 1968), pp. 404–405.

14. Henry Kissinger, *The White House Years* (London: Weidenfeld and Nicolson and Michael Joseph, 1979), pp. 586–587; Dan Hofstadter (ed.), *Egypt and Nasser*, vol. 3, 1967–72 (New York: Facts on File, 1973), p. 235.

15. Ibid., p. 238; *Yediot Ahronot*, 18 Nov. 1987.

16. Rafael, p. 230.

17. Gazit, p. 10.

18. Walter Laqueur and Barry Rubin, *The Israel-Arab Reader*, revised ed. (London: Penguin, 1976), p. 140.

19. Walter Eytan, *The First Ten Years* (New York: Simon and Schuster, 1958), p. 58.

20. *USNA* 674.84A/5–650, 6 May 1950.

21. Sharett, vol. 1, p. 81.

22. "How to Speak to the Arabs," *The Middle East Journal*, vol. 18 (1964), p. 149.

23. Eytan, pp. 30–31.

24. *USNA* 674.84A/2–250, 2 Feb. 1950.

25. Ibid., 674.84A/2–750, 7 Feb. 1950; 674A.84A/2–1450, 14 Feb. 1950; 674.84A/4–2550, 25 Apr. 1950.

26. *ISA* 2453/12, 5, 29 Mar. 1952.

27. *USNA* 674.84A/9–852, 8 Sept. 1952.

28. Ibid., 674.84A/9–1053, 10 Sept. 1953.

29. Sharett, vol. 4, pp. 1086–1087, 1090, 1133.

30. Princeton University Library, John Foster Dulles Oral History Project, Francis H. Russell interview.

31. David Ben Gurion, *My Talks with Arab Leaders* (Jerusalem: Israel Universities Press, 1971), pp. 279, 290.

32. Ibid., p. 289.

33. Moshe Dayan, *Story of My Life* (London: Sphere Books, 1976), pp. 149–153.

34. E. L. M. Burns, *Between Arab and Israeli* (London: George C. Harrap, 1962), pp. 76–77.

35. Ben Gurion, p. 289.

36. Ibid., p. 313.

37. Ibid., pp. 297, 314. Also see Miles Copeland, "Nasser's Secret Diplomacy with Israel," *The Times* (London), 24 June 1971.

38. Gazit, p. 17.

39. Mahmoud Riad, *The Struggle for Peace in the Middle East* (London: Quartet Books, 1981), p. 80.

40. Ibid., pp. 78–80; Rafael, pp. 196–197; Yitzhak Rabin, *The Rabin Memoirs* (Boston: Little, Brown, 1979), p. 155.

41. Dayan, *Breakthrough*, pp. 44, 79.

42. Interview with Menachem Begin, *Yediot Ahronot* weekly supplement, 13 Nov. 1987; Weizman, p. 66.

43. Dayan, pp. 112–113; Cyrus Vance, *Hard Choices* (New York: Simon and

Schuster, 1983), p. 202; Mohamed Ibrahim Kamel, *The Camp David Accords* (London: KPI, 1986), p. 72.

44. Dayan, *Breakthrough*, p. 112.

45. *The Jerusalem Post*, 19 June 1978, p. 1.

46. Vance, pp. 203–204.

47. *FO* 371/115881, 16 Nov. 1955.

48. *USNA* 674.84A/5–650, 6 May 1950. See also *ISA* 2453/12, 27 Feb. 1950, and *FO* 371/82198, 24 Mar. 1950.

49. Hamed Ammar, *Growing Up in an Egyptian Village* (London: Routledge and Kegan Paul, 1954), pp. 21, 22, 24, 39.

50. Anwar el-Sadat, *In Search of Identity* (London: Collins, 1978), pp. 3, 12.

51. "How to Speak to the Arabs," *The Middle East Journal*, vol. 18 (1964), p.149. See also Yehoshafat Harkabi, *Palestinians and Israelis* (Jerusalem: Israel Universities Press, 1974), p. 28.

52. Kathryn B. Doherty, "Rhetoric and Reality: A Study of Contemporary Official Egyptian Attitudes toward the International Legal Order," *The American Journal of International Law*, vol. 62 (1968), pp. 335–364.

53. Sisco interview, 14 Aug. 1985.

54. Copeland, *The Times*, 24 June 1971.

55. Michael K. Blaker, "Probe, Push, and Panic: The Japanese Tactical Style in International Negotiations," in Robert A. Scalapino (ed.), *The Foreign Policy of Modern Japan* (Berkeley: University of California Press, 1977), pp. 59–61.

56. Lucian Pye, *Chinese Commercial Negotiating Style* (Cambridge, Mass.: Oelgeschlager, Gunn and Hain, 1982), pp. 26–27, 40–42.

57. Kissinger, *The White House Years*, pp. 745–748.

58. Ibid., p. 1299.

59. Mohamed Heikal, *Nasser: The Cairo Documents* (London: Nel Mentor, 1973), p. 210.

60. Kissinger, *The White House Years*, p. 1299; Henry Kissinger, *Years of Upheaval* (London: Weidenfeld and Nicolson and Michael Joseph, 1982), p. 823.

61. Dayan, *Breakthrough*, pp. 80–82.

62. Weizman, p. 88.

63. *Newsweek*, 16 Jan. 1978, p. 13; Dayan, *Breakthrough*, p.129.

VII. Deadlock

1. *Yediot Ahronot* (Hebrew), 15 Sept. 1985; Fuad I. Khuri, "The Etiquette of Bargaining in the Middle East," *American Anthropologist*, vol. 70 (1968), pp. 698–706; Edward T. Hall, *The Silent Language* (New York: Doubleday Anchor, 1973), pp. 106–107.

2. William B. Quandt, "Egypt: A Strong Sense of National Identity," in Hans Binnendijk (ed.), *National Negotiating Styles* (Washington: Foreign Service Institute, 1987), pp. 118–120.

3. Shlomo Aronson, *Conflict and Bargaining in the Middle East: An Israeli Perspective* (Baltimore: Johns Hopkins University Press, 1978), p. 56.

4. *The Jerusalem Post*, 8 Feb. 1971.

5. Ezer Weizman, *The Battle For Peace* (New York: Bantam, 1981), p. 186.

6. Moshe Dayan, *Story of My Life* (London: Sphere, 1976), p. 148.

7. *ISA* 2451/b, 14 Dec. 1952; *FO* 371/115885, 7 Dec. 1955.

8. Dayan, *Story of My Life*, pp. 580–581.

9. Yemima Rosenthal (ed.), *Documents on the Foreign Policy of Israel*, vol. 3 (Jerusalem: Government Printer, 1983), p. 254.

10. Henry Kissinger, *Years of Upheaval* (London: Weidenfeld and Nicolson and Michael Joseph, 1982), pp. 800, 816.

11. Lecture at the Hebrew University of Jerusalem.

12. Mohamed Ibrahim Kamel, *The Camp David Accords* (London: KPI, 1986), p. 286.

13. Weizman, p. 353; Moshe Dayan, *Breakthrough* (London: Weidenfeld and Nicolson, 1981), p. 162.

14. Saadia Touval, *The Peace Brokers* (Princeton: Princeton University Press, 1982), p. 269.

15. Yitzhak Rabin, *Pinkas Sherut*, vol. 2 (Hebrew. Tel Aviv: Ma'ariv, 1979), pp. 455–457.

16. Jimmy Carter, *Keeping Faith: Memoirs of a President* (New York: Bantam, 1982), p. 342.

17. Zbigniew Brzezinski, *Power and Principle* (London: Weidenfeld and Nicolson, 1983), p. 237.

18. Kamel, *The Camp David Accords*, p. 245.

19. Kissinger, *Years of Upheaval*, p. 608.

20. Ibid., pp. 538–539, 624.

21. Ismail Fahmy, *Negotiating for Peace in the Middle East* (Baltimore: Johns Hopkins University Press, 1983), p. 161.

22. Weizman, pp. 152, 358, 360.

23. Yitzhak Rabin, *The Rabin Memoirs* (Boston: Little, Brown, 1979), p. 272.

24. Rabin, *Pinkas Sherut*, p. 487.

25. Yitzhak Shamir interview in *The Washington Times*, 1 Mar. 1989; *Yediot Ahronot* (Hebrew), 11 Apr. 1979.

26. Brzezinski, p. 269.

27. Carter, p. 356.

28. Ibid., p. 373; Brzezinski, p. 273.

29. Cyrus Vance, *Hard Choices* (New York: Simon and Schuster, 1983), p. 224.

30. Kissinger, *Years of Upheaval*, pp. 641–654.

31. Meir Rosenne interviewed in *Yediot Ahronot* (Hebrew), 11 Apr. 1979.

32. Weizman, pp. 129–136; Dayan, *Breakthrough*, p. 98.

33. Carter, p. 303.

34. Dayan, *Breakthrough*, p. 140.

35. Ibid., pp. 166, 176.

36. Weizman, pp. 374–375; Touval, pp. 309–312; Ben-Elissar lecture, 20 May 1981, *Tel Aviv University Peace Papers*, p. 24.

37. Dayan, *Breakthrough*, p. 157.

38. See Hamed Ammar, *Growing Up in an Egyptian Village* (London: Routledge and Kegan Paul, 1954), pp. 57–58; Victor F. Ayoub, "Conflict Resolution and Social Reorganization in a Lebanese Village," *Human Organization*, vol. 24 (1965), pp. 11–17; Pierre Bourdieu, "The Sentiment of Honour in Kabyle Society," in J. G. Peristiany (ed.), *Honour and Shame: The Values of Mediterranean Society* (London: Weidenfeld and Nicolson, 1965), pp. 196–197; Abner Cohen, *Arab Border Villages in Israel* (Manchester: Manchester University Press, 1965), pp. 72, 141–145.

39. S.J. Al-Kadhem, "The Role of The League of Arab States in Settling Inter-Arab Disputes," *Revue Egyptienne de Droit International*, vol. 32, 1976, pp. 1–31.

40. Mark Zborowski and Elizabeth Herzog, *Life Is with People: The Jewish Little-Town of Eastern Europe* (New York: International Universities Press, 1952), pp. 234–5.

41. Weizman, p. 126; see also Rabin, *The Rabin Memoirs*, pp. 228–229.

42. *The Jerusalem Post*, 29 Mar. 1985.

43. Kissinger, *Years of Upheaval*, p. 834.

44. *The Jerusalem Post*, 29 Mar. 1985.

45. Kissinger, *The White House Years*, p. 1280; Moshe Dayan, *Avnei Derekh* (Hebrew. Jerusalem: Edanim, 1976), p. 678; Shlomo Aronson, *Conflict and Bargaining in the Middle East* (Baltimore: Johns Hopkins University Press, 1978), p. 140.

46. Gideon Rafael, *Destination Peace* (London: Weidenfeld and Nicolson, 1971), p. 258.

47. Raphael Israeli, *The Public Diary of President Sadat*, part 1 (Leiden: E. J. Brill, 1978), p. 31.

48. Rafael, p. 259.

49. *The Jerusalem Post*, 7, 10 Feb. 1971.

50. *Newsweek*, 6 Mar. 1972.

51. Mordechai Gazit, "The Peace Process, 1969–1973: Efforts and Contacts," *Jersualem Papers on Peace Problems*, no. 35, p. 70.

52. Israeli, pp. 32–33.

53. *Davar* (Hebrew), 17 Feb. 1971; *Yediot Ahronot* (Hebrew), 26 Feb. 1971; *Ma'ariv* (Hebrew), 26 Feb. 1971; Rabin, *The Rabin Memoirs*, p. 193; *The Times* (London), 13 Mar. 1971.

54. Rafael, pp. 255–257, 265; *Ma'ariv* (Hebrew), 26 Feb. 1971.

55. Israeli, pp. 63–64.

56. *Newsweek*, 22 Feb. 1971; Israeli, p. 107. See also pp. 130–133; Gazit, pp. 87–94.

Conclusion

1. Mohamed Ibrahim Kamel, *The Camp David Accords* (London: KPI, 1986), p. 249.

2. *ISA* 2410/2/a, 30 Dec. 1954; *FBIS*, vol. V, no. 195, annex no. 038, 8 Oct. 1985, p. I-2, citing Jerusalem domestic service in Hebrew.

3. *FO* 371/115869, 19 May 1955; *Ha'aretz* (Hebrew), 29 Jan. 1987, p. 1; *The Jerusalem Post*, 30 Jan. 1987, pp. 1–2, 8 Feb. 1987, p. 18.

4. *FBIS*, vol. V, No. 202, annex no. 041, 18 Oct. 1985, p. I-4, quoting *Al-Hamishmar*, 17 Oct. 1985, p. 2.

5. *ISA* 2410/2/b, 19 Feb. 1956, 15 May 1956.

6. Ibid.

7. *The Jerusalem Post*, 1 Nov. 1985.

8. Ibid., 11 Sept. 1986.

9. Sharett diary, vol. 5, p. 1280, 2 Nov. 1955; *ISA* 2456/3, 27 Dec. 1955.

10. *Newsweek*, 9 Apr. 1973, p. 11; Abba Eban, An Autobiography (London: Futura, 1979), pp. 488–489; Gideon Rafael, *Destination Peace* (London: Weidenfeld and Nicolson, 1981), p. 293; Y. Harkabi, *Palestinians and Israel* (Jerusalem: Keter, 1974), p. 234.

11. C. L. Sulzberger, *The Last of the Giants* (New York: Macmillan, 1970), p. 733; Kamel, pp. 27, 133–134.

12. Kamel, pp. 242–243.

13. *ISA* 2453/20, 25 May 1953.

14. Ibid., 2410/2/b, 15 May 1956.

15. Interview with Michael Sterner, 12 Aug. 1985.

16. *Yediot Ahronot*, 27 July 1988, 20 Jan. 1989.

17. *The Jerusalem Post*, 15 June 1988.

18. *The San Diego Union*, 8 May 1989.

19. *ISA* 2410/10, n.d. (ca. 1955).

INDEX

RAYMOND COHEN, Senior Lecturer in International Relations at Hebrew University, Jerusalem, is the author of *Threat Perception in International Crisis, International Politics: The Rules of the Game,* and *Theatre of Power: The Art of Diplomatic Signalling.*